Positive Peace in Schools

Positive Peace in Schools offers a fresh and challenging perspective on the question of conflict, violence and peace in schools. Drawing on the most up-to-date theory and research from the field of peace and conflict studies, this book provides readers with a strong understanding of the concept of positive peace, and how the dimensions of peace-keeping, peace-making and peace-building can be robustly applied in schools.

This accessible book challenges educators everywhere to reconsider the nature of direct and indirect violence in schools, and the structural and cultural factors that sustain it. It engages with global traditions of harmony and balance that are often neglected in Western notions of liberal securitised peace, in order to suggest a model for schools that integrates inner and outer peace. The book also includes practical sections that outline restorative approaches to discipline, peer mediation, circle learning, and classroom activities to promote mindfulness, inclusion and wellbeing. Taken together, these provide a philosophy and a highly effective framework for building conflict literacy and a culture of peace in schools.

Hilary Cremin is a senior lecturer in the Faculty of Education at the University of Cambridge.

Terence Bevington is a freelance conflict consultant and a PhD researcher in the Faculty of Education, University of Cambridge.

Positive Peace in Schools

Tackling Conflict and Creating a Culture of
Peace in the Classroom

Hilary Cremin and Terence Bevington

Routledge
Taylor & Francis Group

LONDON AND NEW YORK

First published 2017
by Routledge
2 Park Square, Milton Park, Abingdon, Oxon OX14 4RN

and by Routledge
711 Third Avenue, New York, NY 10017

Routledge is an imprint of the Taylor & Francis Group, an informa business

British Library Cataloguing in Publication Data
A catalogue record for this book is available from the British Library

Library of Congress Cataloging in Publication Data
Names: Cremin, Hilary, author. | Bevington, Terence, author.
Title: Positive peace in schools : tackling conflict and creating a culture of peace in the classroom / Hilary Cremin and Terence Bevington.
Description: Abingdon, Oxon ; New York, NY : Routledge is an imprint of the Taylor & Francis Group, an Informa Business, [2017]
Identifiers: LCCN 2016044258| ISBN 9781138234987 (hbk) | ISBN 9781138235649 (pbk) | ISBN 9781315304236 (ebk)
Subjects: LCSH: School violence—Prevention. | Conflict management—Study and teaching
Classification: LCC LB3013.3 .C735 2017 | DDC 371.7/82—dc23
LC record available at https://lccn.loc.gov/2016044258

ISBN: 978-1-138-23498-7 (hbk)
ISBN: 978-1-138-23564-9 (pbk)
ISBN: 978-1-315-30423-6 (ebk)

Typeset in Times New Roman
by Swales & Willis Ltd, Exeter, Devon, UK

Contents

Acknowledgements

This book is the fruition of several years of conversation, dialogue, debate and rumination with innumerable peace education workers across the world.

The Cambridge Peace and Education Research Group has provided a valuable and reliable focus and physical space for the ideas in this book to be explored, debated and challenged. We are indebted to its core members who have stuck with it over the years, particularly Sara Clarke-Habibi, Luke Roberts, Noriko Sakade, Kevin Kester, Toshi Tsuruhara and Tim Archer.

Academically, we thank Kathy Bickmore for raising our consciousness of some of the concepts that are central to this book. We thank also Wolfgang Dietrich, Zvi Bekerman, Michalinos Zembylas and so many other peace educators, more than we could name.

Professionally, we owe a debt of gratitude to the people doing the hard work – those staff in schools who keep peace alive in their generous and committed work with children, young people and each other. We would particularly like to acknowledge the commitment made to peace work by the leadership, staff and students at Queensbridge Primary School, Holte Secondary School and Hackney Community College, and also the West Midlands Quaker Peace Education Project.

Personally, Terence is deeply grateful to those people who have helped him to learn the importance of peace – his long-suffering husband Simon, his long-suffered brothers and sister, his fabulous friends and his much-missed mum and dad. Terence also acknowledges the trust given and the confidence gained from his elders: his restorative mentor Marg Thorsborne, his indulgent manager Paul Kelly and his inspiring supervisor (and co-author) Hilary Cremin.

Hilary acknowledges the support of her family and friends, especially when this means that she is not as present as she would like to be. As ever, she acknowledges her deep gratitude to Pat Robinson, who co-authored *Let's Mediate* so many years ago, and who was foundational to the work of Catalyst Consultancy and Change, on which much of this book is based.

Introduction

This book is grounded in Johan Galtung's theory of positive peace.[1] In the book we apply this theory from peace studies to our field of education. The theory contains at its heart the notion that peace can only be achieved if indirect structural violence and cultural violence are addressed, alongside direct violence. This achievement requires activities to make peace and build peace as well as to keep the peace. If peace-keeping alone is used, negative peace will result. There may be a cessation in hostilities, but lasting positive peace requires more than this – it requires the removal of indirect structural and cultural violence. In applying this theory to education, we attempt to develop its practical application.

To come straight to the point – we are arguing here that positive peace in schools can be achieved through the wise and integrated use of peace-keeping, peace-making and peace-building; we are also arguing that all three of these concepts need to be clarified and updated for the twenty-first century. This is an urgent task for peace educators everywhere. As the nature of global conflict and war is evolving, so too is the need for peace, and therefore peace education.

Despite the significant contributions of peace education since the end of the Second World War, the field currently finds itself in crisis. There is a lack of theoretical and conceptual clarity, as well as a need for a stronger research base. Others have noted these needs (e.g. Zembylas, 2007; Harris, 2008; Page, 2008) and have urged the field to find new directions. It is this challenge that we take up here.

The issues for peace education that we will focus on include:

- a lack of engagement with structural and cultural violence in schools;
- a lack of clarity about how peace-keeping, -making and -building fit together holistically in schools;
- a misunderstanding of the role of peace-keeping;
- an unsophisticated application of peace-making;
- an over-reliance on peace-keeping and -making, without due regard for peace-building; and
- an outdated view of peace-building.

These issues are not insignificant, but it is our view that there are adequate responses to be found, which we set out in this book through our framework of positive peace and the iPEACE model.

Drawing on the list above, this framework and model:

- engages with structural and cultural violence in schools;
- clarifies how peace-keeping, -making and -building fit together holistically in schools;
- integrates peace-keeping with more proactive methods;
- enhances peace-making through the concept of 'conflict literacy';
- shifts the balance from peace-keeping and -making towards peace-building; and
- updates notions of what peace-building might entail, including, for example, concepts such as wellbeing and inclusion.

This introduction to the book will first clarify the terms and concepts that will be used throughout, before providing an overview of the book's four parts and eleven chapters.

Defining key terms

As Lewin famously said in 1951, there is nothing more practical than a good theory. For us, Johan Galtung's theories of **peace** and **violence** have been inspirational, and we thank Kathy Bickmore for pointing us in his direction in relation to education and schooling. Galtung is a Norwegian scholar, and one of the most prominent figures in the field of peace studies. In this section, we summarise his theory of **positive and negative peace**, and his notions of **direct, structural and cultural violence**, before relating them more specifically to education. We go on to provide our definition of **postmodernity**, as we will return to this philosophical concept again and again in this book, and it is important to lay out what we mean by it at this early stage. Finally, we provide working definitions of the terms that we consider to be central to peace-building in schools: **inclusion, wellbeing** and **citizenship**.

Violence

In an early paper, Galtung states, "violence is present when human beings are being influenced so that their actual somatic and mental realizations are below their potential realizations" (1969: 168). He then goes on to draw a distinction between **direct violence** and **indirect violence**. **Direct violence** can be understood as physical or psychological acts of aggression directed towards an individual or group. **Indirect violence** comprises both **structural** and **cultural violence**. **Structural violence** can be understood as those aspects of an organisation or a society that indirectly damage people or groups through unjust and inequitable treatment (e.g. lack of access to healthcare for those who cannot pay). **Cultural violence** can be understood as the discourses, narratives and beliefs that enable structural and direct violence to be enacted (e.g. indifference to domestic violence, or the belief that black men are more aggressive than white men). Structural violence and cultural violence are often interdependent, with the structures of society providing mechanisms for cultural violence to be enacted, and cultural values providing support for the continuation of structural violence.

Some have argued that the word **violence** is too strong to use in the context of schools. Becky Francis and Martin Mills, for example, prefer to use the word **damage** rather than violence, as it is "perhaps less emotive and hence less open to accusations of hyperbole" (2012: 253). In this book, however, we have chosen to retain the language of peace studies, and not to shy away from using the term violence in the context of education. We use this term consciously, in order to unsettle and challenge some of the hegemonic thinking and discourses surrounding schools, schooling and school improvement. We do not aim to sensationalise.

Table 0.1 Direct, structural and cultural violence in schools

Type of violence	Direct violence	Indirect violence	
		Structural violence	*Cultural violence*
Definition	Physical, psychological or verbal aggression or attack.	Violence that systematically harms or otherwise disadvantages certain individuals and groups in society.	Violence that is built into the discourses around certain groups of people, their entitlements, capabilities and relative importance.
Examples in schools	Humiliation-based discipline practices. Bullying. Harassment. Verbal abuse. Physical abuse. Sexual abuse of children. Corporal punishment.	Social and disciplinary exclusion of students who do not conform to the normative standards of dominant social groups. Poor infrastructure and provision, lack of access to toilets, clean water, etc. Students becoming ill with stress, excessive homework and testing. Teachers becoming ill with stress and excessive workload. Rote learning and lack of dialogue and engagement in lessons. The reproduction of inequality in and through education.	Students from certain cultural groups not doing as well in school as others. Girls and some boys not having as much space to play as popular boys playing ball games. People not learning about other faiths and cultures, or the achievements of women, indigenous and black people. People not being taught things that will prolong their lives, such as appropriate sex and relationships education. Ideology and colonialism dictating an impoverished and outdated curriculum.

One of the authors has applied Galtung's analysis to direct and indirect violence in schools in other work (Cremin and Guilherme, 2015) and this is reproduced here in Table 0.1. Clearly, direct, structural and cultural violence in schools are linked in many ways, and serve to reinforce each other. Whilst direct violence is easier to detect, the more invidious forms of violence that are contained in structural, cultural and institutional practices can become normalised and hard to spot. Notwithstanding difficulties in teasing out and separating the issues, and in rendering visible that which has become normalised, we set out here to work with concepts of direct and indirect violence in order to integrate theory with practice.

Peace

Galtung's **positive** and **negative peace** are related to his concepts of violence, and can be summarised as follows: negative peace describes a state or condition where there is an absence of direct violence; positive peace describes not only the absence of direct violence but the absence of indirect violence and the presence of harmony and social justice. Positive peace and negative peace are related to the three activities of peace-keeping, peace-making and peace-building in the following ways:

- Direct violence is addressed primarily by **peace-keeping**. This leads towards negative peace.
- Structural violence is addressed primarily by **peace-making** (in reactive mode) and **peace-building** (in proactive mode). This leads towards positive peace.
- Cultural violence is addressed primarily by **peace-building**. This leads towards positive peace.

Peace-keeping, -making and -building are concepts that have often been applied in International Relations, where they are recognised as inter-related. As the UN identifies from its perspective,

> experience has shown that they [peace-keeping, peace-making and peace-building] should be seen as mutually reinforcing. If they are used piecemeal or in isolation, they fail to provide the comprehensive approach required to address the root causes of conflict and hence reduce the risk of conflict recurring.
>
> (UN, 2016)

The same is true in schools.

Thus, we make our foundational case here that these concepts from peace studies can be usefully applied to peace education, and that, just as in International Relations, this needs to be done in an integrated way. Peace education requires a combination of peace-keeping, -making and -building; none is sufficient in itself. We stress the necessity of attending to all three dimensions in schools in order to create a holistic culture of positive peace. Our view is that institutions and individuals become unhealthy if they are stuck in one or other of these ways of responding to direct and indirect violence, and that the answer lies in skilfully and insightfully combining all three.

Table 0.2 summarises definitions of the three dimensions from the perspective of International Relations, and then relates this to schools and education, citing Ian Harris and Kathy Bickmore. The final column of this table clarifies our interpretation of each in a schooling context. In sum, peace-keeping creates conditions of peace *around* the school and *around* people; peace-making occurs *between* people; and peace-building helps to develop peace *within*. Peace within – inner peace – requires (and at the same time builds) outer peace. In the same way, outer peace and security are contingent on (and at the same time enable) peace within: inner peace. Inner peace and outer peace require peace between people(s), and equally peace between people (harmony) builds and strengthens outer peace (security) and inner peace (wellbeing). There is therefore an overarching and underpinning frame for peace work, which is peace itself.

Postmodernity

Having defined violence and peace, we now (rather adventurously!) attempt to define postmodernism. **Postmodernism** is particularly useful for framing the objections that we make in this book to modernist ways of thinking about peace, security, education and justice, and the harm that these ways of thinking cause. **Modernism**'s origins go back as far as the **Enlightenment** at the end of the eighteenth century in the West. In Enlightenment times, the power of reason was seen to be capable of overcoming ignorance, order of overcoming disorder and science of overcoming superstition. Education was the ultimate Enlightenment

Table 0.2 Definitions of peace-keeping, peace-making and peace-building

	International relations/UN perspective	Ian Harris (2000: 20)	Kathy Bickmore (2011a: 42, 45, 2011b: 1)	Our perspective
Peace-keeping	"Peacekeeping refers to the deployment of national or, more commonly, multinational forces for the purpose of helping to control and resolve an actual or potential armed conflict between or within states" (Princeton, 2016).	Peace-keeping strategies can help school administrators deal with physical threats within their schools.	Peace-keeping focuses on "controlling overt aggressive behaviour" through practices such as exclusion.	Peace-keeping in schools uses measures to create order and to limit the likelihood of direct violence occurring. Such measures include the establishment and enforcement of rules with consequences for their infringement. *Peace-keeping activities and measures address the question, how do we keep the members of our school safe from harm?*
Peace-making	"Peacemaking generally includes measures to address conflicts in progress and usually involves diplomatic action to bring hostile parties to a negotiated agreement" (UN, 2016).	Peace-making strategies can help address problems of normative violence within school buildings.	Peace-making is the resolution of conflict once it has materialised, through practices such as mediation.	Peace-making in schools relates to the ways in which the school deals with conflict when it inevitably arises. *Peace-making addresses the question, how do we deal with conflict in our school?*
Peace-building	"Peacebuilding aims to reduce the risk of lapsing or relapsing into conflict by strengthening national capacities at all levels for conflict management, and to lay the foundation for sustainable peace and development" (UN, 2016).	Peace-building strategies are necessary to deal with environmental and structural problems of violence.	Peace-building involves "longer-term, more fundamental processes of redressing injustice, democratization, and nurturing healthy social relationships" through practices such as "collective decision-making, and problem-solving".	Peace-building in schools relates to the broader ambition of social justice, and includes activities that develop pro-social attitudes and behaviours to build a community of care. *Peace-building addresses the question, how do we enable our students and staff to embody and enact peace now and in the future?*

project, and peace education was the ultimate way of working towards world peace. The failure of modernity to bring about world peace through education is the starting point of our considerations in this book.

Postmodernism as a philosophical concept has its historical origins in the late 1970s among French intellectuals. Thinkers such as Lyotard, Derrida and Foucault questioned the idea that society was making progress, and that the modern era, brought in by the Enlightenment two hundred years earlier, continued to hold sway. Their disillusionment with Marxism extended to modernity itself. Not only had the Marxist revolution not materialised, neither had progress in more general terms. The modern era had seen the atrocities of Auschwitz, and brought the world to the brink of nuclear annihilation. This was hardly what early Enlightenment thinkers had in mind!

Lyotard, in his book *La Condition Postmoderne* (1979), first introduced the term postmodernism into philosophy from art, and suggested that knowledge in postmodern society is marked by the end of the *grand narratives*, or *métarécits* of modernity. This was partly a result of new discoveries in science, and partly a result of changing ideas about time, space and language. Lyotard, Foucault and Derrida all write (with different focuses) about the ways in which people are located within history, the effects of globalisation and complexity, and the ubiquity of language games. Their historicist modes of thought, grounded in structural linguistics and anthropology, undermined the logic and body–mind dualism of thinkers such as Descartes; it became ever more untenable to argue, from a humanist perspective, that universal truth was discoverable by rational thought. Foucault, and his analysis of the techniques (technologies) that dictate what counts as truth and knowledge, is particularly useful for this discussion. His core concepts of **regimes of truth** (for example, school improvement discourse), and **the de-centring of the subject**, led to the idea that **power** comes from **knowledge** and **discourse**, and that people (for example, teachers) are situated within discourses of power, rather than possessing power. This offers a fundamental challenge to **humanism** and **humanistic education**. It implies a much-reduced sense of agency for human beings. This also presents challenges for education, and peace education in particular. It is no longer possible to hold on to the idea that there is a universal essence to peace, or even to what it means to be human. These things are always contingent on time and place, and it becomes increasingly important to take an inclusive view.

Postmodern peace-building, therefore, cannot be a simple matter of imposing a common-sense version of peace on the entire planet. It cannot contain the seeds of modern Western hegemony. Neither can it be grounded in utopian idealism, the fundamentals of the market, or the validation and accreditation of the children of global elites. It needs to involve everyone, and it needs to involve risk, humility, solidarity and transformation. It needs to remain open-ended, and subject to adaptation to local circumstances, as well as holding on to inclusive and justice-oriented goals.

Inclusion, wellbeing and citizenship

Finally, we define here some terms that are central to our discussion of peace-building. They are terms that are in more regular usage in schools than in peace education, but often refer to the same notions. In combination, they provide a fairly solid grounding for peace education in schools. These are our own working definitions. We find them useful, but, as with all of our work, we encourage our readers to work together to formulate their working definitions.

Inclusion is the process whereby a school makes it possible, acceptable and desirable for every child and young person in the population to receive a quality education in the same place, regardless of ability, need or identity such as gender, sexuality or ethnicity. Unlike segregation or integration, the focus shifts from the need of the individual to fit in, to the need of the school to provide an environment that allows all young people to flourish. Inclusion can be procedural (in theory there are no barriers to anyone coming to the school, despite over-/under-representation of certain groups); pragmatic (attempts are made to promote inclusion within the boundaries of what seems possible and responsible); or full (inclusion is a core value, and the school is organised accordingly).

Wellbeing implies a state of inner peace, where there is dynamic balance in interpersonal relationships and in the various aspects of intra-personal life (including body, mind, heart and spirit). In a school context, this means that individuals experience warm, challenging and inspiring relationships; and that they have feelings of curiosity, belonging, awe and wonder. These experiences and feelings are enabled through structural aspects of the school (such as provision for meditation, prayer, private study and exercise); through the quality of relationships (such as outstanding teachers, mentors, personal tutors and arts and sports coaches); and through the curriculum (such as strong personal, social, health, mindfulness, sex and relationships education).

Citizenship education enables young people to recognise the personal, social and political contributions of others and to make an active and informed contribution themselves. This may be at the family or local level (such as helping out with childcare); it may be at the level of the school (such as being a member of the school council); it may be at the national level (such as learning about how laws are made and lobbying government); or it may be at the global level (such as linking with schools overseas or participating in a global initiative such as Friends of the Earth or Amnesty International).

Overview of the book

Having defined key terms and concepts used throughout, we now provide an overview of this book. In Part I, we engage with the first of the issues highlighted at the beginning of this introduction – the presence of structural violence and cultural violence in schools. We ask whether the current focus in the media and elsewhere on direct violence (e.g. bullying and fights) is helpful. We ask whether this is a form of cultural violence, especially given the inequalities that persist within systems of education. We also ask whether the current obsession with school improvement, in the UK and elsewhere, is a manifestation of cultural violence of a different kind. To do justice to the transformative potential of positive peace, we argue that schools need to grapple with these significant structural and cultural issues, while recognising that they have their origins beyond the school gates.

In Part II of this book, we turn to peace education itself. We provide an overview of the field, noting particular historical phases and philosophical traditions. We are particularly critical of modernist ways of thinking about peace education, suggesting that postmodern perspectives are more useful. We identify some emergent concepts that hold much promise for the field: notably the need for dynamism, wisdom and flexibility; and the need for more embodied, affective, aesthetic and inclusive models of peace education. To this end, we set out our iPEACE model for positive peace education in schools.

In Part III of this book, we go into more detail about where our iPEACE model for positive peace has come from. We review peace-keeping -making and -building in turn, with a chapter each. We argue that peace-keeping measures in schools – be they enhanced security, school discipline policies or rules and sanctions – do have a place, despite the legitimate concerns of many peace educators. We also argue that peace-making (conflict resolution) in schools is vital for a healthy school community, but that a lack of sophistication in the ways that it is implemented often reduces its effectiveness. What is more, it can be used in rather technocratic ways, ignoring the deep issues of indirect conflict and violence in schools through a pre-occupation with presenting problems. For a more sustainable and holistic approach, peace-building is required. We review this in the final chapter of this part of the book. We argue that peace-building in the twenty-first century has lost the clarity and logic of modernity, that peace-building in times of postmodernity needs to engage more with affect, embodiment, spirituality and complexity, and that it needs to shift from a pure focus on outer (interpersonal and global) peace to an integrated focus on inner and outer peace. Postmodern peace-building needs to take global traditions of peace from the East and South into account, and not draw purely on Western securitised notions of peace.

In Part IV, we bring together the arguments, theories and thinking explored up to that point and present ways in which they can be applied in practice. The first chapter of this part addresses the question of research and how schools and aligned organisations can engage with established evidence in ways that promote rather than denigrate the experiences, knowledge and judgements of the professionals working in schools. This chapter also presents examples of methods that schools can employ to engage in their own action research in developing a culture of positive peace. The subsequent chapter contains five case studies, where staff from schools that have been engaging in peace work share their stories in their own words. The final chapter of this part is a compendium of practical activities that can be used with staff and with students to promote and develop the attitudes, knowledge and skills required for a school culture of positive peace.

Conclusion

Thus, the aim of this book is to work with Galtung and the perennial and elusive concept of peace in order to render peace practicable without compromising or commodifying its essence. We do not underestimate the difficulties of working towards positive peace in schools, but neither do we give up hope. We argue fundamentally that more attention needs to be given to peace-building, but that this is a process: an attitude, a leaning-towards, a never-giving-up. It is not an end state. The builder of peace does not have to be perfect, neither does peace reside in utopia; but peace-building does fundamentally involve a life-long process of working, as much as possible, for positive peace. This may sometimes be more about transformative moments than transformed institutions, but this is not important; peace-builders across the planet each start their journey from where they are currently located.

Note

1   Galtung first introduced the concept of positive peace in his 1967 submission to UNESCO, *Theories of Peace: a synthetic approach to peace thinking.* He later expanded discussion of the concept in his 1969 paper, *Violence, Peace, and Peace Research.*

References

Bickmore, K. (2011a). Keeping, making, and building peace in school. *Social Education*, 75, 40–44.

Bickmore, K. (2011b). *Location, Location, Location: restorative (educative) practices in classrooms.* Presented to ESRC 'Restorative approaches to conflict in schools' seminar 4, Moray House School of Education, University of Edinburgh, Scotland, 16 February 2011.

Cremin, H. and Guilherme, A. (2015). Violence in schools: perspectives (and hope) from Galtung and Buber. *Educational Philosophy and Theory*, 48(11), 1123–1137.

Francis, B. and Mills, M. (2012). Schools as damaging organisations: instigating a dialogue concerning alternative models of schooling. *Pedagogy, Culture and Society*, 20(2), 251–271.

Galtung, J. (1967). *Theories of Peace: a synthetic approach to peace thinking.* Unpublished. [online] Retrieved 11 September 2016 from www.transcend.org/files/Galtung_Book_unpub_Theories_of_Peace_-_A_Synthetic_Approach_to_Peace_Thinking_1967.pdf

Galtung, J. (1969). Violence, peace, and peace research. *Journal of Peace Research*, 6(3), 167–191.

Harris, I. (2000). Peace-building responses to school violence. *NASSP Bulletin*, 5(84), 5–24.

Harris, I. (2008). History of peace education. In M. Bajaj (Ed.), *Encyclopedia of Peace Education*, 15–24. Charlotte, NC: Information Age Publishing.

Lewin, K. (1951). Problems of research in social psychology. In D. Cartwright (Ed.), *Field Theory in Social Science: selected theoretical papers*, 155–169. New York: Harper & Row.

Lyotard, J.-F. (1979). *La Condition Postmoderne.* Paris: Les Editions de Minuit.

Page, J. (2008) *Peace Education: exploring ethical and philosophical foundations.* Charlotte, NC: Information Age Publishing.

Princeton. (2016). *Encyclopedia Princetoniensis.* [online] Retrieved 16 January 2017 from https://pesd.princeton.edu/?q=node/259

United Nations. (2016). *Peace and Security.* [online] Retrieved 5 August 2016 from www.un.org/en/peacekeeping/operations/peace.shtml

Zembylas, M. (2007). *Five Pedagogies, a Thousand Possibilities: struggling for hope and transformation in education.* Rotterdam: Sense.

Part I

Violence in schools

Introduction

This first part of the book sets the scene for the subsequent parts. It reviews some of the fundamental questions and problems that the positive peace framework and iPEACE model set out to address. It asks about the extent of conflict and violence in schools, and where they originate. Does violence come from young people, teachers, parents, members of the community or the media? Or does it rather originate in systems and cultures of schooling at local, national and international level? These questions are important, because the ways in which violence is framed have a significant impact on its responses. If violence is attributed to the wrong origins and causes, interventions will ultimately fail. This part of the book will suggest that many of the initiatives targeting violence in schools may well be misguided, due to an overly simplistic understanding of what is involved.

Chapter 1

School violence

I was threatened by a pupil wielding a hammer.

(former teacher Ian Corcoran)

Introduction

This alarming quote came from the BBC's *Victoria Derbyshire* television series on 24 September 2015. This chapter reviews the extent to which such incidents have become common in schools in the United Kingdom (UK) and elsewhere. Are schools really such violent places, and is violence increasing? The media certainly creates this impression. No matter what the situation is, however, the perception of violent students is not without effects, and this chapter will end with discussion of the ways in which these discourses impact on the lives of young people and teachers in schools.

Violent students?

The *Victoria Derbyshire* television series, cited above, drew on a freedom of information request to 32 police forces in the UK. The reporter Nicola Beckford wanted to know how many alleged crimes linked to schools were reported to police in 2014. The results are worrying – 30,000 incidents in one year. This is equivalent to 160 allegations per school day, with theft and violent crime the most common types of offence to be reported. This is doubly concerning, considering that most schools probably avoid contacting the police because of the damaging effects of negative press.

The statistics collated by the BBC show that theft was the most common offence, with 13,003 incidents reported. There were 9,319 reports of violent crime, 4,106 reports of criminal damage or arson and 754 drugs-related offences. Some forces did not provide data on sexual offences, but in the 25 that did, 1,502 crimes were recorded. The largest number of alleged crimes was reported to the Metropolitan Police, the Greater Manchester Police and the West Midlands Police. The figures for 2014 showed a slight increase in the total number of crimes linked to schools from 2013.

A key concern is that violence seems to be increasing amongst primary-aged (4–11-year-old) children. In July 2012, *The Independent* newspaper reported that in the UK around 89 youngsters aged between 5 and 11 were excluded from school each day for assaulting or verbally abusing their classmates and teachers. The figures drew on 2010/11 Department for Education (DfE) government statistics, and showed that 10,090 children up to the age of 8 were given one or more fixed exclusions in 2010/11, compared to around 9,520 the year before. The 2010/11 figures include 670 children aged 4 and under, who were excluded at least once, along with 1,470 5-year-olds.

Still more alarming are the violent deaths that occur in schools. In the United States of America (USA) this has become almost normalised. Speaking after the Oregon school shooting in the USA in 2015, in which nine people were killed and seven injured before the assailant was shot dead by police, the American president Barack Obama spoke with evident frustration and distress about how "Somehow this has become routine". The BBC news item that covered this event reported that there had been 62 shootings in US schools in 2015. In the UK, this is thankfully not a common phenomenon, but the incidents catch media attention when they do occur. There have been two teachers killed by students in the last thirty years: the first, headteacher Philip Lawrence, was stabbed to death by a teenager in December 1995 outside the gates of St George's Catholic School while he was trying to protect a 13-year-old boy; the second, 61-year-old Ann Maguire, was stabbed repeatedly by a 16-year-old in front of a classroom of students at Corpus Christi Catholic College in Leeds in April 2014. Incidents involving students include: Bailey Gwynne, aged 16, who died after being knifed in the stomach during an altercation with a classmate at Cults Academy in Aberdeen; and a 15-year-old student who was stabbed to death during his lunch hour in a row over £10 in Newham, London in 2001.

The headlines – dramatic though they are – belie the reality for most teachers and students in schools. Student-related 'violence' tends to be much more about everyday indiscipline, bullying and disruption. Teachers cite pervasive indiscipline as a reason for leaving the profession more often than fear of serious or dramatic incidents. Students also report the misery of verbal, psychological and cyber-bullying more often than serious physical attacks. This is not a situation that is limited to the UK. In 2003, Peter Smith carried out a review of violence in all fifteen (then) member states in Europe, and two associated states, under the EU Fifth Framework programme of research activities. It showed, for example, that: 12 per cent of students admitted to bullying other students regularly or often in Belgium and Austria; 22 per cent of students had been victims of sexual harassment by boys at least once in the Netherlands; and, in Spain, 72 per cent of teachers considered a lack of discipline in schools to be a serious problem.

According to a survey carried out by a UK teachers' union, the Association of Teachers and Lecturers (ATL), low-level disruption is endemic in UK schools. The survey investigated behaviour in schools, and was distributed to over 1,108 primary, secondary and further education staff working in state and independent schools and colleges in the UK between 15 February and 12 March 2010. It found that 89 per cent of the teachers surveyed had dealt with disruptive behaviour in that academic year, and that almost half of them felt that disruption was getting worse. Other data from the survey indicate that low-level disruption is only slightly higher in secondary schools (91.2 per cent) than primary (86.2 per cent), and that physical aggression is higher in primary (48.3 per cent) than in secondary schools (19.8 per cent). In the independent sector, low-level disruption occurs at a similar level to the state sector, but physical aggression is significantly less (9.5 per cent as opposed to 31.7 per cent). All of the above suggests that, although serious violence in schools is very rare, low-level disruption and indiscipline are resulting in unacceptably high levels of stress among the teaching profession. This is, of course, a cause for concern.

The key questions that remain, then, are: is violence in schools getting worse; and, if so, what can be done about it? Reviewing the European research cited above, Smith (2003) notes that it is not clear whether violence is getting worse, although many people perceive it to be so. The role of the media in this was highlighted by the Portuguese contributors, who noted that "the excessive media attention, and the use of school violence as a political argument, makes the phenomenon appear larger than it really is and contributes to the growing feeling of insecurity, which is not really supported by data" (Sebastião *et al.*, 2003: 133). There were similar findings in France. Although statistics about violence in schools in France look shocking (with a total of 240,000 incidents registered with central government in 1999), in actual fact there was less reported violence in schools than in the communities they served. School was thus one of the safest places to be.

It is perhaps interesting to note that every generation of parents and teachers seem to continue the discourse that young people are not as polite/cooperative/respectful as they used to be. The feeling that things have recently got worse in schools is an oft-repeated mantra. For example, the *Elton Report* (DES, 1989) was commissioned at the end of the 1980s because of public concern that violence and indiscipline in schools were getting worse. The report did not show this, but did find that low-level disruption was an issue. Although the survey methods make it hard to compare, the percentages appear quite similar to more recent statistics over 25 years later. The overall picture is thus one of stability, not of deterioration.

A piece of research that is particularly useful for this topic is Brown and Winterton's *Insight* review into violence in schools for the British Education Research Association (BERA) in 2010. It reports on a meta-analysis of studies in UK schools at the time. Evidence was reviewed from a variety of sources, including youth surveys funded by government agencies such as the Youth Justice Board and the Office for Standards in Education (Ofsted), smaller qualitative studies of young people known to be at risk of violence and victimisation, and large-scale surveys undertaken by academics and teaching unions. The findings support the view that violence in schools is not as serious as many would fear, although the authors are cautious in their claims because of the methodological difficulties in carrying out this research. For example, definitions of bullying vary between studies, as do research methods, sample sizes and timeframes. This makes it difficult to compare and synthesise data. Also, much of the survey data is self-reported, which risks error due to exaggeration, lack of memory or differences in perspectives between researchers and respondents about what counts, for example, as intimidation or sexual harassment.

Research commissioned by teachers' unions may over-represent levels of stress, threat and violence due to the need to improve working conditions. Likewise, school exclusion data needs to be treated with caution, because of political pressure to reduce exclusions at various times. In addition, there are gaps in research about topics that are less likely to attract funding (such as violence by adults against young people), and a confusing array of studies in those areas that are highly fundable (such as levels of bullying among young people, especially those who are socially excluded). The caution of the authors of the BERA report is necessary; these are contested areas that should be acknowledged. Nevertheless, the report reveals some interesting findings.

The key findings from the BERA review are shown in Table 1.1. Overall, they corroborate other studies which suggest that extreme cases of violence, including severe bullying leading to death, are very rare in UK schools. By contrast, low-level disruption, verbal aggression (for example, between students and towards teachers) and cyber-bullying appear to be areas that warrant further attention.

Table 1.1 Key findings from BERA review into violence in schools

- Most children and young people say they feel safe inside schools, particularly in teacher-controlled spaces.
- Extreme and serious incidents of violence, including violent assaults, are very rare in UK schools.
- About 16 young people commit suicide every year as a result of being bullied at school.
- In large-scale surveys, about 50 per cent of primary students report that they have been bullied, compared with 25 per cent of secondary students.
- Children from marginalised and potentially vulnerable groups are more likely to say they are bullied than their peers.
- Many teachers say low-level disruption, such as students being noisy in class, is the biggest challenge to teaching and learning.
- Boys, and especially black Caribbean boys, are disproportionally represented in statistics on school exclusion.
- Girls are more likely to self-exclude and truant than be excluded from school.
- The level of permanent exclusion from UK schools is low, but this may reflect national policies rather than improvements in student behaviour.
- The incidence of weapon carrying in schools is low, but some teachers have recently reported increases.
- Cyber-bullying appears to be on the rise, particularly among teenage girls. Teachers also report increased exposure to cyber-bullying.
- Some forms of identity-based bullying appear to be on the increase.
- Teachers report that they regularly witness verbal aggression between students and an increasing proportion say they have been aggressively confronted by parents.

These findings suggest that violence in schools, damaging as it is for those who experience it, is not as prevalent as many would claim.

Policy to address violence in schools

It is unfortunate that public perception seems to be at odds with reality. It is doubly unfortunate that this has been allowed to drive policy and funding. Interventions to reduce perceptions of violence in schools are not without effect. They often set a climate of fear, suspicion and intolerance. The negative effects of these initiatives are particularly felt by socially excluded groups in society, but they affect all students through the climate that they establish. This constitutes a form of cultural violence.

For example, in 2010, the UK's Conservative–Liberal Democrat coalition government responded to concerns about violence in schools through its DfE White Paper *The Importance of Teaching*, followed by the Education Act 2011. In it they start from the premise of violent students, and outline measures to ensure that teachers will have new powers, which are akin to those of the police and security forces:

- Teachers will be given greater authority to discipline students, including an expansion of search powers, a removal of the need to give 24 hours' notice of detentions and clearer instructions on the use of force.
- Teachers will be granted anonymity when they are accused by students.
- Headteachers will be given new powers to maintain discipline beyond the school gates.

- Headteachers will be expected to take a strong stand against bullying, particularly prejudiced-based racist, sexist and homophobic bullying.
- Ofsted inspections will focus more heavily on behaviour and safety, including bullying.
- The system of independent appeals panels for exclusions will be changed so they take less time, and students who commit serious offences cannot be re-instated.
- A new approach to permanent exclusions will be piloted, giving schools the power, money and responsibility to secure alternative provision for excluded students.

The tenor of the White Paper is that adults must regain control and replace softly-softly approaches with increased disciplinary measures. The implication is that teachers have lost authority and the power to ensure a safe and productive working environment for students (Stanfield and Cremin, 2013). Another more recent example is an incident in which the UK government Department for Education issued guidance on exclusion, only to be forced to with-draw it a few weeks later. It had attempted to further reinforce a headteacher's right to exclude, and the ease with which this could be done, but the guidance was found to have been introduced without the required consultation. The increasingly authoritarian tone of government guidance, here and elsewhere, is concerning, especially when it leads to increased security and surveil-lance, and to new powers to exclude young people who may already be socially excluded.

Another strategy suggested in the 2010 White Paper to decrease levels of violence in schools is the fast-tracking of ex-soldiers into the teaching profession through the 'Troops to Teachers' programme. Section 2.15 says:

> We will also encourage Armed Forces leavers to become teachers, by developing a 'Troops to Teachers' programme, which will sponsor service leavers to train as teachers. We will pay tuition fees for PGCEs for eligible graduates leaving the Armed Forces and work with universities to explore the possibility of establishing a bespoke compressed undergraduate route into teaching targeted at Armed Forces leavers who have the rel-evant experience and skills but may lack degree-level qualifications.
>
> (DfE, 2010: 2.15)

Leaving the recruitment and training issues aside, the implications here are deeply prob-lematic, in our view. The idea that out-of-control youth need to be educated by trained soldiers is misinformed, and further promotes the militarisation of schooling (Stanfield and Cremin, 2013). It is as if teachers who have lost authority need to borrow the author-ity of the soldier in order to be able to control unruly teenagers. Little thought is given to the transferability (or desirability) of the authority of the armed forces in civilian settings. Writing about this in the context of the USA, Lagotte and Apple (2011) raise concerns about the ways in which the military have perhaps too much access to young people in schools serving diverse urban communities. They are worried about the ways in which this may be used for controlling urban populations, and for recruitment into the armed forces. More importantly, however, schools are not army camps, and the young people in them are not enlisted. Despite the undisputed need for structure, routine and safety in schools, it is nevertheless the case that the process of gaining an education does not automati-cally require authoritarian discipline, or fear. Schools that are overly militarised rely on extrinsic, rather than intrinsic, motivation. As we will show later in the book, this impedes self-discipline – the putative goal of any education system. For now, it is sufficient to ask whether this is really how education in the twenty-first century should be conducted. And, if so, whose interests are served by the discourse of out-of-control youngsters whose regular acts of violence in schools need to be curtailed by trained soldiers?

Conclusion

The debate about whether young people are vulnerable or dangerous will continue to run, but there is no doubt that perceptions of inflated levels of violence in schools have harmful effects. When headteachers take on powers to increase surveillance and exclusion – with reduced levels of accountability and processes of appeal – their role shifts from managing learning towards policing. Dealing with challenging behaviour in isolation from other factors removes the links among behaviour, motivation and learning and can result in an impoverished curriculum. Inadequate pedagogy and poor quality teaching should not be shored up by enhanced capacities to exclude students who struggle to cope or who challenge. Framing young people as violent is a form of cultural violence that makes it easier to justify those policies that advantage some groups in society at the expense of others. These discourses of violent students contain their own seeds of structural violence.

References

British Educational Research Association. (2010). *Insight 1. Violence in UK Schools: what is really happening?* London: British Educational Research Association.

Department for Education (DfE). (2010). *The Importance of Teaching: the schools White Paper 2010.* London: DfE.

Department for Education and Skills. (1989). *Discipline in Schools: report of the committee of inquiry, chaired by Lord Elton.* London: DES.

Lagotte, B. and Apple, M. (2011). Educational reform and the project of militarization. In P. Trifonas and B. Wright (Eds), *Critical Issues in Peace and Education*, 8–20. New York: Routledge.

Sebastião, J., Campos, J. and Tomas de Almeida, A. (2003). Portugal: the gap between the political agenda and local initiatives. In P. K. Smith (Ed.), *Violence in Schools: the response in Europe*, 119–134. London: Routledge.

Smith, P. K. (2003). *Violence in Schools: the response in Europe*. London: Routledge.

Stanfield, J. and Cremin, H. (2013). Importing control in Initial Teacher Training: theorizing the construction of specific habitus in recent proposals for induction into teaching. *Journal of Education Policy*, 28(1), 28–37.

Chapter 2

Schooling as violence?

Introduction

Having reviewed violence in schools from the point of view of public discourse and the media, this chapter now switches focus to the idea that schooling itself might constitute a kind of violence. There is, of course, something seemingly perverse in talking about schooling as violence. In many ways, education and its most universally formalised manifestation – schools – are intended to be a mechanism of personal and social progress. Indeed, it is rare to meet a teacher who has not entered the profession with some idea about how they might impact positively on young people's lives. The present authors have both been teachers and continue to commit their energies to education and schooling. Education and schools are – at least in their intention – a force for good. The aim of this chapter, however, is to discuss the extent to which schools individually, and the school system more generally, embody and enact violence. This is not to say that schools are intentionally violent, but rather to acknowledge that there are elements of schooling that have come to work against the wellbeing and the flourishing of the intended beneficiaries.

In the introduction to this book, we outlined the three forms of violence, taken from Galtung, that are central to our theoretical analysis in this book. To recap, Galtung makes a distinction between direct violence and indirect violence. Direct violence is often physical, and leads to harm in relatively straightforward ways. Indirect violence can be structural or cultural. Structural violence is present in unequal societies, and cultural violence masks structural violence. The harm that is caused by indirect violence is less straightforwardly evident than the harm that is caused by direct violence.

Viewing the phenomenon of indirect violence from a different theoretical perspective, Brigitte Scott uses Bourdieu and Passeron's (1977) construct of symbolic violence to discuss the school cultures, structures and practices that enact violence against teachers. She found that "tracking and defining instances of symbolic violence brings us face-to-face with specific institutional practices that are unfair, damaging, and manipulative" (2012: 531). This is also our task here – to use Galtung's constructs of cultural, structural and direct violence to review practices in schools. The aim is to 'bring us face-to-face' with what may have become unseen manifestations of violence in order to render them visible again. The rest of this chapter focuses on evidencing and discussing indirect structural and cultural violence. The subsequent chapter will explore how one particular form of cultural violence – technocratic 'school improvement' – has pernicious effects in schools

Structural violence in schools

Various authors have identified the role that schools play in the reproduction of societal inequalities as one of the most invidious forms of structural violence (Bajaj and Brantmeier, 2011; Francis and Mills, 2012; Harber, 2004). These authors discuss issues of access and quality, and the ways that schools can serve to limit resources and opportunities for certain groups and thus reproduce inequalities in broader society.

This is not how schools are often viewed, however, in mainstream public discourse on education. They are seen as mechanisms for widening opportunity and providing social mobility. This has the result that many have become inured to the iniquity of the education system. In this section, we throw light on this by putting two aspects of on-going educational inequality under the spotlight: attainment and disciplinary exclusion. We set this analysis within the context of the English educational system, but it could equally be applied to other education systems throughout the world.

First, the differential rates of attainment among different ethnic groups present a complex and concerning picture. Analysis by the UK's Department for Education (2015) of the current (but soon to be replaced) measure of five GCSEs including English and maths at grades A*–C shows some ethnic groups, such as Indian and black African, achieving at a higher level than their white English peers in 2014 (72.9 and 56.8 per cent respectively over 56.6 per cent white English).[1] The same analysis shows that other ethnic groups, such as black Caribbean (47 per cent) and Pakistani heritage (51.4 per cent), fare markedly worse. It is troubling that there are such wide discrepancies for certain ethnic groups.

The discrepancies between different socio-economic groups are even wider. In 2013, only 37.9 per cent of students who were entitled to free school meals (the most commonly used proxy for poverty) achieved five GCSEs including English and maths at grades A*–C, compared to 64.6 per cent of their more affluent peers. What is perhaps most alarming is that the gap between these two groups was stubbornly resistant to change over a ten-year period (28 per cent difference in 2004 and 26.7 per cent in 2013). It would therefore appear that, while there has been a rise in attainment for both groups, the gap in attainment between poorer and richer students has remained fixed. In light of these figures, it is important to interrogate what is happening in schools and wider society to enable this inequality to persist, despite repeated political claims that things will change.

Thus, the evidence that schools are failing to enable social mobility is more or less irrefutable. From the government's own research (Social Mobility and Child Poverty Commission, 2015) to the Organisation for Economic Co-operation and Development's statistical analysis (2015), the biggest predictor of educational achievement in the UK is a person's social class. This is not what is presented in popular education discourse, however. As Pring (2013) points out, education has been 'sold' to young people and their parents for several decades as a way of achieving better jobs, greater social mobility and rising living standards. The dream of 'knowledge work' within an information-driven economy has not materialised, however, for those at the bottom of the social scale, and it is perhaps time to acknowledge that something else is going on here.

The second area that we wish to put under the spotlight is the disquieting differential in the rates of disciplinary exclusion from school. Both fixed-term and permanent exclusion have been shown to have significant and lasting damaging effects on the life opportunities of young people (Scott *et al.*, 2001). Strand and Fletcher (2014) have conducted an impressive and robust longitudinal analysis of exclusions from English secondary schools.

The data from this study provide an enlightening picture of how disciplinary exclusion is applied differentially according to a variety of characteristics. There is a significant degree of disproportionality, for example, according to students' ethnic group: students of black Caribbean and mixed white and Caribbean heritage have over a 30 per cent chance of experiencing exclusion, compared to 15 per cent for white British students and 9 per cent for students of Indian heritage.

Further interrogation of these data reveals a subtle but significant distinction in how white British students are treated compared to those of other heritages. Strand and Fletcher report that on average white British students receive more fixed-term exclusions (FTEs) before they are permanently excluded than nearly every ethnic minority group, and that the FTEs given to white British students are of shorter duration. The evidence therefore indicates that schools punish students from ethnic minority groups with longer FTEs, and also give more chances to white British students before permanently excluding them. The conclusion drawn by the authors of that study is that "[t]hese data are consistent with a degree of systemic discrimination" (2014: 18). Such examples of systemic discrimination are what we refer to here as manifestations of structural violence.

A comparison of attainment and exclusion data is salutary: those groups who are most likely to attain well are least likely to be excluded, and vice versa. These factors intersect in pernicious ways. For example, as schools vie for the most academic and least problematic students, those with social, emotional and behavioural difficulties may well find themselves on the wrong end of the exclusion process, with little recourse to appeal. As Shaughnessy (2012) points out, the UK's 2010 White Paper *The Importance of Teaching* incentivises schools to exclude those students whose needs are complex and expensive to meet. Thus, some of the most socially excluded young people become further marginalised. These young people find themselves out of school, with little supervision or support, and with alternative provision hard to access. As the National Children's Bureau points out:

> If a child is missing education they are at significant risk of failing academically, and of being out of education, training and employment (NEET) in later life. They may be at risk of physical, emotional or psychological harm, particularly if their whereabouts become unknown or they are taken off the school roll. Recent high-profile cases of child maltreatment involving sexual exploitation have included children who were missing education.
>
> (NCB, 2014: 3)

These effects are devastating for the young people involved. In acting in these ways, schools risk badly letting down some of the most vulnerable young people in their area. If education moves away from concerning itself with social justice and inclusion, and towards more limited concerns of competition and academic performance, then everyone loses.

Cultural violence in schools

The discussion now moves to a consideration of cultural violence in schools, revisiting concerns about militarisation discussed in the previous chapter, and bringing in two new areas of cultural violence: neglect and omission; and non-recognition and intolerance.

Cultures of surveillance and militarisation

As already stated, we find ourselves alarmed by schools which pride themselves on a climate of control and compliance that is more akin to a military context than to a school. We have argued that schools are not army camps; here we argue that they are not prisons either. Despite this, we have seen zero-tolerance discipline regimes celebrated for not allowing physical contact between students, for example, or gatherings of more than three or four during break and lunch times. In these schools, it is commonplace to administer an additional punishment automatically to those who question an existing sanction. Such systems of control and compliance are not only anti-educational; they risk creating schools in the image of a prison.

Corporal punishment in state schools in the UK ceased to be legal in 1986, and in private schools in 1998. However, examples of students being subjected to verbal, psychological and physical acts of violence continue (Harber, 2004). Michel Foucault's searing critique of the evolution from the physical punishment of the prisoner through to psychological punishment (indirect violence) in *Discipline and Punish* (1977) can be applied to the school context without too much effort. Increased surveillance and security in schools can make them feel like prisons, as McCluskey points out:

> Bells that ring to time work and control play, rules that govern movement round and between buildings, regulated access to toilet facilities, uniform codes, public address systems, electronic absence monitoring, systematized rewards and punishments, high security perimeter fences, CCTV, alarm systems and swipe access, short rests and long periods of work . . . These are all features more often associated with incarceration than with education.
>
> (McCluskey, 2013: 132)

These things serve to promote a way of being in school that is devoid of responsibility, joy and the love of learning. Put simply, if students are treated as criminals through the everyday fabric of school life, it makes it more likely that they will respond in kind. The very technology that is supposed to diminish violence and deviance in schools serves to amplify it.

Neglect and omission

While there will forever be appalling examples of adults in schools deliberately and wilfully causing harm to their students, these cases are thankfully rare. There are, however, many more indirect ways in which adults enact violence onto their students. Cultural violence can be present through acts of omission as well as through acts of commission. Where there is a lack of care, trust and positive regard for young people, their development and possibilities for self-actualisation are damaged.

Concerns about structural and cultural violence in schools are to be found in the rapidly increasing numbers of parents choosing to home educate their children. The proportion of young people experiencing emotional and mental health difficulties is higher than ever, according to headteachers (NCB, 2016) and mental health organisations (Young Minds, 2016). There are two sides to this picture: the first is the extent to which schools can actively damage the emotional and mental health of their pupils through their priorities and practices (such as over-burdening pupils with homework and placing them under excessive pressure to perform in public examinations); the second is through acts of omission, through failing to promote and develop the wellbeing of their students. We will return in detail to the broad question of wellbeing later in this book, when we argue that promoting wellbeing is a cornerstone of positive peace-building practice.

Another omission from many systems of schooling throughout the world is the opportunity to develop autonomous and critical thinking. Talking about her insider experiences as a teacher in Mossbourne Academy, for example, Christy Kulz states that "There is little space for critical thinking, innovation or creativity in the neoliberal school; instead there is obedient reproduction where students, parents and teachers learn to accept Mossbourne's approach is the only option" (2013: 216). Systems of compliance and control rely on reduced levels of criticality among students. By criticality we refer to what John Dewey termed reflective thinking, which is regarded as the precursor to the modern understanding of critical thinking: "Active, persistent, and careful consideration of a belief or supposed form of knowledge in the light of the grounds which support it and the further conclusions to which it tends" (Dewey, 1909: 6). Critical thinking has at least two distinct functions: it involves understanding processes of learning in order to improve it; and it involves challenging what may be presented as knowledge or facts. While the former function is more common in schools under the label of meta-cognition and self-regulation, the latter function appears to be actively discouraged.[2] Essentially, schools seem to value learning how to learn, but do not value learning how to think. It is this second function of critical thinking that is more closely aligned with Paulo Freire's concept of *conscientização*.

The work of Freire and his contribution to the creation of cultures of positive peace rooted in a socially just society are expanded upon later in this book. For the moment, we consider the failure to develop critical faculties as a form of cultural violence through omission. It impedes the flourishing of young people as they grow into adulthood and begin to shape the world in which they live. Critical thinking enables young people to discriminate between fact, opinion and promotion in an increasingly information-rich world. It would appear that critical thinking is increasingly at odds with standardised models of schooling that have been actively promoted by successive governments in the UK and elsewhere in the world. Disallowing the potential for young people to challenge the world not only goes against one of the fundamental roles of education, in our view, but also enables inequality and privilege to be sustained and reproduced through cultural violence.

Non-recognition and intolerance

In their analysis of how schools damage students, Francis and Mills present three ways: through the reproduction of social inequalities; through "institutional structures of discipline and surveillance" (2012: 251); and by allowing and at times legitimising pupils brutalising each other through violence and bullying. Having reviewed the first two, we now turn to this final area of brutalisation and bullying. It will be recalled that we argued earlier that student violence in schools is not as extensive as is often claimed in the media. We made the point, however, that low-level disruption and bullying create misery for young people and adults alike.

Francis and Mills draw an insightful parallel between the systems of hierarchisation and social exclusion within schools, and pupil-to-pupil brutalisation, arguing that school as an institution "actively produces these behaviours [among pupils]" (2012: 259). They cite numerous studies, many of them ethnographic, which depict disturbing examples of how *schools → violence?* (handwritten margin note)

pupils punish difference in others. Of course, this is not a new phenomenon, but the question that they raise is about the extent to which processes of 'othering' and punishing difference might be actively produced by contemporary cultures of schooling.

In an increasingly standardising and competitive education system, it is both unsurprising and unacceptable that 'otherness' becomes a threat rather than an asset. Pupils who require more resources and attention can be perceived as taking away from other pupils. Students who challenge the authority of the school can be regarded as deviant, and required to move into line or be excluded. These values are communicated to children and young people through behaviours, practices and systems.

John Paul Lederach, a peace theorist, has developed a model and theory of conflict transformation, which "views the presenting issues as an expression of the larger system of relationship patterns. [Conflict transformation] moves beyond the 'episodic' expression of the conflict and focuses on the relational and historical patterns in which the conflict is rooted" (2003). Lederach proposes that it is essential to look beneath and behind the presenting incident of violence to understand better the factors that may have contributed to its enactment. In this way, it is important to address both individual incidents of violence and the patterns of relations, practices and structures that lead to acts of violence. Cultures of schooling need to be predicated on the need to reduce structural and cultural violence. This will lead to reductions in direct violence, as young people learn different ways of being and relating.

Conclusion

This chapter has reviewed both structural and cultural violence in systems of education. The differing experiences and outcomes of different ethnic and socio-economic groups are one source of evidence for this. As Francis and Mills make clear, schools and school systems exist as "institutional expressions (albeit often heightened expressions) of discourses and resulting structural arrangements perpetuated by society" (2012: 254). In our analysis of schooling as violence, we also seek to acknowledge the influences of their social context. It is not, however, sufficient to argue that schools are powerless because of larger structural and cultural pressures. Our argument is that schools could be better supported to use the agency they have in informing and forming the lives of the young people with whom they work. The differential experiences of young people from different ethnic and socio-economic groups, for example, should give school leaders reason to pause for thought on the decisions they make on a daily basis: decisions about whether or not to give a student another chance; and on whether or not to prioritise the needs of the school over the needs of an individual. While phrasing this discussion in terms of violence may seem extreme to some, we argue that many young people experience this as violence, and that it is unbalanced to focus only on the direct violence that occurs as a result. It is the aspects of structural and cultural violence outlined above that contribute to the under-achievement, disenfranchisement and alienation of significant groups of young people. In such a situation, young people are prevented from achieving their potential, to their own detriment and to the detriment of society at large. Following on from this, it will be evident that staff working in schools are themselves subjected to the pressures and priorities that are manifested through structural and cultural violence. The ways in which teachers and others are injured by these systems and structures will be explored in detail in the next chapter, which looks at the broader discourses around schooling.

Notes

1 GCSE (General Certificate of Secondary Education) examinations are taken by the vast majority of 16 year olds. Currently graded from A* (highest) to G (lowest). Achievement of 5 GCSEs at grades A*–C including English and maths is the generally recognised threshold of success at this level. The percentage of students achieving this threshold is a very significant criterion by which schools are judged. From 2017 onwards, the grades will be signified by number 9 (highest) to number 1 (lowest).

2 "Meta-cognition and self-regulation approaches (sometimes known as 'learning to learn' approaches) aim to help learners think about their own learning more explicitly . . . Meta-cognition and self-regulation approaches have consistently high levels of impact." The Education Endowment Foundation, www.educationendowmentfoundation.org.uk.

References

Bajaj, M. and Brantmeier, E. (2011). The politics, praxis, and possibilities of critical peace education. *Journal of Peace Education*, 8(3), 221–224.

Bourdieu, P. and Passeron, J. (1977). *Reproduction in Education, Society and Culture*. London: Sage Publications.

Department for Education (DfE). (2010). *The Importance of Teaching: the schools White Paper 2010*. London: DfE.

Department for Education (DfE). (2015). *A Compendium of Evidence on Ethnic Minority Resilience to the Effects of Deprivation on Attainment*. London: DfE.

Dewey, J. (1910). *How We Think*. Lexington, MA: D. C. Heath.

Foucault, M. (1977). *Discipline and Punish: the birth of the prison* (A. Sheridan, Trans.). London: Penguin.

Francis, B. and Mills, M. (2012). Schools as damaging organisations: instigating a dialogue concerning alternative models of schooling. *Pedagogy, Culture and Society*, 20(2), 251–271.

Harber, C. (2004). *Schooling as Violence*. London: Routledge Falmer.

Kulz, C. (2013). *'Structure Liberates?': making compliant, consumable bodies in a London academy*. Doctoral thesis, Goldsmiths, University of London.

Lederach, J. (2003). *Conflict Transformation*. [online] Retrieved 15 September 2016 from www. beyondintractability.org/essay/transformation

McCluskey, G. (2013). Challenges to education: restorative approaches as a radical demand on conservative structures of schooling. In H. Cremin, G. McCluskey and E. Sellman (Eds), *Restorative Approaches to Conflict in Schools: interdisciplinary perspectives on whole school approaches to managing relationships*, 132–141. London: Routledge Falmer.

NCB. (2014). *Not Present, What Future? Children missing education in England*. London: NCB.

NCB. (2016). *Keeping Young People in Mind: findings from a survey of schools across England*. [online] Retrieved 19 September 2016 from www.ncb.org.uk/sites/default/files/field/attachment/news/ascl_and_ncb_findings_from_survey_briefing_final_footnotes.pdf

OECD. (2015). *In It Together: why less inequality benefits all*. Paris: OECD Publishing.

Pring, R. (2013). *The Life and Death of Secondary Education for All*. London: Routledge.

Scott, B. (2012). Caring teachers and symbolic violence: engaging the productive struggle in practice and research. *Educational Studies*, 48(6), 530–549.

Scott, S., Knapp, M., Henderson, J. and Maughan, B. (2001). Financial cost of social exclusion: follow up study of antisocial children into adulthood. *British Medical Journal*, 323: 191–194.

Shaughnessy, J. (2012). The challenge for English schools in responding to current debates on behaviour and violence. *Pastoral Care in Education*, 30(2), 87–97.

Social Mobility and Child Poverty Commission. (2015). *State of the Nation 2015: social mobility and child poverty in Great Britain*. London: Social Mobility and Child Poverty Commission.

Strand, S. and Fletcher, J. (2014). *A Quantitative Longitudinal Analysis of Exclusions from English Secondary Schools*. Oxford: University of Oxford.

Young Minds. (2016). *Mental Health Statistics*. [online] Retrieved 16 September 2016 from www. youngminds.org.uk/training_services/policy/mental_health_statistics

Chapter 3

School improvement as violence

Introduction

The previous chapter discussed Galtung's structural and cultural violence, and the ways that these relate to schooling. This chapter sets out the case for school improvement as an example of cultural violence. We have argued that cultural violence in schools creates mechanisms of structural violence, leading to acts of direct violence against school staff and students. This chapter discusses the current hegemonic discourse around school improvement, and assesses the cultural, structural and direct violence that can result from it.

On the one hand, school improvement is hard to argue against; it is one of the new orthodoxies of the education world. It is one of a number of related concepts, alongside the 'standards agenda' and 'evidence-based practice', that have become "regimes of truth" (Foucault, 1991), with their own sets of technologies and practices. They each hold a strong rhetorical appeal – for who can argue against schools being improved, standards being raised or practice being based upon evidence? On the other hand, as with any immediately appealing rhetoric, it is essential to probe beneath the surface and to question how rhetoric contributes to the evolution of discourse. In line with the postmodern perspective discussed throughout this book, we draw in this chapter on Foucault's notion of discourse, which "defines and produces the objects of our knowledge" and "governs the way that a topic can be meaningfully talked about and reasoned about" (Hall, 1997: 44). Here, we critically analyse school improvement discourse to reveal the assumptions on which it is based, the mechanisms that sustain its influence and the implications of the priorities that it sets. This analysis brings to light some of the ways in which school improvement has come to embody cultural violence enacted through institutional structures and practices.

A brief history of school improvement

School improvement as a movement (and latterly as an industry) evolved from research into school effectiveness in the 1970s. Initially, school effectiveness provided a framework for academic researchers to investigate how schools do what they do, and how they might do it better. An important cornerstone for school improvement in the UK was the Education Reform Act 1988, and in the USA it was the No Child Left Behind Act 2001. Since the 1970s, school improvement discourse has become increasingly hegemonic and globalised. It can no longer simply be considered at the micro-level of the school, district or even state. Education has become yet another aspect of people's lives that has effectively shrunk at the same time as expanding globally, so that it is now possible to compare what happens in schools in Hackney and Hong Kong. Not only is it possible; it is desirable, and is an influential driver of change.

Writing in 2014, Pasi Sahlberg discussed the phenomenon of the global education reform movement (GERM), grounded in the Programme for International Student Assessment (PISA) tables:

> GERM is an unofficial education policy orthodoxy that many formal institutions, corporations and governments have adopted as their official program in educational development. This global movement includes some welcome elements that have strengthened the focus on learning, encouraged access to education for all, and emphasised the acquisition of knowledge and skills that are relevant in the real world. But GERM also has symptoms that indicate it may be harmful to its host; driving education reforms by competition, standardisation, test-based accountability, fast-track pathways into teaching and privatisation of public education.
>
> (Sahlberg, 2014: 50)

Thus, in communicating notions of harm, Sahlberg uses language of germs and infection, where we use the language of direct and indirect violence. Both refer to the same phenomena. In the UK, the Education Reform Act 1988 "articulated six key elements of neoliberal and neoconservative advocacy around education policy" (Ball, 2013: 89) which included: the establishment of a national curriculum and its associated external assessment mechanisms with testing at ages 7, 11 and 14; budgetary devolution from local authorities to schools through the local management of schools; and the enshrinement in law of parents' right to express a preference about which school their children would attend. In 1992, this was supplemented by the creation of Ofsted and local league tables of schools. It is not hard to see how these factors operated together to work towards the marketisation of schools. From then onwards, devolution of budgets to schools and the establishment of per capita funding meant that income was overwhelmingly driven by recruitment of students. In a market place where parents can 'choose' which school to send their child to, Ofsted ratings, examination results and league tables take on new and increased importance. School improvement has become increasingly conflated with improved attainment in public examinations.

This narrow definition of school improvement has become rather monolithic, and (rather ironically) stunts creativity and growth. In the UK, Barbara MacGilchrist of the UCL Institute of Education has said of this "the government's definition of an improving school as being one with a linear, continuous, upward trajectory of test and examination results has passed its sell-by date" (2003: 1). We would go further to claim that it sows the seeds of structural and cultural violence.

Theoretical perspectives on school improvement discourse

There are three main critiques of school improvement discourse that tie it in with structural and cultural violence: that it serves political interests; that it serves market interests; and that it harms teachers and students. We will now review each of these perspectives in turn.

School improvement discourse and political interests

While it is of course both warranted and necessary to seek to improve schools, this can never take place in a political vacuum. Goldstein and Woodhouse (2000) present an engaging overview of the history of school improvement and argue that successive governments have used research evidence selectively in service of their own ends. School improvement research often (though not always) presents an over-simplified diagnosis and intervention plan for improving schools and can be lacking in theoretical depth and rigour. Politicians tend to warmly welcome (and fund) initiatives that fit with their political ideology, and to ignore or reject findings that contradict their preferred strategies.

Another source of evidence that governments use for political ends is school inspections. In England, inspections are carried out by Ofsted – a non-ministerial department of government. Ofsted has been used by successive governments to influence school practice without the need to undergo the usual parliamentary scrutiny and ratification. "When the Government wants schools to do something but feels constrained from making it statutory, it announces that it will be inspected by Ofsted" (ATL, 2007). The result of such indirect political influence is that Ofsted has become the de facto arbiter of what matters in schools and what counts as quality. School improvement has in many ways become a euphemism for Ofsted-readiness. The terminology deployed by Ofsted "has become normatively accepted as the means by which to describe successful and failing education in England" (Clarke and Baxter, 2014: 481). This is problematic "if this means decisions are being made that run counter to decisions the school would have otherwise made in the interests of pupils" (Policy Exchange, 2014: 44). While it may seem illogical to argue against inspection and accountability, it is important to review the extent to which they may have become a vehicle for structural and cultural violence. What some have called 'the new accountability' is termed by Biesta "technical–managerial accountability", which he contrasts to "professional–democratic accountability" (2010: 51). Biesta highlights how "systems, institutions and individual people adapt themselves to the imperatives of the logic of accountability, so that accountability becomes an end in itself, rather than a means for achieving other ends (2010: 59). In England this translates into schools making 'what Ofsted wants' the primary (if not exclusive) focus of their work to 'improve'. In a context of growing social and global inequality, which is at best resistant to decades of reforms in education and at worst perpetuated by education, these systems of accountability become part of the problem rather than part of the solution.

There are other ways that governments use school improvement discourse for their own ends. It can, for example, be used to deflect criticism from other policies. It is in the interests of ministers and policy makers to hold schools responsible for the effects of wider social problems. Holding schools accountable passes the blame and makes the solutions look simpler than is really the case (Hamilton, 1996; Bauman, 2000; Pring, 2013). School improvement discourse can serve to " 'pathologise' schools by implying that economic and other problems of society can be ascribed to the failings of education and those who work in the system, especially teachers" (Goldstein and Woodhouse, 2000: 354). This assumption essentially removes from politicians their responsibilities for contributing to structural violence, such as through unequal distribution of wealth and the degradation of social cohesion wrought by anti-immigration posturing, for example. As previously discussed, this masking of structural violence is one of the key functions of cultural violence.

School improvement discourse and market interests

In addition to political concerns, there are related concerns about the undue influence of the market on education systems, enacted through school improvement discourse. One element of the philosophy underlying school improvement can be traced back to the New Public Management (NPM) movement of the 1980s (Clarke and Newman, 1997). The essential assumption of NPM is that what works in the private sector should be successful in the public sector. The enactment of this way of thinking can be seen perhaps most clearly in the ways that schools have become marketised in alignment with capitalist principles. David Marquand (cited in Apple, 2005) has summarised and critiqued this discourse:

> The language of buyer and seller, producer and consumer, does not belong in the public domain; nor do the relationships which that language implies. Doctors and nurses do not 'sell' medical services; students are not 'customers' of their teachers; policemen and policewomen do not 'produce' public order. The attempt to force these relationships into a market model undermines the service ethic, degrades the institutions that embody it and robs the notion of common citizenship of part of its meaning.
>
> (Apple, 2005: 33)

As both Marquand and Apple point out, the language of the market has replaced the language of social justice and progressive education. This language is expressed both through notions of utility and outputs, and notions of 'value for money' and the 'efficiency and effectiveness' of providers (Clarke and Baxter, 2014: 485). The impression is created that school improvement relates primarily to raising standards of educational performance, and that this is quantifiable, measurable and comparable in the same way that other products and outputs of markets are. David Reynolds, for example, celebrates the new "'technological' orientation" of education, which "is simply concerned to deliver 'more' education to more children" and thus "eschews the values debate about goals" (1997: 99). The Dutch education philosopher Gert Biesta gives short shrift to such a position:

> The means we use in education are not neutral with respect to the ends we wish to achieve. It is not the case that in education we can simply use any means as long as they are 'effective' . . . education is at heart a moral practice more than a technological enterprise.
>
> (Biesta, 2007: 10)

We would agree, arguing that a position that attempts to mask ideology through the 'common sense' of the market place or through manipulation of performance markers and test scores is a position of structural and cultural violence. The positioning of school improvement as a technological exercise directed towards increasing productivity and efficiency has real and harmful effects on students and teachers. Biesta challenges a technocratic conceptualisation of teaching and teachers; he argues that the drive for standardisation has the effect of rendering teachers as technicians who need only to learn and apply predetermined policy and practice. From this perspective, individual professional judgement is not to be trusted and successful outcomes (invariably test grades) can be attributed to the fidelity of the teacher's implementation of evidence-based practices. Ironically, this leads to an impoverished idea of what schooling can achieve.

School improvement discourse and harmful effects

Biesta and Sahlberg among others (e.g. Hammersley, 2013) contend that the current focus on technical–managerial accountability has a number of harmful effects and dangers. For example, the drive for external accountability has created an obsession with evidence, which means that teachers spend time and energy proving what they have done rather than doing it. This limits their effectiveness, as the Association of School and College Leaders points out: "the requirement for evidence at a particular time and in a particular form may inhibit achievement of that which is to be measured" (ASCL, 2010). It also places an additional workload burden on school staff. In the DfE's own consultation, the *Workload Challenge* (2014), 53 per cent of teachers reported accountability and the perceived pressures of Ofsted as the main driver of workload (DfE, 2015: 5). The harmful effects of Ofsted on schools and school staff are well documented by individual teachers through media such as the *Times Education Supplement* community forum, by the teaching unions (NASUWT, 2012; NUT, 2015) and in the research literature (Courtney, 2012).

Technical–managerial accountability has damaging effects on professional identity and on professional relationships. Francis and Mills (2012) name the unrelenting focus on standards, accountability and evidence as the driver of the 'aggressive practices' to which teachers are subjected. They identify burnout, stress and poor quality of life as some of the results of these practices but they also identify more indirect psychic and existential effects. These can be summarised as "accountability terrorizing teachers into becoming what they do not want to become" (2012: 262). Here, they draw on Stephen Ball's characterisation of reform as not changing what teachers do, but changing who they are:

> Ball suggests that reforms grounded in a performative culture represent "a struggle over the teacher's soul" . . . within this culture: "We become ontologically insecure: unsure whether we are doing enough, doing the right thing, doing as much as others, or as well as others".
>
> (Francis and Mills, 2012: 262)

In addition to the negative effects of school improvement discourse on teachers, there are significant negative effects for students. High-stakes, test-based accountability regimes enacted through league tables and Ofsted inspections are not without consequence for young people. Based on analysis of more than 9,000 students as part of the *Longitudinal Survey of Young People in England*, Foliano et al. (2010) concluded that an increased emphasis on test score performance was adding to student disengagement. In seeking to improve outcomes for young people by creating the conditions in which the highest examination grades can be attained by the highest proportion of students, school can become unpleasant and irrelevant for many. In a report on the number of students at risk of what they term 'drop-out' (a term designed to include those who absent themselves from school for their own reasons, as well as those who are excluded), Stamou et al. (2014) found that many factors contribute to disengagement from school. Students' reports include "the structure of lessons in school, the low level of activity they involved, their relations with teachers and other school staff as well as their own difficulties with behaviour and anger management" (2014: 1). These research findings correlate with what we and others hear repeatedly in our regular visits to schools: that the narrow focusing on test results leads to an impoverished curriculum; standardised, uninspiring lessons; and more rigid relations between staff and their students.

Thus, school improvement discourse has real-life implications for teachers and students, and for what is taught, measured and valued in schools. The crucial point here is that school improvement has come to be understood and engaged with as a technological exercise, one that not only silences discussion of the fundamental purposes and aims of education and of schools, but actively excludes consideration of alternative, and perhaps more inclusive, peaceful and humane ways of seeing and doing things in education.

Positively peaceful school improvement

The premise of this book is to contrast cultural, structural and direct violence in schools with an alternative view, grounded in positive peace and the potential of young people to become fully functioning, compassionate, cooperative and contributing members of society. Our position is that the current hegemonic steamroller of school improvement discourse and its ensuing priorities, structures and practices are at best neglecting to create the conditions for students to flourish, and at worst actively damaging the life chances of certain young people.

We argue that the first challenge for developing peaceful schools is to rethink what is meant by school improvement. Here, we support the conclusions of a paper from the Institute of Development Studies (IDS). The authors' principal recommendation is that

> [t]he assessment of 'effective' education needs to be expanded to include broader education outcomes that reflect this goal, including individual and social transformation, empowerment and learners' retention rates, rather than simple test scores.
>
> (IDS, 2009: 26)

This seemingly radical declaration may be useful in challenging and expanding current thinking around what constitutes good education and how we measure it in both developing and developed contexts. It is possible to imagine a new conceptualisation of school improvement based on the criteria identified by the IDS – one that privileges trust over suspicion, professional judgement over standardised judgements and collaboration over competition.

The second challenge is to rethink what is meant by accountability. Drawing on the experience of Finland and other Nordic countries, Pasi Sahlberg makes the point that

> [t]he question is not whether schools, teachers and students should be held accountable or not. The challenge is how to establish an accountability system that would support worthwhile learning, increase social capital and thereby help schools to be active players in developing our societies.
>
> (Sahlberg, 2010: 58)

Sahlberg builds on the work of bodies such as the Scottish Executive (2006) and the Secondary Heads Association in England (2003) in promoting 'intelligent accountability', which he defines as "accountability policies that balance qualitative with quantitative measures and build on mutual accountability, professional responsibility and trust" (2010: 53). Biesta proposes a refocusing of accountability onto its professional–democratic rather than its technical–managerial function. Following Bauman, he argues persuasively that "the culture of accountability ultimately makes relationships of responsibility impossible" (2004: 250). He suggests that individuals' sense of professional responsibility is eroded by the damaging practices of technical–managerial accountability. Reclaiming the professional–democratic focus and function of accountability, as Biesta proposes, would enable accountability to serve more effectively and justly as a mechanism for improving teachers' professional sense of responsibility and the quality of their professional relationships with their colleagues and managers. This is the first step towards positively peaceful schools.

Conclusion

To summarise, we have argued here that the main way in which discourse around school improvement functions as a form of violence is that it establishes priorities, which then exert pressure on the actors within the school system to behave in ways that are to the detriment of their own and each other's optimum state. This top-down pressure is an example of what Galtung referred to as cultural violence. To counteract this, it is important to propose alternative conceptualisations and practices of school improvement that would contribute to positive peace. It is to this proposal that the remainder of this book now turns.

Note

1 See the then UK new Labour government's dismissal of the findings of the *Cambridge Primary Review* (2009) for a stark example of political selection of educational research evidence: www.cprtrust.org.uk/wp-content/uploads/2014/06/Simon_lecture_in_FORUM_53_1_web.pdf and www.theguardian.com/education/2009/oct/16/cambridge-primary-review-government-reaction.

References

Apple, M. (2005). Schooling, markets, race and an audit culture. In D. Carlson and C. Gause (Eds), *Keeping the Promise: essays on leadership, democracy and education*, 27–44. New York: Peter Lang Publishing.

ASCL. (2010). *Assessing Assessment: politics or progress?* High Wycombe: ASCL.

ATL. (2007). *New Accountability for Schools*. London: ATL.

Ball, S. (2013). *Global Education Inc: new policy networks and the neoliberal imaginary*. London: Routledge.

Bauman, Z. (2000). *Liquid Modernity*. Cambridge: Polity.

Biesta, G. (2004). Education, accountability and the ethical demand: can the democratic potential of accountability be regained? *Educational Theory*, 54(3), 233–250.

Biesta, G. (2007). Why 'what works' won't work: evidence-based practice and the democratic deficit of educational research. *Educational Theory*, 57(1), 1–22.

Biesta, G. (2010). Why 'what works' still won't work: from evidence-based education to value-based education. *Studies in Philosophy and Education*, 29(5), 491–503.

Clarke, J. and Baxter, J. (2014). Satisfactory progress? Keywords in English school inspection. *Education Inquiry*, 5(4), 481–496.

Clarke, J. and Newman, J. (1997). *The Managerial State: power, politics and ideology in the remaking of social welfare*. London: Sage.

Courtney, S. (2012). *Ofsted's Revised Inspection Framework: experiences and implications*. Paper presented at BERA Conference, Manchester. [online] Retrieved 16 September 2016 from www.leeds.ac.uk/educol/documents/216133.pdf

Department for Education (DfE). (2015). *Government Response to the Workload Challenge*. [online] Retrieved 16 September 2016 from www.gov.uk/government/uploads/system/uploads/attachment_data/file/415874/Government_Response_to_the_Workload_Challenge.pdf

Foliano, F., Meschi, E. and Vignoles, A. (2010). *Why Do Children Become Disengaged from School?* [online] Retrieved 15 September 2016 from www.repec.ioe.ac.uk/REPEc/pdf/qsswp1006.pdf

Foucault, M. (1991). *Discipline and Punish: the birth of a prison*. London: Penguin.

Francis, B. and Mills, M. (2012). Schools as damaging organisations: instigating a dialogue concerning alternative models of schooling. *Pedagogy, Culture and Society*, 20(2), 251–271.

Goldstein, H. and Woodhouse, G. (2000). School effectiveness research and educational policy. *Oxford Review of Education*, 26(3/4), 353–363.

Hall, S. (1997). Representation, meaning, and language. In S. Hall (Ed.), *Representation: cultural representations and signifying practices*, 15–30. Thousand Oaks, CA: Sage.

Hamilton, D. (1996). Peddling feel-good fictions. *Forum*, 38, 54–56.

Hammersley, M. (2013). *The Myth of Research-Based Policy and Practice*. London: Sage.

IDS. (2009). *Transforming Children's Lives Through Innovation in Quality Education: implications for policy and practice*. IDS practice paper 4. [online] Retrieved 12 September 2016 from www.ids.ac.uk/files/dmfile/pp4.pdf

MacGilchrist, B. (2003). *Has School Improvement Passed Its Sell-by Date?* Inaugural lecture. London: Institute of Education.

NASUWT. (2012). *Ofsted Inspection: the experiences of teachers and school leaders*. [online] Retrieved 16 September 2016 from www.nasuwt.org.uk/consum/groups/public/@press/documents/nas_download/nasuwt_009171.pdf

NUT. (2015). *The Impact of Accountability Measures on Children and Young People*. [online] Retrieved 16 September 2016 from www.teachers.org.uk/sites/default/files2014/exam-factories_0.pdf

Policy Exchange. (2014). *Watching the Watchmen: the future of school inspections in England*. London: Heron, Dawson and Sawyer.

Pring, R. (2013). *The Life and Death of Secondary Education for All*. New York: Routledge.

Reynolds, D. (1997). School effectiveness retrospect and prospect. *Scottish Educational Review*, 29(2), 97–113.

Sahlberg, P. (2010). Rethinking accountability for a knowledge society. *Journal of Educational Change*, 11(1), 45–61.

Sahlberg, P. (2014). A conversation on lessons from Finland with John Graham. *Professional Voice*, 10(1), 46–53. [online] Retrieved 20 September 2016 from www.aeuvic.asn.au/pv_10_1_complete_web.pdf

Scottish Executive. (2006). *A Curriculum for Excellence: progress and proposals*. Edinburgh: Scottish Executive.

Secondary Heads Association. (2003). *Towards Intelligent Accountability for Schools, Policy Paper 5*. Leicester: Secondary Heads Association.

Stamou, E., Edwards, A., Daniels, H. and Ferguson. L. (2014). *Young People at Risk of Drop-Out from Education: recognising and responding to their needs*. Oxford: Department of Education, University of Oxford.

Part II

Peace in schools

Introduction

The first part of the book reviewed direct, structural and cultural violence in schools, including the violence that is inherent in systems of schooling and in discourses of school improvement. We now move to the opposite of violence – peace. We retain notions of direct and indirect violence in this discussion, but now point towards Galtung's positive peace, which provides a framework for our work and for our iPEACE model. So, to recall, positive peace describes a state or condition absent of both direct and indirect violence, and where there are present harmony and social justice.

This second part of the book provides an overview of peace education and suggests why we believe it holds much promise for responding to the issues that we have identified here. It will become clear from our review of the field in this part of the book that we feel that proactive peace-building has become even more important over time, but that there is less and less agreement about what this should look like. This presents challenges for the field. The certainties of modernity are now largely in the past, and both war and peace look very different in postmodern times.

We present our case here that peace education in modern times was about the drive to avoid war and promote global justice and international understanding. The field grew and experienced a certain degree of success, but it was held back, in our view, by its ties with modernity. An over-reliance on science, rationality and reason limited its ability to respond to complexity, and it has been overly concerned with binaries and linear thinking. It has largely ignored ways of thinking and knowing that emanate from the global East and South. The liberal peace agenda, promoted by international actors working for global security and economic growth, has had undue influence on the field, thus limiting its ability to embrace different traditions of global peace.

We go on to argue that peace education in postmodern times needs to respond to growing complexity and globalisation. It needs to recognise that 'how' matters more than 'what', and that the quality of the learning relationship is key. Peace education needs to involve active, participatory and relevant learning facilitated by committed and inspirational educators. It also needs to respond in more sophisticated ways to complexity and globalisation. Models for peace education need to allow for the multiple realities that make up the everyday life of schools, and the need to embrace paradox and contingency. We do not shy away from this, arguing that practical solutions to real problems need to be found in the here and now, despite the risks of complicity with structural and cultural violence.

We turn to these challenges in this part of the book, and offer our framework of positive peace and our iPEACE model as a possible response. Chapter 4 provides a theoretical and historical overview of the case that we make here, while Chapter 5 is more geared towards policy and practice. In Chapter 5, we set out our iPEACE model and our framework for positive peace. Part III of the book presents more detail about the peace-keeping, -making and -building activities and frameworks that we propose, while Part IV grounds itself in the classroom and in research and evaluation.

The next chapter begins with a definition of peace education.

Chapter 4

Peace education

Introduction

One of the prime purposes of this book is to translate thinking and theory from peace and conflict studies into the school context. This chapter therefore draws directly on writing from peace studies, as well as other fields, in order to review theoretical perspectives and evidence that support the development of positive peace in schools. We provide an overview here of peace education, including historical perspectives following the Second World War. We provide a definition and a typology, before discussing some of the ways in which a changing landscape of peace and violence globally has impacted on peace education, and the ways in which it is viewed. But first, it is necessary to define what is meant by peace education.

Purpose of this book [handwritten annotation]

Defining peace education

Many definitions of **peace education** assume a context of global conflict. Fountain, for example, defined peace education for UNICEF:

> Peace education in UNICEF refers to the process of promoting the knowledge, skills, attitudes and values needed to bring about behaviour changes that will enable children, youth and adults to prevent conflict and violence, both overt and structural; to resolve conflict peacefully; and to create the conditions conducive to peace, whether at an intrapersonal, interpersonal, intergroup, national or international level.
>
> (UNICEF, 1999: 1)

This is a useful and comprehensive definition that applies beyond its original context of post-war settings.

Peace education has been defined by Betty Reardon (2000: 401) as

> planned and guided learning that attempts to comprehend and reduce the multiple forms of violence (physical, structural, institutional and cultural) used as instruments for the advancement or maintenance of cultural, social or religious beliefs and practices or of political, economic or ideological institutions or practices.

The primary focus of peace education for Reardon, therefore, is the reduction of violence.

It is interesting to note that most definitions of peace education (and peace for that matter) mention conflict and violence. Indeed, following Galtung, we ourselves began this book with a discussion of violence. As an exercise, we often ask our students to define peace at the start of our lectures on peace education and we find that the majority of them are unable to do so without referring to conflict. The exception often comes from students from Africa and South East Asia who do not have a history of Pax Romana – peace as cessation of hostilities. For them, peace is about balance, harmony and inner processes of connection with nature, humanity and creation. We will return to this later, but in the meantime it is sufficient to note that most definitions of peace education in the West concern the reduction of destructive conflict and violence and the promotion of constructive conflict resolution, social justice and educational inclusion (however conceived). Work in schools to promote inner peace is usually carried out under the banner of wellbeing, and not peace education.

Ian Harris (2009: 11) grounds his definition of peace education in the processes that are involved when communities (within and beyond formal education) work together towards peace:

> Peace education is the process of teaching people about the threats of violence and strategies for peace. Peace educators strive to provide insights into how to transform a culture of violence into a peaceful culture. They have to build consensus about what peace strategies can bring maximum benefit to the group.
>
> (Harris, 2009: 11)

It is this process-oriented definition of peace education that we find most useful.

A typology of peace education

Having provided definitions of peace education, we now go on to review the different aspects of peace education and the thinkers and philosophers who have influenced it. This is a complex process. Given the global, cultural and political nature of peace education and its orientation towards justice and freedom, it is not hard to see why it is multi-faceted and contested. Several commentators have attempted to create a typology of peace education (and related concepts of peace and conflict) in an attempt to synthesise some of these debates and to create conceptual and thematic clarity. Table 4.1 draws on some key commentators in order to present the ideas that seem to come up time and again. It is interesting to note that, although these commentators have gone about this in different ways, referring variously to curriculum, approaches, types, ethical traditions, contexts and families of peace, they all converge around core themes of justice and equality, conflict resolution, global citizenship, affect and care, spirituality and aesthetics and postmodern peace education.

The most common themes in the field of peace education are the first three: justice and equality; conflict resolution; and global citizenship and human rights. These have traditionally made up the bulk of the content of peace education in the last century and have been core to its development. The final three – affect and care; spirituality and aesthetics; and postmodern peace education – have emerged more recently, and less has therefore been written about them. This book has been written partly as a response to that gap.

Page's five ethical traditions that underpin peace education in Table 4.1 (virtue ethics; consequentialist ethics; conservative political ethics; ethics of care; and aesthetic ethics) are particularly pertinent to the definition and framing of peace education and are thus worth briefly expounding here. They, and the philosophers they draw upon, overlap. Together they provide an integrated view of the philosophical roots of peace education.

Table 4.1 Typologies of peace education

	Harris and Morrison, 2003 (Curriculum)	Galtung, 1969 (Approaches)	Cremin, 2010 (Types)	Page, 2008 (Ethical traditions)	Salomon and Cairns, 2009 (Contexts)	Dietrich, 2012 (Families of peace)
Justice and equality	Peace, social justice and environmental awareness	Peace-building	Violence reduction in schools	Virtue ethics	Intergroup conflict (not interpersonal)	Moral peace (justice)
Conflict resolution	Peace as a process of non-violent conflict management	Peace-making	Conflict resolution	Consequentialist ethics	Interpersonal and psychological (not political)	
Global citizenship and human rights	Human rights, development, war, security and international understanding	Peace-building	Post-conflict and human rights education	Conservative ethics	Ethno-political conflict, relating to a threatening adversary	Modern peace (security)
Affect and care	Respect for life and addressing fears	Peace-building		Ethics of care		
Spirituality and aesthetics	Appreciation of the concept of peace and a 'futures' orientation			Aesthetic ethics	Relative tranquillity	Energetic (dynamic) peace, trans-rational peace
Postmodern peace education		Peace-building	Transformative peace education			Postmodern peace (truth)

Virtue ethics are grounded in the work of religious figures and philosophers such as St Augustine, Aristotle, Thomas Aquinas, Hume and Kant. Page points out that there are weaknesses in linking virtue ethics with peace (as they can also be used to support violence) but that virtue ethics reinforce the importance of personal integrity and autonomy. In a world of direct, structural and cultural violence, virtue ethics are linked with practice. They help to create settled dispositions of peace, resilience and commitment to justice. Dietrich refers to this as moral peace.

Consequentialism suggests that ethics should be concerned with the consequences of actions and can be seen in the work of Hume, Jeremy Bentham, John Stewart Mill, Marx, Freire, Gandhi and R. S. Peters. An important idea for peace is that non-violence ought to be adopted, due to its utility. As Page (2008) points out, if we want to avoid the disastrous and painful consequences of violence and injustice in the future, we need to educate for peace today.

Conservative ethics suggest that peace can be brought about through gradual change; revolutions risk undoing the social fabric upon which peace relies. Conservative political philosophers include Hobbes, Hume, Hegel and, more latterly, Oakeshott and Scruton. Dietrich's modern peace is related to this, despite the apparent paradox, as both modern and conservative perspectives are grounded in faith in science and reason and in the ability of humans to use their knowledge and ingenuity to work towards peace. Education is seen as integral to this process.

Ethics of care hold that truth cannot be objectified, only experienced in relationship. They therefore contain elements of existentialism (e.g. Heidegger and Kierkegaard). Historic philosophers in this tradition include Augustine, Aquinas, Levinas, Buber and Ricoeur. More recently, Carol Gilligan (1993) and Nel Noddings (2003) provide a much-needed feminised perspective. They suggest that trust and caring are the natural order of things, especially for women, and that the inclination towards war has to be actively developed through propaganda and social and political structures that tend to favour men. Nodding's commitment to caring is very similar to Gandhi's *ahimsa* or non-violence.

Aesthetic ethics historically draw on the work of philosophers such as Plato, Augustine, Aquinas, Hume and Adam Smith, and on religious writings from Hebrew, Islamic and Buddhist traditions. They are concerned with beauty, harmony and holism and have been on the resurgence in recent times, perhaps because of increased planetary awareness and the images of 'Gaia' that were sent back to Earth from space (Page, 2008; Midgeley, 2004). Dietrich (2012) refers to this as 'energetic' peace (which we translate as dynamic peace), meaning peace that is grounded in the notion of energy flow, such as is found in Tao and Tantra, and in pre-modern religions in the West that worshipped the great Goddess. This way of conceptualising peace currently survives mainly in the global East and South, but its influence is found throughout the modern world, including in practices of meditation, prayer, music, shamanism, martial arts and mindfulness. Many peace workers and peace educators engage in these practices in their personal or spiritual lives but do not feel able to integrate them into their professional lives. This is despite the fact that spiritual and esoteric experiences are often the motivation for their work. Page (2008) sums up with a powerful case for grounding peace education in aesthetic ethics:

In summary, I argue that all of education is undergirded by aesthetic judgements or judgements as to what is beautiful or desirable. If we believe that peace, that is, harmonious and co-operative relations between individuals and societies, is a beautiful thing, a valuable thing in itself, then we should not be reticent in encouraging this as a stated objective for education.

(Page, 2008: 158)

We find value in all of these traditions of peace ethics, but it is this last that we find most inspiring. It seems strange to us that anyone should contest that peace is a beautiful and desirable thing or dispute that it should make up the core of any educational enterprise. We recognise, however, that this view is not universally shared, and that peace education needs to shake off the negative associations it has attracted. To do this, we argue, it is necessary to update it as a concept. Peace education in postmodern times needs to allow for diversity in the ways in which it is understood and enacted, alongside unity in its core aims and values. For us, this involves a deep engagement with aesthetic peace.

their new aesthetic peace

Peace education in modern and postmodern times

Having provided definitions and a typology of peace education, we now end this chapter with a historical perspective. One of the key arguments in this book is that peace education has been hampered by its association with modernist discourse: both discourse surrounding peace and discourse surrounding education. We argue here that, just as war is changing in the twenty-first century, so is peace, and that peace education needs to evolve to fit with postmodern times.

Wars now are just as likely to be waged on abstract issues such as terror or radicalisation, and within-state conflict is just as likely as between-state conflict (Pinker, 2011). The most likely victims of violence are no longer those involved directly in the conflict, but those who suffer its effects indirectly. Issues of forced migration, terrorism, drones and civilian 'collateral damage' continue to exercise the international community, while new state and corporate systems of violence seek to assert control and externalise risk and harm (Wiist *et al.*, 2014). All of this requires new ways of thinking about peace, and new ways of thinking about security, international relations and reconciliation.

Thus, the peace education that arose in response to the Second World War is no longer fit for purpose in postmodern times. Changing ideas of time, place, identity and epistemology are unsettling the hegemony of US-driven global politics. It will be clear by now that the authors wish to locate peace-work in an aesthetic tradition and in the creativity and spontaneity of the arts and the natural world, but, first, it is necessary to provide a brief insight into the early days of peace education, when its aims and values were much less contested.

Peace education after the Second World War

Peace education began in earnest after the Second World War. A visionary document from that time merits particular attention (despite occasional dated language and concepts). It is called *The Teacher and World Peace: a preliminary survey of the fundamentals*, and was written by the New Educational Fellowship (NEF) for UNESCO in 1948. It was drawn up in response to a request from UNESCO (in its early days of inception) to provide techniques for schools to challenge parochial attitudes and reduce tensions between nations. One of its authors, Alex Bloom, was headteacher at St George-in-the-East secondary school in London between 1945 and 1955. He ran his school on the principles of radical democratic education and was deeply committed to peace education after his experiences during the First World War. Michael Fielding has written extensively about his work (e.g. Fielding, 2014) and we are grateful to him for introducing us to it.

What is striking about this document and much of the early peace education work is that it was surprisingly radical and optimistic. It was clearly grounded in proactive peace-building, and not just in peace-keeping or peace-making. There was evidently a hope at the time that education, science and reason would result in more enlightened attitudes towards international relations, and that a body of knowledge would gradually be built up that was adequate to the needs of the modern world. The authors drew on child and human development theory to argue that, just as a child must let go of immature ways of acting and being, the world must let go of international tension and war. Education is seen as an important means of achieving this. War is presented as the problem, and "education has an essential contribution to make to its solution" (NEF, 1948: 1).

A clear belief in the power of education is evident throughout. The core argument is that, if schools are to prepare young people with the skills, values and knowledge needed for adult life, this should be done in ways that promote peace, rather than its opposite. Thus, traditional competitive and academic styles of learning should not be used as they risk alienating the child and creating personality traits that are not desirable for later life (or for world peace). In their place, the authors call for: teachers who are self-aware; learning that is experiential, relevant, cooperative and creative; schools that are democratic; and discipline that is based on self-discipline rather than imposed from above.

This kind of education (reminiscent of Dewey's 1916 work *Democracy and Education*) is holistic, and grounded in affect and creativity:

> It is the total personality that matters. No amount of information, no wealth of gadgets or equipment, can compensate for poverty or disintegration or a festering sore within the personality. We educationalists do wrong if we regard as frills on the timetable the activities which foster emotional, social, aesthetic and religious experience, which cultivate the imagination and the aptitude for creation and appreciation. They should rather be regarded as foundation, for they go deeper and have more lasting effect than what we offer on the intellectual plane.
>
> (NEF, 1948: 7)

The arts, creativity and 'aesthetic and religious experience' are thus seen as fundamental to teaching and learning. The beliefs, values and interpersonal skills of the teacher are central to these processes. This could not be more different than contemporary discourses of school improvement and the role of the teacher, reviewed in the first part of this book. According to Bloom and his co-authors, not everyone can, or should, enter the profession of teaching. Care needs to be taken in selecting future teachers, and those who are already in the profession (especially people who might be suffering psychologically because of their experiences of war) "should increase their awareness of their own motives, through group analysis and other techniques" (NEF, 1948: 2). They go further to say that "What the teacher *is* matters more than anything else in bringing about desirable attitude development on the part of the child" (1948: 12). We find this truly radical, despite some of the rather conservative assumptions elsewhere in the document. It is a theme that we take up in our own work, almost 70 years later. Notions of affect, relationship, identity, spirituality, creativity and authenticity have re-emerged for us as central to peace education, although for us, with the hindsight of intervening years, modernist discourses of science, rationality and reason are part of the problem, and not part of the solution.

For the moment, however, it is important to recognise that peace education at this early stage was about peace-building through engagement with structural and cultural violence in systems of schooling. It was holistic and oriented towards everyday relationships in the here and now, not on performance targets, abstract knowledge, skills training or bolt-on projects. It was, above all, a response to the urgent need to ensure that there would never be a third world war.

Paulo Freire

Thus, from its early inception, peace education has been about peace-building – preventing war and promoting justice and global citizenship. Perhaps the most notable educator for justice of the twentieth century was Paulo Freire (1921–1997). Freire's influence on peace education (as well as critical literacy, and non-formal education) has been immense. For the purposes of this chapter, we will primarily refer here to his 1973 book *Education for Critical Consciousness*, which builds on his earlier and most famous book *Pedagogy of the Oppressed* (1970).

Freire's philosophy of education has much in common with Alex Bloom (although Freire's particular emphasis is on oppressed adult learners). It too is concerned with peace-building through the removal of structural injustice and cultures of oppression. It too is radical: it replaces schools with 'culture circles'; teachers with co-ordinators; and 'I do' with 'I wonder' (Freire, 1973). Projects inspired by this philosophy are not based on any set curriculum. Each new group creates the topics and themes for discussion out of their own contexts and desire for cultural participation. The starting point for Freire was that all people, including those who cannot read, are already literate in the symbols, themes and ideas of their cultures. Reading is a technical process that follows from being conscious of this. Learning to read enables the oppressed to engage with the ideas and practices of those who would oppress them, and thus to liberate themselves.

Both Freire and Bloom see education as supremely relational and grounded in spirituality, creativity, love and reflexivity. For Freire, educators need to be in dialogue with learners in such a way that they also continue to learn – the humbler they are, the more they will learn. Educators need to problematise the realities they seek to communicate. Those who do not engage with learners in this way are guilty of empty formalism, repeating texts (doxa) without knowing them and transmitting the harmful myths of oppressors. Freire sees the traditional curriculum as disconnected from life: lacking in concrete activity and incapable of developing critical consciousness. Its words and concepts are "emptied of the reality they are meant to represent", with the result that "its own naïve dependence on high-sounding phrases, reliance on rote, and tendency towards abstractness actually intensifies our naïveté" (1973: 37). These words resonate uncomfortably with some of the discussion of structural and cultural violence in schools reviewed in the first part of this book.

To follow Freire is to be a particular kind of educator. As with Bloom, values and justice-oriented ways of being in the world are more important than subject knowledge to be a successful teacher. Preparing teachers in a technical sense is not hard: "the difficulty lies rather in the creation of a new attitude – that of dialogue, so absent in our own upbringing and education" (1973: 52). The coordinators (teachers) need to use dialogue "in order to carry out education rather than domestication". Using language that is similar to Buber (1928), Freire talks of dialogue as "an I–Thou relationship", between two subjects. "Each time the 'thou' is changed into an object, an 'it', dialogue is subverted and education is changed to deformation" (1973: 52). The Freirian educator is able to maintain I–Thou relationships, and avoids turning the learner into an object to be filled with de-contextualised knowledge (the banking education model promoted through contemporary regimes such as PISA).

Just as Alex Bloom built his school around radical democratic education, Freire built his work around supporting people to be radical (but not sectarian). The radical takes up a stance that is

> [p]redominantly critical, loving, humble, and communicative, and is therefore a positive stance. The [person] who has made a radical option does not deny another [person's] right to choose, nor does [s/he] try to impose [his/her] own choice . . . . The radical does, however, have the duty, imposed by love itself, to react against the violence of those who try to silence [her/him] – or those who, in the name of freedom, kill [his/her] freedom and their own.
>
> (Freire, 1973: 10)

Thus, peace for Freire is of a particular kind. It is not passive or lacking in conflict; it is grounded in struggle and in solidarity with oppressed groups. Commitment to peace comes from a spiritual, humanistic and ethical stance, and education is "an act of love, and thus an act of courage" (1973: 38). There is no end-state; process is everything. In this, Bloom and Freire perhaps part company. Freire expressly rejects what he refers to as the 'technical aid' conception of education. Thus, he leans towards postmodernity.

In contrast, Bloom is powerfully grounded in discourses of modernity, science and psychology and has a clear end goal in mind. War-loving attitudes are seen as an ailment: "a festering sore within the personality" (1948: 7) that the approaches advocated can cure. While recognising that the home environment has a role, the authors claim that teachers lay the foundations of young people's personalities and that their work can "secure happiness and fulfilment in childhood" (1948: 3) that will bring long-term psychological benefits. There is a faith in educational processes here that has since fallen out of favour. The aspirations for peace education remain, but theorists such as Bronfenbrenner (2005) Vygotsky (1980) and Bourdieu and Passeron (1977) have shown that eco-systemic and structural factors introduce a good deal of complexity into processes of development, learning and social justice. Peace education in the intervening years has become more cautious in its claims and methods.

Freire was quite visionary and postmodern in this respect. He is dismissive of medical language when it is applied to social or educational settings. Indeed, he sees this use of language as a tool of oppression. He criticises the ways in which the elite describe people who wish to liberate themselves as 'unwell' and requiring 'medicine' – "whereas in fact their 'ailment' is the wish to speak up and participate" (1973: 14). He also sees scientific neutrality as a form of oppression: "those who talk of neutrality are precisely those who are afraid of losing their right to use neutrality to their own advantage" (1973: 147). Again, discussion in Part I of this book about the cultural violence inherent in the political use of school improvement discourse resonates powerfully here.

Critical peace education in postmodern times

Freire's view of peace education as radical and critical has been foundational to the field. It has inspired a whole raft of work in this genre (e.g. Hicks, 1988; Reardon and Cabezudo, 2002; Diaz-Soto, 2005; Toh and Cawagas, 2010; Bajaj and Brantmeier, 2011; Duckworth, 2011; Jenkins, 2013; Bajaj, 2015; Bajaj and Hantzopoulos, 2016). Indeed, there have been increasing calls over the past decade for peace educators to become more critical. Bajaj (2015), for example, argues for stronger integration between theory and practice, with critical peace educators drawing on 'pedagogies of resistance', and working directly with social movements and community organisations who are addressing social and economic hierarchies in highly unequal contexts. She feels that university-level peace education teacher training programmes that offer courses in the global 'North' have much to learn from the context-specific praxis in the global 'South'.

Thus, it becomes evident that, for critical peace education in postmodern times, the 'who' is as important as the 'what' (if not more so). The primary target group is learners on the margins. The 'how' of critical peace education is also vital. It needs to be grounded in praxis and in education that is accessible, engaging and democratic. It should not be purely academic and it should link with larger social movements that work for equity and social justice.

This creates challenges for peace education in schools and universities in postmodern times. Bajaj would like university-level critical peace education to "counter the sometimes-decontextualized learning and preparation of assignments in peace education courses, and connect learning with actual programs and social conditions" (2015: 160). She proposes a set of core competencies for critical peace education students in higher education, while warning that their tutors should resist "regulation, universalization, and the development of rigid norms and standards for what peace education ought to be" (2015: 156). There is a tension here that is felt throughout the field. As Reardon and Snauwaert ask, how can peace education within the modern university avoid taking on the values of corporate culture and global markets, where

> [k]nowledge has become a commodity, the currency of success in the market; critical analysis is an exercise in perfecting technique for increasing material value; and wisdom is relegated to history and philosophy, realms that do not enjoy high-value in a market-centred academy?
>
> (Reardon and Snauwaert, 2015: 168)

It is no doubt the case that, while the early critical peace educators remained close to those who were living and working directly with 'the oppressed', peace educators that come after do not necessarily draw on the same sense of vocation, identity or religious values. Critical peace education is supposed to benefit socially and politically excluded groups, but all too often the main beneficiaries are elite students, researchers and academics (Cremin, 2015).

It is our argument here that, if university-level peace education is compromised by an exam-driven curriculum, standardised core competencies and de-contextualised learning, this is all the more so for schools. This raises a number of questions: can peace education only take place in schools that enable oppressed groups to set their own agenda for peace, freedom and democratic participation? Do young people in schools, constrained by structurally and culturally violent systems of schooling, automatically count as 'oppressed'? If so, how do peace educators work with them in ways that do not reproduce violent relations? These are tricky to answer, and in some ways it depends on whether an idealist or a pragmatist stance is adopted. We argue here that it *is* possible to do valuable peace education work with young people in schools, and that the answer lies in occupying the space between idealism and realism. Indeed, the purpose of this book is to provide both a philosophical and a practical basis for doing so. It is important, however, to avoid treating peace education as a kind of humanities curriculum that can be taught as an academic enterprise, empty of real world engagement, and yet capable of transforming social relations. This is to promote peace-building as a sham, and devalues the deep potential of positive peace education.

The UN, global citizenship and human rights

As already discussed, the early roots of peace education were to reduce tension between nations after two world wars through peace-building, and this drive for international understanding, global citizenship and universal human rights has continued to this day. This is despite the fact that some of the certainties of modern times have given way to the complexity of postmodernity.

Over the past seven decades, global institutions such as the UN, UNESCO and the World Bank have played a role and have issued a variety of international frameworks and documents about peace education. Among these (and in addition to the Charter of the United Nations, and the Universal Declaration of Human Rights), two documents stand out. These are: *Recommendation Concerning Education for International Understanding, Cooperation and Peace and Education Relating to Human Rights and Fundamental Freedoms* (UNESCO, 1974); and the *Declaration and Integrated Framework of Action on Education for Peace, Human Rights and Democracy* (UNESCO, 1995). The 1974 recommendations state that education at all levels should include global perspectives and that young people should be taught that they have responsibilities towards people in other nations, as well as rights. Education for peace should teach communication skills and the values and attitudes that make it more likely that young people will engage in problem-solving at local, national and international scales. The 1995 guidelines go further, to suggest that all teaching should take an international approach and that young people should learn about forms of conflict, their causes and effects; human rights and international standards; democracy and civic participation; development, de-colonisation and globalisation; and the UN and international institutions.

Significantly, these two documents span the end of the Cold War, and the differences between them reflect some of the global changes that took place at this time. The collapse of Soviet communism brought about an increased confidence in Western liberal capitalism; improved communication, travel, and information technology opened up global markets. During the Cold War, peace education was focused on the threat posed by nuclear proliferation but, after the Cold War, it was more concerned with democracy and human rights.

Later, the UN responded to the end of the Cold War with a fresh drive for preventive diplomacy, peace-making and post-conflict peace-building. Writing a UN report in 1992, at the start of his term as Secretary-General of the United Nations, Boutros Boutros-Ghali could detect "an increasingly common moral perception that spans the world's nations and peoples" (1992: 15). He felt that this was finding expression in international laws, universal human rights and an expansion of Western-style democracy, justice and prosperity. Education was seen as an important part of this.

All was not as it seemed, however. Like Bloom in 1948, Boutros-Ghali in 1992 used modernist language that implies universal and technical solutions to complex global problems.

He spoke of the UN's obligation to provide "technical assistance" for the transformation of "deficient national structures and capabilities", as well as new democratic institutions. Consensus was seen to underlie the work of the UN at every level, from the local to the global (despite the complicity of the West in global inequalities). Scaling-up, it appeared, was just a matter of time, provided that everyone came to the table, and was willing to be democratic and prosperous:

> The authority of the United Nations system to act in this field would rest on the consensus that social peace is as important as strategic or political peace. There is an obvious connection between democratic practices – such as the rule of law and transparency in decision-making – and the achievement of true peace and security in any new and stable political order. These elements of good governance need to be promoted at all levels of international and national political communities.
>
> (Boutros-Ghali, 1992: 59)

The UNESCO guidelines for peace education, human rights and democracy make sense in the light of these sentiments. If there is global consensus about a universal moral order, then education in every country of the world needs to reflect this consensus. Thereby world peace is brought that much closer.

There are of course problems with this. Not everyone in the world has such faith in global markets and in Western-style liberal democracy, as the events of the twenty-first century have demonstrated. The structural adjustment policies of the World Bank and the International Monetary Fund in the 1980s did not have the 'trickle down' economic effects that were hoped for, and there is no reason to believe that 'trickle-down justice' will be any more effective (Novelli et al., 2015). Many current intractable conflicts have their roots in the imposition of Western-style democracy on countries whose traditions and infrastructure do not support it. Peace education needs to reflect the contestation and complexity of postmodernity; it should not attempt to impose a hegemonic and homogenised view of global peace. To do so is structurally and culturally violent (Gur-Ze'ev, 2011).

It is interesting at this juncture to go back to the question of the 'how' of peace education. It is notable that (unlike critical peace education) international guidelines for peace education tend to be made up of descriptions of the 'what' rather than the 'how'. The 'what' of peace education through global citizenship and human rights covers such themes as: universal human dignity and universal moral inclusion; democratic deliberation and social transformation; understanding the root causes of war; international humanitarian and human rights law and institutions; and disarmament and human security. It is not, however, always the case that this content is taught in ways that support the core messages. An anecdote from our own experience is the perfect illustration of this. One of the authors was involved in an initial teacher education programme with citizenship trainees a few years ago. As part of her role, she found herself one day observing a lesson on children's rights. The trainee was clearly anxious, and had set the class a task that held the minimum potential for disruption – copying in silence from the board. After several minutes, one of the students who was clearly in discomfort put up her hand and asked if she could leave the room to go to the toilet. The trainee answered that she could not, and that she should return to her work copying out her rights as a child. This is a classic case of the 'what' of peace education being in conflict with the 'how'.

Thus, when peace education is grounded in curriculum and practice that is de-contextualised, hegemonic and lacking in reflexivity, the result is education *about* peace rather than education *through* peace. It repeats the mistakes of modernity, applying pseudo-science and false rationality to processes that are deeply embedded within the affective and contextualised aspects of life (Noddings, 2011). It also risks reproducing structural and cultural violence and diminishing processes of peace-building.

The history of peace education in the second half of the twentieth century, then, has been about the drive to avoid war, promote global justice and international understanding and engage with peace-building through education. The field has grown and has experienced a certain degree of success. We have argued here, however, that it has been held back by its ties with modernity. An over-reliance on science, rationality and reason has limited its ability to respond to complexity. It has been overly concerned with binaries, linear thinking and Enlightenment principles and has thus lost touch with ways of thinking and knowing that emanate from the global East and South. While peace education places recognition of the 'Other' at the heart of its work, this all too often involves integration into Western norms. The liberal peace agenda, promoted by international actors working for global security and economic growth, has had undue influence on the field, thus limiting its ability to embrace diverse traditions of peace.

Two key ideas emerge from the history of peace education in the last century. The first is that the 'how' matters more than the 'what'; pedagogy is important and so is the quality of the learning relationship. Peace education needs to involve active, participatory and relevant learning, facilitated by committed and inspirational educators. The second is that peace education needs to embrace the conditions of postmodernity.

Peace education in times of postmodernity

While modernity and postmodernity coexist in time, it is nevertheless the case that the twenty-first century marks an acceleration in the conditions of postmodernity. We argue here that postmodernity increasingly provides a useful way of thinking about peace education (and indeed education as a whole). Many peace educators are influenced by the modernist and functionalist assumptions of the institutions in which they work; they do their best in environments that are patently not supportive of positive peace. Current systems of education operating in most parts of the world are heavily influenced by discourses of marketised school improvement as discussed in Part I of this book. This does not bode well for the transformation of schools, despite (or because of) constant calls for reform. The field of peace education might do well to respond to Gur-Ze'ev's (2011) call for a response to poststructural (postmodern) critiques. We do not expect a paradigm shift within education, or even peace education, any time soon.

Postmodernism implies massive changes for education, but schools have been remarkably resilient to change so far, and it is hard to embed positive peace education into modern systems of schooling. Although postmodernism is associated with a shift from modern methods of production (sometimes called Fordism because of the mass production techniques used by the Ford motor company) to more consumer-led, dynamic and flexible methods, education has not made this shift and remains stuck in the industrial age. As Richard Pring points out, in the UK, despite decades of universal secondary education and innovation in school buildings, "we still retain the Victorian idea of formal education taking place within a single establishment which therefore should provide the resources, facilities and teaching expertise across the curriculum and across the range of learners" (2013: 166). This might perhaps have been appropriate for educating people to work in factories, offices (before the advent of information technology) and the army, but it is not a good model for developing the kinds of ethical and creative thinking that are necessary in the twenty-first century. With the decline of the industrial society, and the rise of the knowledge society, workplaces are now characterised by computers, information technology, design and global marketplaces, as well as transience, risk and insecurity. Gone are production lines and jobs for life, and in their place are home-working, processes of "responsibilisation" (Rose, 1996) and portfolio lifestyles. Schools are slow to catch up with this, with structurally and culturally violent consequences for young people and wider society.

Postmodernism has challenged modernist assumptions in the field of peace studies too (Dietrich, 2012). In the early days after the Second World War, peace research focused predominantly on international relations, international law and behaviourism, but between the late 1960s and 1980s many peace researchers took on postmodern perspectives. They were able to embrace "a rainbow of approaches, methods, and teachings that allow us to speak of something like a praxeology of postmodern peace research" (Dietrich, 2012: 183). Much of this research was inter-disciplinary in nature. In 1954 the Society for General Systems research was established at Stanford University by the biologist Ludwig von Bertalanffy, the mathematician and systems theorist Anatol Rapoport, the physiologist Ralph Gerard and the economist Kenneth Boulding. The guiding principles of this school were the general observation that 85 to 90 per cent of all social interactions are non-violent and that ecological systems provide a useful way of thinking about peace.

How should education systems respond to this, and what are the implications for peace education? In one sense, it could be argued that peace education offers a tantalising vision of postmodern education, grounded in relationships, interest, inquiry and peace-building. This is not just a good vision of peace education; it is a good vision of education as a whole. There is not the scope here to discuss what education might look like if schools were not the main modus operandi, but it is interesting to reflect on what might happen if education could take place within institutions that were not constrained by structural and cultural violence.

As we have argued, however, these kinds of radical changes are not likely to happen any time soon. It is therefore worth reflecting on how some of the theories and tools of postmodernism can be applied to peace education. One of the key tools of postmodernism is deconstruction. This involves making explicit the ways in which discourses of power operate in society. Postmodernists have long given up faith in progress but they feel that it is nonetheless important to deconstruct structurally and culturally violent discourses. Deconstruction is at least a first step towards peace-building. For example, we have gone some way towards deconstructing discourses of school improvement in the early part of this book. We feel that doing this could create the conditions for change. Many peace educators and advocates for social justice use deconstruction as a positive method, unveiling the oppressive and unjust ways that discourses favour the interests of power in societies. It will be recalled that Freire's notion of peace-building contained conflict, conscientisation and struggle at its heart. When false logic and cynical manipulation of information are challenged, then spaces for disruption, solidarity and resistance are created. This has always been at the heart of peace education.

Peace education itself is not inured, however, to processes of structural and cultural violence. These can even be reproduced in its name. Thinkers who have taken a postmodern/deconstructive stance, not only on power relations within education as a whole, but also on peace education, include Ilan Gur-Ze'ev, Claire McGlynn, Peter Trifonas, Brian Wright, Michalinos Zembylas, Zvi Beckerman and Ana Ferreira. McGlynn (2009) for example, reflects on peace education in 'post' conflict settings. She is particularly critical of perspectives that assume that people experiencing conflict are in need of some kind of psychological treatment. She highlights the inadequacies of education for peace, multiculturalism and human rights when it ignores the constraints of broader economic and social policies, and the complexities of dealing with conflict in different societies. She considers the limitations of contact theory as a framework for peace education grounded in psychology and proposes theoretical perspectives from the fields of sociology and political science. She is hopeful that certain pedagogical practices, such as critical emotional praxis and deliberative communication, might begin to reinforce the affective and relational elements of peace education, and that they might make more explicit the inequalities that sustain conflict and violence in 'post' conflict societies.

Bekerman and Zembylas point to romanticism and misrepresentation within peace education, and a lack of theorising which leads to "functionalist, psychologised and often idealised perspectives" (2012: 26). They suggest that advocates of peace education need to approach critically the epistemological and metaphysical certainties of western modernity and the global inequalities that sustain conflict, violence and injustice. Peace educators need to be aware of for whom they speak, and for whom they do not. They need to question how world peace can be brought about when so many people remain unrepresented, and when there is no global agreement about what it would look like.

Another aspect of postmodern thinking is complexity. In the field of peace studies, complexity allows the insight that the monolithic categories of 'oppressor' and 'oppressed' are not useful. In many ways, we are all both oppressor and oppressed to different degrees in different situations. For example, women may be oppressed by men (in most countries earning on average 60–75 per cent of men's wages, according to World Bank Statistics, accessed in September 2016 from www.data.worldbank.org) but poor women are oppressed by rich women who employ them to do the childcare and housework that poor women cannot afford to do in their home country. This has been referred to as "intersectionality" by various theorists (e.g. Brah and Phoenix, 2004) who argue that various factors of disadvantage intersect with each other, creating consequences that are greater than the sum of their parts for any one individual. It is no longer possible to sustain the view that particular and recognisable groups in society are at the root of all problems, and that the oppressed can or should rise up in revolution against them. Labelling particular groups as oppressed and fighting for their emancipation through critical theory runs the risk of reproducing a "counter-violence of the oppressed" that takes its legitimacy from past injustices (Gur-Ze'ev, 2011: 119). This recreates the flawed logic of broken modernist grand narratives. Interpersonal, local and global relations are much more complex and interrelated than this would imply.

Complexity teaches peace educators that there is no enemy out there to be conquered – even peacefully – the enemy is within as well as 'out there' and a certain degree of reflexivity and self-awareness are crucial to avoid dramatic over-simplification and hypocrisy. Schools that wish to embrace positive peace need to take account of this complexity, and of the need for inner as well as outer peace. They need to reject the false enterprise of modernist schooling and to dare to work with young people in open-ended, exploratory, diverse and networked ways.

We do not pretend that this is easy. Indeed, the crisis in the field of peace education is testimony to the fact that many struggle to find new ways of thinking that do not reproduce structural and cultural violence. We propose that part of an adequate response lies in balancing idealist and realist perspectives. In the past, these have been seen as in conflict with each other (Page, 2008), with some arguing that peace education cannot function in contexts where there is direct and indirect violence, and others arguing that peace education needs to operate within the conditions where it is located, even if these reproduce structural and cultural violence. We find Zembylas and Ferreira's (2009) notion of heterotopic spaces in education and peace education particularly useful here. Dominant relations in schools will no doubt persist for some time yet, but it is nevertheless important to create spaces where different ways of being and relating are enabled.

Heterotopia

Heterotopia is a concept developed by the poststructuralist/postmodern thinker Michel Foucault, and refers to transgressive spaces that exist within dominant power relations. We have been intrigued in our review of postmodern conceptions of peace education in the literature that 'utopia' is often mentioned and subverted in some way. It has variously been referred to as 'utopian realism', 'negative utopia' and 'heterotopia'. The word utopia literally means both everywhere and nowhere. It is a place that can never be pinned down. Sir Thomas More first used the word in 1516. It contains an intriguing pun on the Greek language. The Greek *ou-topos*, meaning 'no place' or 'nowhere', is almost identical to the Greek word *eu-topos*, meaning a 'good place'. So at the very heart of the word are a paradox and the vital question: can a perfect world ever be realised? The same question resounds throughout the field of peace studies.

Giddens (1994) refers to utopian realism, which he sees as endemic within late modern times. It hints at the tantalising possibility of bridging the idealist–realist divide that has so hampered the field to date (Page, 2008). Gur-Ze'ev (2001) also plays with the ambiguity of utopia and puts it to use through his concept of 'negative utopia'. Negative utopia goes beyond the idealised thinking that Gur-Ze'ev sees as worse than ineffective in the field of peace education. He contrasts negative with positive utopia, characterising the latter as involving "naïve universalistic essentialism" (2001: 333) and thus structural and cultural violence. In contrast, negative utopia leaves peace undefined. It contains the possibility of standing in solidarity with those who suffer oppression and injustice. Thus, negative utopia is a 'place' or a positionality, where someone might stand ready to address conflict and violence whenever it manifests itself. It does not involve imposing a particular view of peace on the 'Other'. Negative utopia is not the same as dystopia. Just as in mathematics, it is a double negative that becomes a positive.

Taking the concepts of utopian realism and negative utopia one stage further, Zembylas and Ferreira (2009) talk about heterotopic spaces in education and peace education. As Klaus (2014) points out, in 1986 Foucault described heterotopias as spaces that "have the curious property of being in relation with all the other sites, but in such a way as to suspect, neutralize, or invert the set of relations that they happen to designate, mirror, or reflect" (Foucault, 1986: 3). These spaces are sites of oppositional discourse, or counter-narrative, and are capable of juxtaposing in a single real space several realities that are incompatible with each other. Heterotopic spaces are bound by rules that give them a particular identity. They serve either to highlight the illusionary character of normative or dominant spaces, and/or to create an alternative reality that can begin to offer some form of compensation. Foucault mentions cemeteries, brothels, boarding schools, fairgrounds, prisons and ships as examples of heterotopia. Of ships (his heterotopia par excellence) he says that "in civilizations without boats, dreams dry up" (cited in Klaus, 2014: 9). In a lecture on heterotopia as a short 12-minute radio broadcast, Foucault also counted the space of children's imaginative games in dens, tents and beneath the bedclothes as heterotopias.

Fortunately or unfortunately, Foucault did not elaborate on this concept of heterotopia, which has left the fields of philosophical enquiry and peace education with some intriguing possibilities for further exploration.

Writing about peace education, Zembylas and Ferreira (2009) argue that heterotopic spaces enable alternative understandings of identity and belonging. They offer the possibility of transgressive identities – those that create new identities and alliances across conflicting groups. Teachers who wish to work with this concept see themselves as critical design experts, creating small openings for alternative consciousness and moving from macro to micro and back again. They try to make sense of the troubled knowledge that affects both sides of a divided society, as they question the ontological position of normative epistemologies.

Conclusion

We hope that it is evident in this discussion that peace education needs to evolve to take account of the fact that we are living in postmodern times. The truisms of the past, from both religion and science, no longer hold true for all times and all places. Education in general, and peace education in particular, need to embrace a more mature, complex and inclusive idea of what it means to live and thrive in peace in the twenty-first century. Postmodernity is not a concept that can be adopted as a particular approach – it just is!

Leaving the last word to Elavie Ndura and colleagues (2011), it is important to take note of grassroots voices of hope in times of postmodernity. She remains optimistic and aspirational alongside the educators and students who are educating for peace in post-conflict Burundi. Ndura argues that:

> Educators must become transformative intellectuals who possess the dispositions, knowledge and skills necessary to develop a discourse that unites the language of critique with the language of possibility. They must speak up against economic political and social injustices within and outside of schools. They must also become ethnic border-crossers who understand the impact of their ethnic identities on their classroom practices and interactions. In addition they must become critical pedagogues who can transform classrooms into critical spaces that question the obviousness of taken-for-granted assumptions. Educators must also become social activists who are at the forefront of the pursuit of true independence and national self-determination.
>
> (Ndura, 2012: 39)

We find this an apt quote for the conclusion of this chapter. Here, the Freirean tradition of keeping those at the grass roots at the heart of peace-building can be seen. This is a form of peace-building that is fraught with risk and that contains an embodied sense of what it is to be of service to those who suffer the effects of armed conflict. There are no guarantees in times of postmodernity, no grand plan, no building on bodies of knowledge and research that will ultimately lead to world peace. This is about creating transformational moments, one at a time, through solidarity, witnessing and the co-creation of heterotopic space that nestles within dominant ways of being. This applies as much to the UK as it does to Burundi.

References

Bajaj, M. (2015). 'Pedagogies of resistance' and critical peace education praxis. *Journal of Peace Education*, 12(2), 154–166.

Bajaj, M. and Brantmeier, E. (2011). The politics, praxis, and possibilities of critical peace education. *Journal of Peace Education*, 8(3), 221–224.

Bajaj, M. and Hantzopoluos, M. (Eds) (2016). *Peace Education: international perspectives.* London: Bloomsbury.

Bekerman, Z. and Zembylas, M. (2012). *Teaching Contested Narratives: identity, memory and reconciliation in peace education and beyond.* Cambridge: Cambridge University Press.

Bourdieu, P. and Passeron, J. (1977). *Reproduction in Education, Society and Culture.* London: Sage.

Boutros-Ghali, B. (1992). *An Agenda for Peace: preventive diplomacy, peacemaking and peacekeeping.* Report of the Secretary-General pursuant to the statement adopted by the Summit Meeting of the UN, A/47/277–S/24111, 17 June 1992.

Brah, A. and Phoenix, A. (2004). Ain't I a woman? Revisiting intersectionality. *Journal of International Women's Studies*, 5(3), 75–86.

Bronfenbrenner, U. (Ed.) (2005). *Making Human Beings Human: bioecological perspectives on human development.* Thousand Oaks, CA: Sage Publications.

Buber, M. (1928 [2004]). *I and Thou.* London: Continuum.

Cremin, H. (2010). Restorative approaches to conflict in schools: injustice or transformation? Unpublished presentation at Queens University Belfast, contact hc331@cam.ac.uk.

Cremin, H. (2015). Peace education research in the twenty-first century: three concepts facing crisis or opportunity? *Journal of Peace Education*, 13(1), 1–17.

Dewey, J. (1916). *Democracy and Education.* New York: Macmillan.

Diaz-Soto, L. (2005). How can we teach peace when we are so outraged? A call for critical peace education. *Taboo: The Journal of Culture and Education*, Fall–Winter, 91–96.

Dietrich, W. (2012). *Interpretations of Peace in History and Culture.* London: Palgrave Macmillan.

Duckworth, C. (2011). Restorative writing: critical peace education in a juvenile detention home. *Peace and Conflict Studies Journal*, 18(2), 234–262.

Fielding, M. (2014). Radical democratic education as response to two world wars and a contribution to world peace. *Forum*, 56(3), 513–529.

Foucault, M. (1986). Of other spaces. *Diacritics*, 16, 22–27.

Freire, P. (1970). *Pedagogy of the Oppressed.* New York: Continuum.

Freire, P. (1973). *Education for Critical Consciousness.* New York: Continuum.

Galtung, J. (1969). Violence, peace, and peace research. *Journal of Peace Research*, 6(3), 167–191.

Giddens, A. (1994). *Beyond Left and Right: the future of radical politics.* Cambridge: Polity Press.

Gilligan, C. (1993). *In a Different Voice: psychological theory and women's development.* New York: Harvard University Press.

Gur-Ze'ev, I. (2001). Philosophy of peace education in a postmodern era. *Educational Theory*, 51(3), 315–336.

Gur-Ze'ev, I. (2011). Improvisation, violence and peace education. In P. Trifonas and B. Wright (Eds), *Critical Issues in Peace and Education*, 104–120. New York: Routledge.

Harris, I. (2009). A select bibliography for peace education. *Peace and Change*, 34(4), 571–576.

Harris, I. and Morrison M. L. (2003). *Peace Education* (2nd edn). Jefferson, NC: McFarland.

Hicks, D. (Ed.) (1988). *Education for Peace.* London: Routledge.

Jenkins, T. (2013). The transformative imperative: the National Peace Academy as an emergent framework for comprehensive peace education. *Journal of Peace Education*, 10(2), 172–196.

Klaus, P. (2014). *Becoming Sumerhillian*, Master's Thesis, Faculty of Education, University of Cambridge.

McGlynn, C. (2009). Negotiating cultural difference in divided societies: an analysis of approaches to integrated education in Northern Ireland. In C. McGlynn, M. Zembylas, Z. Beckerman and A. Gallagher (Eds), *Peace Education in Conflict and Post-conflict Societies: comparative perspectives*, 9–25. New York: Palgrave Macmillan.

Midgeley, M. (2004). *The Myths We Live by*. London: Routledge.

Ndura, E., Meyer, M. and Atiri, J. (2011). *Seeds Bearing Fruit: pan-African peace action for the twenty-first century*. Lawrenceville, NJ: Africa World Press.

New Education Fellowship (NEF). (1948). *The Teacher and World Peace: a preliminary survey of the fundamentals*. London: New Education Fellowship.

Noddings, N. (2003) *Caring: a feminine approach to ethics and moral education*. Berkeley, CA: University of California.

Noddings, N. (2011). *Peace Education: how we come to love and hate war*. Cambridge: Cambridge University Press.

Novelli, M., Lopes Cardozo, M. and Smith, A. (2015). *A Theoretical Framework for Analysing the Contribution of Education to Sustainable Peacebuilding: 4Rs in conflict-affected contexts*. University of Amsterdam. [online] Retrieved 19 September 2016 from www.learningforpeace. unicef.org/partners/researchconsortium/research-outputs

Page, J. (2008). *Peace Education: exploring ethical and philosophical foundations*. Charlotte, NC: Information Age Publishing.

Pinker, S. (2011). *The Better Angels of Our Nature: why violence has declined*. New York: Viking Books.

Pring, R. (2013). *The Life and Death of Secondary Education for All*. London: Routledge.

Reardon, B. (2000). Peace education: a review and projection. In B. Moon, S. Brown and M. Ben Peretz (Eds), *International Companion to Education*, 397–425. New York: Routledge.

Reardon, B. and Cabezudo, A. (2002). *Learning to Abolish War*. New York: Hague Appeal for Peace.

Reardon, B. and Snauwaert, D. (2015). *Betty A. Reardon: a pioneer in education for peace and human rights*. Basel: Springer International Publishing.

Rose, N. (1996). Governing 'advanced' liberal democracies. In A. Barry, T. Osborne and N. Rose (Eds), *Foucault and Political Reason*, 37–64. Chicago, IL: University of Chicago Press.

Salomon, G. and Cairns, E. (2009). Peace education. In G. Salomon and E. Cairns (Eds), *Handbook on Peace Education*. London: Routledge.

Toh, S.-H. and Cawagas, V. (2010). Peace education, ESD and the earth charter: interconnections and synergies. *Journal of Education for Sustainable Development*, 4(2), 167–180.

UNESCO. (1974). *Recommendation Concerning Education for International Understanding, Cooperation and Peace and Education Relating to Human Rights and Fundamental Freedoms*. Paris: UNESCO.

UNESCO. (1995). *Declaration and Integrated Framework of Action on Education for Peace, Human Rights and Democracy*. Paris: UNESCO.

UNICEF. (1999). *Peace Education in UNICEF*. New York: UNICEF.

Vygotsky, L. S. (1980). *Mind in Society: the development of higher psychological processes*. New York: Harvard University Press.

Wiist, W. H., Barker, K., Arya, N., Rohde, J., Donohoe, M., White, S., Lubens, P., Gorman, G. and Hagopian, A. (2014). The role of public health in the prevention of war: rationale and competencies. *American Journal of Public Health*, 104(6), 34–47.

Zembylas, M. and Ferreira, A. (2009). Identity formation and affective spaces in conflict-ridden societies: inventing heterotopic possibilities. *Journal of Peace Education*, 6(1), 1–18.

iPEACE education

Introduction

Having discussed some of the limitations and possibilities of peace education from a theoretical and historical perspective, in this chapter we now go on to present how the framework of positive peace offers new possibilities for building a culture of peace in schools. Of necessity, this chapter takes on a more structured and direct style, as it attempts to outline our framework and model. This is not to belie the complexity and challenges involved. Rather we hope to integrate theory with practice in ways that teachers and others will find useful. In this, we draw on Aristotle's concept of *phronesis* – practical wisdom, the integration of *techne* (technical ability) and *episteme* (knowledge) with virtue (or in our case an aspiration towards peace). For peace educators, this involves deepening understanding of the processes involved, increased proficiency, reflexive practice and the ability to embrace complexity, contingency and transience. It also involves deepening connection at all levels and creating new heterotopic spaces in which structural and cultural violence in schools and elsewhere can be unsettled and transformed.

We suggest here that positive peace in schools can be achieved through an approach that we have characterised as the iPEACE model. The iPEACE model is two-fold. The first element is responsive and is connected with **peace-keeping** and **peace-making**; the second is proactive and is connected with **peace-building.** Table 5.1 outlines how the model fits together and how it relates to our previous discussion. It names the different conflict resolution processes and peace-building focuses and the learning that might result from engagement with each one. It works towards both inner and outer peace.

The responsive iPEACE model shown in Table 5.1 begins with peace-keeping, which, as we discussed earlier, relates to negative peace and the maintenance of safety and human rights. The processes named in this part of the table maintain order and ensure that rules and laws are kept but they do nothing to work towards positive peace. For this reason, strategic avoidance is included as a responsive aspect of peace-keeping, although it is clearly much less directive than the other two methods. The responsive iPEACE model also includes a range of different forms of peace-making which provide constructive and appropriate responses to conflict in schools.

The proactive iPEACE model shown in Table 5.1 concerns itself exclusively with peace-building. The focus in these rows involves everyone in the school community and builds towards peace in the longer term. It works to address wider issues of structural and cultural violence in schools. Together, the responsive and proactive iPEACE models create the conditions for positive peace in schools. Next we outline in more detail what is involved within each model.

Table 5.1 iPEACE model of peace-keeping, -making and -building

Mode	Conflict resolution process or peace-building focus	Learning	Peace-keeping/-making/-building
Responsive iPEACE	**Legal procedures**	Respect for the law	Peace-keeping
	Punishment	Respect for school rules	
	Strategic avoidance	Resilience and diplomacy	
	Restorative approaches	How to heal/repair a relationship after harm *Responsibility and reconciliation*	Peace-making
	Peer mediation	How to resolve conflict with a peer *Empowerment and wider perspectives*	
	Negotiation	How to be assertive *Compromise*	
Proactive iPEACE	**Relationships**	How to build and sustain peaceful relationships *Reciprocity, friendship, solidarity*	Peace-building
	Wellbeing (inner peace)	How to balance body, mind, heart and spirit *Holism, gratitude, joy*	
	Inclusive policy and practice	How to value and engage with difference *Tolerance, cooperation, curiosity*	
	Education for global citizenship	Awareness of global connectedness *Compassion, advocacy, excitement*	

The responsive iPEACE model

The responsive model enables complexity and synthesises different forms of conflict resolution. It proposes that there is no right or wrong approach: only the right approach for the situation. Thus, even legal procedures, punishment and avoidance have a role; they simply need to be applied in the correct circumstances. All too often, schools rely on punishment when this is not the best strategy to meet the needs of all involved (including victims), or else restorative interventions or mediation are used when it is clear they will not work. The key is to become 'conflict literate', which means: being aware of the various characteristics of conflict; being able to select the best strategy; and being proficient in using the various strategies.

Conflict literacy is essential for positive peace in globalised postmodern times. In our work over the years, we have noticed that conflict resolution training tends to be built around one or other method of conflict resolution, and that this unitary approach can have the effect of setting people into rather unpeaceful opposing camps. The conditions of modernity and marketisation prevail, so that peace work becomes grounded in professional and commercial interests manifested in the selling of solutions to problems that have been naïvely formulated and in one-dimensional training packages. The world of restorative justice, for example, tends to see itself as an umbrella that subsumes mediation, but those who have trained as mediators often see things rather differently. Certain forms of conflict resolution, such as avoidance or punishment, traditionally get a bad name, and teachers can be given a confusing array of partisan information about which strategy is supposed to work best. Those teachers who are temperamentally suited to more authoritarian approaches to discipline can feel dismissed and alienated and often subvert positive peace initiatives in schools because they feel that they are being asked to give up control. Peace educators who become evangelical about a particular approach, or who put pressure on those who do not share their values to change or leave, or who build empires, are resorting to the methods of war, not of peace.

The lack of rigorous evaluation and research evidence in general in the field of peace studies and peace education (discussed elsewhere in this book) does not help. For these reasons, we seek to bring clarification to this field by drawing clear distinctions between the different approaches and practices. Our framework for positive peace and our iPEACE models are not intended to imply that simple solutions exist to these problems. Rather, we offer them as a means of navigating complexity while accepting that no solution will ever be permanent or complete.

Both the responsive and the proactive iPEACE models are acronyms, although they each stand for something slightly different. The responsive iPEACE model stands for:

- identify conflict
- Pick the right strategy
- Enable voices to be heard
- Attack problems not people and Acknowledge feelings
- Create options
- Evaluate.

The responsive iPEACE model begins with the important initial issue of identifying the conflict in the first place.

Identifying the conflict

Conflicts between adults and students are often easy to spot, but conflict between students or between adults can be more diffuse. Sometimes one or more people in a team or a class know that there is a conflict, but the person or people involved cannot see it, or may not want to admit it. Conflicts cannot be resolved unless they are identified in the first place, so this is the important first step in the responsive iPEACE model. In order to identify conflict the facilitator might ask:

- How do I know that something is not right?
- Is harm being done? (If so, by whom and to whom, and in what way?)
- Are there things that could be done better?

If a conflict has been identified, the next stage is to consider the people involved. In particular, it is important to notice who is, or is not, talking about it. The consequences of resolving (or not resolving) the conflict may differ for each of the parties. In addition, people outside the main conflict may have more of a stake in whether or not it is resolved than the parties themselves. Power differences, and people's personalities, identities, values, levels of support and life circumstances, all have an influence on how likely people are to respond positively to attempts at conflict resolution. Some forms of conflict resolution are voluntary and will not work if both parties are not willing to participate or do not recognise the conflict in the first place/ Thus, consideration of the people involved helps make the decision about which strategy to use.

Picking the right strategy

Conflict resolution literature identifies the following forms of peace-keeping and peace-making. The list below has been adapted to reflect the language and practices of schools:

- legal and formal procedures (exclusion, warnings, dismissal)
- punishment
- restorative approach
- mediation
- problem-solving circles
- negotiation
- avoidance.

These strategies range from being oriented around security and procedural justice to what Lederach would call 'elicitive' or person-centred approaches. Avoidance is the clear exception here. It is included because it is sometimes a positive act of diplomacy and wisdom.

The role of the person attempting to resolve the conflict will be different with each strategy. The best strategy in each situation depends on several factors, including the consequences of acting/not acting. These factors can be legal or practical or they can be about prioritising teaching and learning or student wellbeing. It is important to reflect on whether there is someone who is clearly in the wrong, according to legal, social or cultural norms, and what someone in a position of authority might be expected to do about it.

Another significant factor is the nature of the facilitator's relationship with the conflict and with the people involved. Is the resolution of the conflict more important to the facilitator than to the parties themselves? If so, there is a need to proceed with care. Also, the nature of the relationship between the parties is significant. How are people connected to each other and to the facilitator? Who is accountable to whom? Where does power lie?

A final set of considerations is to do with harm. It is important to reflect on whether harm has been done and, if so, whether both parties have been harmed or whether there is someone who feels that they have been victimised. Does the other party recognise this and have they expressed acknowledgement and/or remorse?

Table 5.2 outlines a checklist that can be used as a prompt to help identify the best strategy in any given situation. If legal procedures and punishment are not necessary, then it is often preferable to use negotiation, mediation or restorative interventions. It is sometimes even wise to use avoidance and to strategically ignore the situation, especially if there are other aspects of the situation that require attention.

The following sections relate to selecting the right strategy for particular conflicts. More detail about what is involved in each is included in Part III of the book.

Legal procedures

In serious cases where the law has been broken, the decision about whether to involve the authorities is straightforward. In less serious cases, it might help to consider:

Table 5.2 Responsive iPEACE peace-keeping and -making checklist

	Legal procedures	Punishment	Restorative approach	Mediation	Problem-solving circles	Negotiation	Strategic avoidance
Background	The law has been broken – there is a victim and an offender	Clear infringement of school rules – there is someone in the wrong and (often) a victim	Someone has been harmed – there is a clear wrong-doer	Dispute between two people needing a mediator	Someone has a conflict that they would like to resolve	Conflict between two people who need to sort it out	A problem that may be solved naturally
Needs of the school	Legal compliance or redress	To reinforce authority, consistency and school rules	Restoration of relationships, inclusion and learning from mistakes	Student and staff wellbeing and learning how to resolve conflict	Student and staff wellbeing and learning how to support others experiencing conflict	Student and staff wellbeing and learning how to be assertive and caring	Discretion, avoidance of confrontation
Power	Power with the State and legal institutions	Power with the school	Power re-balanced to support the person harmed	Power shared between all people in dispute	Power with the person experiencing conflict	Power shared	Power issues avoided
Timescale	Can be lengthy and messy	Can be messy and counterproductive	Groundwork can take time, but quick resolution possible	Groundwork can take time, but quick resolution possible	Often quickly leads to ideas for resolution	Can be lengthy, depends on skills of those involved	Can take no time or can take time if issues are not addressed
Accountability	To the courts	To the school	To the school and the person harmed	To each other	To each other	To each other	N/A
Outcome	Decided by courts	Decided by someone in authority	Decided by people involved	Decided by people in dispute	Decided by the person experiencing conflict	Decided by people involved	Unknown

- Who in the school is responsible for decisions like this?
- Could a child be harmed if I (or the child-protection officer) do not inform police?
- Do I have a statutory duty to report this incident?
- Am I bound by ethical guidelines?
- Am I morally culpable if I do not pass information on to someone in authority?

Punishment

Although many people who promote positive approaches to discipline in schools have ambiguous feelings towards punishment, it cannot always be avoided. Punishment can be appropriate when there has been a clear infringement of basic school rules, when people are put at risk and when there is a refusal to comply following reasonable reminder and warning.

Rules with consequences protect the rights of students to learn and of teachers to teach. They enable everyone in the school community to feel safe and respected. Despite the reservations expressed in the first part of this book, it may sometimes be necessary to exclude someone temporarily, or even permanently, if others are at risk or if the situation or relationship has reached a point of no return. While mediation or a restorative response to an incident may be preferable, they are sometimes neither appropriate nor possible. Sometimes people do not agree that harm has been caused, or they blame the victim or they choose not to participate in these voluntary methods. Punishment sends a clear message that, regardless of the views of the person who has caused harm, certain behaviours will not be tolerated, and that it is ultimately the prerogative of those responsible for safety and wellbeing in school to make those decisions on behalf of everyone.

It is important to remember, however, that punishment takes the responsibility for resolving conflict out of the hands of the people involved and places it with those in authority. In many ways, it is in students' interests to work against the process rather than with it. This can lead to missed opportunities for conflict transformation. At the very least, it is our view that punishment is over-used in schools, to the detriment of the other methods. Punishment is also often confused with discipline, and we draw out the important distinction between the two in more detail in Chapter 6.

Restorative approach

It is sometimes difficult to decide between restorative approaches and mediation. Both processes are voluntary. Restorative approaches are useful when harm has been done to someone. Mediation is useful when two people disagree. Restorative approaches uphold clear institutional or ethical principles, while mediation enables disputing people to come to a mutually acceptable resolution. Both processes enable local, common-sense solutions that are grounded in the needs and interests of the people involved.

Mediation

Mediation is appropriate where there is a dispute or a disagreement and where the school does not need to take action other than to support the people involved to arrive at a solution. Schools often train a group of peer mediators to resolve the disputes of their peers.

Problem-solving circles

Circle processes involve a group supporting someone experiencing a conflict to find a resolution. Unlike other peace-making methods, problem-solving circles do not necessarily include all parties directly involved in the conflict and may not concern interpersonal conflict at all. It may well be that someone is experiencing inner conflict or is unsure what to do in a given situation.

Circle processes can be very powerful and often reward time invested with real benefits for both the person experiencing conflict and the group members who are supporting her or him. Although it is important to bear in mind that these processes cannot serve as a substitute for therapy, a teacher who is aware of issues of safeguarding and the mental health needs of her students should be able to support her class to explore together some important issues for development and growth.

Negotiation and strategic avoidance

These strategies are useful when there is no need for a third party or no need to take any action at the present time. In negotiation, many of the principles of mediation and restorative approaches apply, but without third-party intervention. When entering upon a negotiation it is important to prepare. On leaving, it is equally important to ensure that the basic needs of all parties are met. Non-violent communication provides a useful framework for this.

If a decision is made to avoid any direct action, it is useful to consider:

- Could things escalate?
- Is someone expecting action?
- What needs to be communicated to whom?
- How will it become evident that it is time to act?

The next parts of the iPEACE model (EACE) are especially important for restorative interventions, mediation, problem-solving circles and negotiation. They are not as relevant for legal procedures, punishment or avoidance. To recap, these parts are:

- **E**nable voices to be heard
- **A**ttack problems not people and **A**cknowledge feelings
- **C**reate options
- **E**valuate.

Enabling voices to be heard

Enabling voices to be heard is central to mediation and restorative conversations. Conflicts are often complex and can involve more people than is at first apparent. One of the initial tasks is to find out who is involved and to enable them to speak. It is important, however, to avoid blame, gossip, detective work, mischief-making or power play. Rather, people need the opportunity to say from their perspective what has happened, how they have been affected and what they need to happen next.

The initial stages of enabling voices to be heard are best carried out in a series of one-to-one conversations. These conversations need to:

- gain consent for a process to take place;
- find out what happened;
- clarify feelings involved, harm that has been done and any misperceptions;
- enable each person to feel heard;
- reinforce each person's right to have their own feelings and perspectives, even if others do not agree with them;
- identify the needs of the different parties;
- set out the parameters of the conflict, including the needs of the school;
- clarify roles, expectations and how to proceed;
- gain agreement about respecting everyone's needs and next steps.

It is often the case that these initial meetings clear up any misunderstanding and problems in communication and that conflicts can be resolved at this early stage without the need for a face-to-face meeting. Many people find encounters in situations of conflict difficult or upsetting and prefer this more indirect approach. A judgement needs to be made, however, about whether to push for a face-to-face meeting (people may benefit from being in the same room) or whether to continue to act as an intermediary. Shuttle communication does not provide facilitated support for people coming together for the first time after a solution has been found. It can be successful, provided that it is time limited and targeted to the issues at hand. There may need to be follow-up meetings at a later date to check on progress.

Whether or not the process of enabling voices to be heard takes place with all people in the same room, there are a few key things to take into account. Expectations about confidentiality (or its limits) need to be established from the start and agreed with all parties. Also, all parties need to agree to speak respectfully to (and about) each other. If these initial meetings take place separately, a decision will need to be made about if and when to bring the parties together – they may need to calm down and let off steam first. The facilitator is responsible for physical and emotional safety, and this starts with the choice of timing and venue.

Emotional safety comes through the careful use of language. Parties can be encouraged to talk about themselves, beginning sentences with 'I' rather than 'he' or 'she', and avoiding blaming each other. The skilful facilitator is assertive if necessary, ensuring that people listen respectfully. She or he uses language that is neutral, even if the parties use inflammatory or judgemental words, and summarises in ways that take the heat out of provocative statements without altering the overall meaning. Facilitators avoid taking sides, however unconsciously or subtly, and focus questioning on feelings and harm caused, without being directive. There is an added dimension in restorative conversations, where an early judgement has been made about who has been harmed and may need reparation. Facilitators using these processes avoid surreptitiously giving advice though the use of questions (for example: "Have you tried . . . ?" or "Why didn't you . . . ?") and ground their practice in elicitive methods, which place the people involved at the heart of the process and support them to find their own solutions to their own problems. Advice, guidance and suggestions have their place, but not as part of enabling voices to be heard.

Attacking problems not people

Often in a conflict situation, people attack each other rather than the problem. This goes back to the ways in which people are socialised to think about conflict, especially in Western cultures. Boys and girls are taught to think and act differently in conflict situations. From early childhood people are taught about goodies and baddies and the importance of competing. The dominant culture glorifies fighting in all its forms through films, computer games and popular media. Unfortunately, this way of thinking about conflict often carries forward into areas of life that cannot be impacted through force, manipulation or aggression. New problems are piled on top of old unresolved ones, and things can go from bad to worse. Even if things appear to have settled down, and people are quiet or fearful, history is littered with cases of conflict resurfacing when the power balance shifts, whether this is in international relations, institutions such as schools or family life.

This approach to conflict has been referred to as an adversarial approach – it treats the other party as an enemy. In an adversarial approach to conflict, people attack each other rather than the problem.

In a non-adversarial approach, people attack the problem rather than each other. This can be summarised as: "be hard on the problem, soft on the people" (Fisher *et al.*, 1991) and would look like this:

The shift that takes place when people move to non-adversarial conflict resolution is transformational. It is not, however, beyond the capacity of most people. Blame has been removed, and people feel safe to collaborate because they are no longer fighting for their emotional, reputational or physical survival. Skilful facilitation makes this possible. Changing the direction of people's energy and language while enabling them to feel heard and respected is certainly a process that can take a lifetime to perfect! Having said that, it is important to recognise that processes such as mediation and restorative facilitation can be taught and practised, and most people can learn how to use them in the right situation to get better results than would otherwise have been achieved.

A final thing to consider is how to change the focus towards areas that have traction. Some things are not negotiable, such as the need to be free from violence, but others have more room for manoeuvre. This can be summarised as:

- Positions
- Interests
- Needs (PIN).

It is possible to negotiate around interests, but not around positions or needs. Positions are unhelpful. Someone might say, for example, that they are never going to work in the same classroom as another person again. Often this is a starting position when someone feels threatened. This leaves no room for negotiation, however, and whatever interests lie beneath the surface then remain unexplored.

Interests are the stuff of conflict resolution. The role of the facilitator is to find the interests that lie beneath the positions that have been taken. For example, interests in the above example might be to have a positive classroom environment or to be spoken to with courtesy. Often these interests are underpinned by needs, also non-negotiable, but universal and much easier to understand and empathise with. Needs are often connected with human rights. In the above example, the underlying need might be for respect, personal space or dignity. Negotiating around interests, underpinned by needs, will enable facilitators to support the parties to move from attacking each other to attacking the problem together.

Creating options

There is a pivotal point in a restorative conversation or mediation when it becomes clear that the energy has shifted, and the focus needs to move from the past to the future. This usually comes when feelings and perspectives have been acknowledged. The first part of a mediation or restorative process can feel like hard work, but this second part often flows well. Creating options involves being as free as possible. It is good to get parties to generate lots of ideas, offers and requests and then to evaluate their relative merit before arriving at a solution – or rather solutions, as conflict is often multi-faceted.

At this stage it is important to consider:

- Who is making offers/requests? Are they balanced, appropriate and realistic?
- Are people thinking creatively?
- Does the agreement reflect the short, medium and long term?
- Is the agreement fair to all involved, including people not in the room?
- Who will monitor the agreement?
- What will happen if the agreement is broken?
- How will conflict be avoided in future?

Evaluating

The final stage of any peace-keeping or peace-making process is to evaluate success and, where appropriate, to acknowledge or celebrate the contributions of everyone involved. Essentially, this involves asking "has it worked?" and "what other benefits did it bring?" This may be harder to determine than it sounds. For example, it may well be that the parties themselves feel that the process has worked for them, but others may feel that it has not worked overall, because of different objectives. Change may take time, and other factors might come into play in the meantime. It is useful to reflect, even before the process has started, on how it will become evident whether or not the process has worked. It may be necessary to set up a review meeting once an agreement has been reached, to give everyone a chance to evaluate whether things really are working out as people want.

As stated from the start, conflict is not always bad. Sometimes it is constructive and brings unexpected gifts. It can be transformational and shift people and organisations into new, more healthy ways of working and relating. From this point of view, after engaging in any process of peace-making, it is worth reflecting on what has been learned about the school. Has the process merely kept the peace or has it contributed to positive change? Has it contributed to the removal of structural or cultural violence, and are there ways that this could be extended into peace-building? Has the process identified any wider training, technical or relational needs? The answers to these questions begin to feed into processes of peace-building.

The proactive iPEACE model

The previous section used an iPEACE acronym to focus on peace-keeping and peace-making, and this section now moves on to use the same term as an acronym for peace-building. To a certain extent, the iPEACE peace-building model mirrors the iPEACE peace-making model, but this time the focus is on being proactive in order to work towards a positive school culture, rather than being responsive and focusing on a presenting conflict. The proactive iPEACE model, like its responsive counterpart, does not imply simple solutions to complex problems in times of postmodernity; rather it provides a framework for schools to formulate their own responses, and to reflexively work together to build positive peace. The iPEACE peace-building model stands for:

- identify what peace-building means for the school
- Plan for peace-building
- Enable multiple and holistic perspectives
- Accept complexity and diversity
- Embrace Creativity
- Evaluate and grow.

Table 5.3 provides an outline of the processes, questions and activities that make up the proactive iPEACE model and which can be undertaken as part of building and reviewing a culture of positive peace. As we discussed in Chapter 4, the *how* of peace education is at least as important as the *what*. Therefore, it is essential to employ methods and methodologies that are congruent with the values and aims of positive peace education. We now go on to review each aspect of the proactive iPEACE peace-building model in turn.

Identify what peace-building means for the school

The first question in identifying points for development for peace-building is, predictably, "what do we mean by peace-building?" This can quickly be followed by the question "what do we mean by peace?" As discussed in earlier chapters, not everyone will be in agreement about this. For example, is peace a philosophy or a process? Is it a journey or a state? Is it mainly an absence of destructive conflict or violence or does it have meaning in its own right?

There are two main ways to respond to this uncertainty. The first, quite simply, is to ask people – the more the better. These people might be located at a distance from the school, or they might be in close proximity. They might be in school all the time, such as teachers, students or non-teaching staff, or they might be involved more occasionally, such as business people, global charity workers or local residents. It may be that their relationship with the school is reciprocal, such as parents, or it may be that their relationship is unilateral, such as policy makers or school inspectors. This latter group may not respond directly to questions about peace, but their beliefs and assumptions will be clear from the documentation that they send out. The second way to respond to this uncertainty is to keep returning to values and to the ethos of the school. These provide an anchor for schools, as they navigate changing priorities.

Table 5.3 The proactive iPEACE peace-building model

iPEACE	Phase	Questions to consider	Mechanisms and actions
Identify what peace-building means for the school as a community	Conceptualisation	What is our vision of positive peace in our school?	Read research
		What are the things that are already contributing to a culture of positive peace?	Attend conferences
		What are the things that we wish to continue?	Engage in dialogue with other schools
		What are the things that we wish to change?	Facilitate staff reflection, debate, dialogue, discussion
		What are the things that we wish to create?	Use appreciative inquiry methods
		What does building a culture of positive peace mean in practice?	Surveys (staff, pupil, parents) and photo-voice
		How will we know when we have been successful?	
Plan for peace-building (e.g. inclusion, wellbeing and citizenship)	Formulation	How do we achieve our vision?	Staff, parent and pupil champions' group
		What do we need to do to enact peace-keeping, peace-making and peace-building activities?	Individual interviews and focus groups
		What practices, systems, routines require attention?	Appreciative inquiry
Enable multiple and holistic perspectives		What are the needs of different parties – knowledge, skills, training, empowerment, voice, etc?	Participatory methods
		How can we respond to these needs?	
Accept complexity and diversity	Implementation	How are we doing?	Put the plan into practice
		What early changes do we need to make?	Iterative continuous review
Embrace creativity			
Evaluate and grow	Evaluation	What has changed?	Repeat surveys, appreciative inquiry and participatory methods
		What has not?	Engage multiple parties in processes of reflection and dialogue about the implementation, impact and influence of what has been done
		What do we need to do next?	Celebrate!

Our proactive peace-building iPEACE model has inclusion, wellbeing and citizenship at its heart (these will be discussed in more detail in Chapter 8 on peace-building in Part III), but schools may of course identify a different focus. We have chosen inclusion, wellbeing and citizenship for several reasons: they are grounded in values; they provide well-recognised frameworks for education research and development internationally; they build peace beyond schools in wider society and family life; and they provide for both outer and inner peace. We recognise that they are not, however, the only hooks for peace-building work in schools.

Once the focus for peace-building in the school has been identified, the next stage is to begin to think about planning for development as a whole-school community.

Plan for peace-building

Having identified what peace-building means to as many people as possible in the school community, the next stage is to agree the overarching aims and objectives and to plan for change. Overarching aims come from values and lead into specific objectives and targets. The skilful peace-builder will balance multiple perspectives and synthesise broad areas for development and growth, as well as creating clear objectives and targets. As will be clear by now, this is an iterative process that is continually subject to review and change, but it is necessary to start somewhere.

A set of questions that might help to formulate a short-, medium- and long-term plan include:

- What level to begin with?

    - students
    - parents
    - school leadership
    - heads of year/department/phase
    - community.

- What groups need to be engaged?

    - a cross-institution champions group with an evolving but defined purpose
    - groups of parents, community members
    - groups of students
    - existing groups within school (e.g. year heads)
    - governors.

- What are the areas for development?

    - curriculum development
    - staff training
    - school policy and practice
    - pedagogy
    - peer support
    - staff and student voice
    - excellence and achievement
    - parental links
    - buildings and facilities.

- What is the timescale?

  o   short and intense
  o   medium term, over a school year, for example
  o   long term, involving several years to build.

- What resources might be needed?

  o   time
  o   money
  o   staffing.

- What formal processes might need to happen?

  o   risk assessment
  o   inclusion on school development plan
  o   support from the governing body.

Having created a shared vision, clarified values and developed an action plan, the stage is set for a peace-building process that will sit hand in glove with peace-making processes and that will work towards a culture of positive peace.

Enable multiple and holistic perspectives

As has already been established, peace-building work relies on multiple perspectives and on multiple aspects of school life, such as the physical environment, the quality of relationships, everyday practices and routines and the nature of teaching and learning. These different voices and areas of school life are in relationship with each other and create a complex web of interactions, both across different groups and across the various aspects that make up an individual's experiences. Engaging with this complexity in a holistic way is vital for the health of a peace-building institution.

In order to do this, it is necessary to gather, analyse and discuss a range of data that might inform action. These data might come from existing databases, from surveys, interviews and focus groups or from alternative methods of accessing student voice, such as arts-based methods, photo-voice or drama projects. These more creative methods will be explored in Part IV of this book. The richer the data, the more it will be possible to respond in sensitive and informed ways to the peace-building needs of members of the whole-school community.

Accepting complexity and diversity

It is important at this stage once again to reinforce the idea that no project is linear. Change happens in both positive and negative directions, and conditions on the ground have just as much influence on outcomes as actions taken. If there is one thing that is predictable, it is that a peace-building project will never achieve predicted outcomes! This is to be embraced, celebrated and worked with; it is not to be denied. As already discussed in Chapter 4, however, many psychologists and social scientists continue to ignore this psycho-social reality and act as if the conditions of modernity continue to hold sway. The resulting flawed thinking can undermine feelings of achievement and growth in schools working to build peace in times of postmodernity.

It is more realistic and productive to see schools as complex ecosystems embedded within local, national and global networks that influence them in complex ways. How can any intervention be the same, or even broadly the same, when it hits the ground? Real schools in real settings have dynamics that are dependent on the individuals within them and on the ways in which these individuals interact with each other and with factors outside the setting. Even if complexity within a school were captured, it would only ever be momentarily, as these dynamics are constantly shifting.

While we advocate involving the whole-school community in reviewing and building positive peace, it is also important to question the nature of this "community". Schools have porous walls – the individuals within them come and go and have overlapping but different communities of belonging. Some individuals who have influence on what happens are located at a distance (relatives in Pakistan, policy makers in Whitehall) and some are closer at hand (parents, local employers). People at each of these levels influence each other, as well as influencing people located within the school, and so the pattern of interactions becomes infinitely complex. This complexity occurs equally at an individual level. Whether someone strives to keep a young person in the classroom or sends them out following disruptive behaviour might be as much a function of whether they have had an argument with their significant other that morning as it is a function of whether or not they value inclusion. Change is rarely linear or predictable in people's lived experience.

None of this is to imply that the checklists and models in this chapter are without their uses – the reverse is the case. They provide insights and processes for engaging in peace-making and peace-building, but they are not to be used mechanically or unthinkingly. They, as everything else, are contingent and are only as useful as the actions of the people who interpret and apply them. No doubt they will evolve over time, and we look forward to hearing from our readers about ways in which they can be adapted and improved.

Thus, complexity and contingency are not to be feared or contained. They are to be celebrated as part of the dynamics of life! Stress does not come from awareness of these dynamics; it comes from their denial. We have seen project after project falter in schools, despite noble aspirations and intentions, because project implementers have failed to take account of schools as complex ecosystems. Complex ecosystems are beautiful: they are dynamic, organic and capable of breathtaking transformation. They are not amenable to manipulation or control, and they are so much the better for it.

Embracing creativity

One positive response to complexity, unpredictability and constant change in school is to embrace creativity. Creativity enables adults and young people in school to locate themselves within complex frameworks and to find a voice that might otherwise be hard to articulate. One method of embracing creativity is to use "photo-voice" as a way of investigating how students feel about conflict and peace in the school. Photo-voice has been used extensively in community health settings to access marginalised voices that may not otherwise be heard and will be discussed in more detail in Part IV of this book.

Another way of embracing creativity is to work with John-Paul Lederach's concept of the moral imagination (2005). Lederach introduces notions of affect, spirituality and aesthetics into peace-building, and uses concepts of turning points, complexity, time, Haiku, spiders' webs, yeast, serendipity, Pied Pipers, risk and imagination! In his book, he explores possibilities for giving birth to new ideas, while remaining rooted in the challenges of the real world. The moral imagination is akin to Freire's conscientisation. When this is applied to peace-building, it is supremely creative. It involves imagining constructive responses that transcend and ultimately break the grip of destructive patterns and cycles of violence. Violence often arises from the inability of individuals and groups to imagine themselves in a web of relationships that includes their enemies. Violence can be transcended by the awareness of this complex web. While violence is often familiar, peace is unknown and therefore often perceived as risky. This is why imagination is so important.

Lederach works within an aesthetic tradition, talking about the creativity and spontaneity of the arts and the ability of a story, a poem or an image to transform conflictual relationships. He also uses metaphors from the natural world in order to deepen understanding of the complexity of conflict, violence and peace-building. He is critical of social movements for peace that rely on simplistic linear thinking. For Lederach, reconciliation is not "forgive and forget"; it is "remember and change".

From a practical point of view, we advocate working with the arts in as many ways as possible while working proactively to build peace in schools. This can include the creation of works of art for an interactive exhibition, community art and craft work, drama, dance, digital media and music. Art brings people together and enables the sharing of perspectives and emotions surrounding conflict and peace.

Lederach ends his book with a delightful suggestion for a plaque over the door of a school for moral imagination. The plaque would read:

> Reach out to those you fear.
> Touch the heart of complexity.
> Imagine beyond what is seen.
> Risk vulnerability one step at a time.

There are few exigencies for peace education that have more potency, in our view.

Evaluate and grow

Evaluation of peace-building needs to sit in congruence with the aims and objectives of peace education. Evaluation of the 'what works' variety is not only unsuitable, but actively antithetical to the aims of peace education. As we explored in Chapter 3, this reductionist, technological view of education is part of the discourse around schooling and school improvement that feeds the culture of accountability, which is responsible for privileging external, standardising pressures over the needs of the children and adults in the school system. In the spirit of peace-building, the focus of evaluation should be at least as much on learning as it is on accountability. It is therefore crucial to adopt methods for evaluation that promote participation of multiple voices and perspectives, capture the affective and emotional aspects of the changes that occur as much as the rational and observable, and in themselves contribute to the building of peace.

Conclusion

This chapter has taken forward the theories developed in the previous chapter and has provided a framework for implementing them in schools. It has built upon our call for transformation: transformation of knowledge about peace and conflict; transformation of perspectives (epistemology); and transformation of relationships, with the self, with other people and with the cosmos. Our contention is that peace education can and should play a core role in the work of schools. Peace has been sidelined for too long in the conflict-ridden societies of the West. Most children and young people living in the UK may not experience armed conflict, but their lives are marked by many other forms of violence: by abuse and neglect; by bullying and harassment in the real and the cyber worlds; and by the preponderance of violent games, films and other media that reach into their bedrooms and homes. The next part of the book now goes on to explain and illustrate how schools can engage with the three dimensions of positive peace that we have highlighted: peace-keeping, -making and -building.

References

Fisher, R., Ury, W. and Patton, B. (1991). *Getting to Yes: negotiating an agreement without giving in* (2nd edn). Sydney: Century Business.

Lederach, J. (2005). *The Moral Imagination*. Oxford: Oxford University Press.

Part III

Peace-keeping, -making and -building

Introduction

In Part I of this book, we argued that structural and cultural violence are endemic in schools and that they create a climate in which direct violence – between students, and between students and adults – can result. In Part II, we argued that much peace education in the twenty-first century is no longer fit for purpose, due in part to its ties with outdated and harmful modernist discourse. We have gone on to present our framework for positive peace and our responsive and proactive iPEACE model as one way of responding to the scale of the criticisms and challenges that we have raised. We do not begin to pretend that this is straightforward, but neither do we give up hope. We hold on to the positive outcomes of our work in schools to date and urge the reader to take heart from the case studies of real schools that we present in Part IV of this book.

This third part of the book goes into more detail about the peace-keeping, -making and -building dimensions of positive peace that we have identified throughout this book. Here and elsewhere, we stand in solidarity with all of the wonderful teachers (and educationalists more generally) reading this. Indeed, our job would be meaningless and incomplete if we did not share a clear vision and research-informed framework for bringing about the changes that we advocate. Once again, this chapter is written in a relatively direct style, and we have included activities that change-leaders in schools could use to facilitate professional development with their teams.

Chapter 6

Education for peace-keeping

Introduction

Peace-keeping is the first level of peace work. It covers those aspects of school life that can be considered fundamental in keeping all members of the school community safe to teach and to learn. Technically, just as in international relations, peace-keeping involves the removal of direct violence. It does not address structural or cultural violence; it keeps warring parties apart. In a school, this often translates into separating or removing students who have become physically violent, as well as ensuring that direct violence does not occur in the first place through physical prevention, rules and punishment. As discussed in Part I of this book, systems of schooling generally remain culturally violent (and create contexts for direct violence) so that it is important to have in place those safeguarding measures that provide the basic sense of security required for more developmental peace work to take place.

Peace-keeping, however, is expedient and not educational. For this reason, many peace educators are wary of it. These peace educators can often struggle to get their message across, as many in schools see a strong need for peace-keeping measures. While we would agree that peace-keeping is often used to the detriment of other more positive measures, we do not reject it altogether. This chapter starts from the premise that schools have a fundamental and inarguable duty of care to keep all members of the school community safe from harm in all its forms. It explores some of the key concepts within the peace-keeping field, including safety, security, rights, rules and discipline. It will illustrate some of the ways in which schools seek to keep the peace, such as behaviour management systems, disciplinary procedures and security measures. It will explore ways in which basic peace-keeping practices can be shifted toward more educational ends through processes of critical thinking, dialogue and inclusion. We begin with issues of security and safety.

Security and safety

At a fundamental level, peace-keeping is enabled through security measures. Security has transformed the look of schools in the past 20 years. It is now the norm for schools in the UK and elsewhere to have an unscalable perimeter fence, segregated entrances for adults and students, double entry doors for visitors and CCTV cameras monitoring outside and inside. Many of these measures were recommendations for schools in the UK following the public inquiry into the shootings at Dunblane Primary School on 13 March 1996. The Dunblane school shootings, a mercifully rare occurrence in UK schools compared to the United States, happened just three months after the headteacher Philip Lawrence was stabbed to death in

West London, and four months before a man entered a primary school in Wolverhampton and attacked three children and four adults. It is therefore completely understandable that security management has become more of a priority for schools in the UK, but there are also risks associated with the over-securitisation of schools. Whilst it is essential that schools do their best to protect those to whom they have a duty of care, "the question is . . . *what kind* of safety is desirable, and at which point does this desire for safety become uneducational" (Biesta, 2014: 2). While technical security, as manifested in physical security measures, plays an important part in keeping potentially dangerous people out of the school premises, it can inadvertently promote feelings of insecurity and a sense of danger for those within. As discussed in the first part of this book, schools should not be made to feel like army camps or prisons. This can in fact contribute to the very problems that these measures set out to address.

As a case in point, in a "photo-voice" study into engagement, disaffection and identity in an urban secondary school in the UK in 2011, Cremin *et al.* found that a surprising number of the students took photographs of gates, fences, locks and CCTV. They expanded on this in their annotated scrapbooks and in their photo-elicitation interviews where they talked about their school as a prison. They disliked the fact that the area of the school where the head-teacher's office and the staffroom were located was protected by electronic locks, and that only adults had access to key fobs. They also disliked the fact that toilets were permanently locked because students could not be trusted to use them responsibly, so that they needed to find an adult with a key before they could go to the toilet. They also criticised the use of CCTV throughout the school and the television screens in the staffroom. They felt watched, mistrusted, contained, diminished.

In a similar study investigating civic action and learning among young people in socio-economically disadvantaged communities, Cremin (2012) found that an initiative to promote 'safer schools' through increased visibility and liaison with the police had the effect of making many students feel further alienated. They felt like 'failed citizens' even before they had had a chance to participate in civic life. One student felt indignant that a police officer in her school was wearing body armour, as if she were a threat to him. She argued powerfully that it is inappropriate for a policeman to act as if he were at risk of being shot on entering a school building.

There is a risk here of the criminalisation of poverty; while certain social groups find themselves subject to increased surveillance, their privileged peers have more autonomy and freedom to 'screw up' as a normal and natural part of growing up. This combines structural with cultural violence. Security may be felt to be necessary by parents and others, but this should not degenerate into creating a climate of mistrust and fear. Peace-keeping needs also to involve other ways of ensuring safety, such as providing positive behavioural support, nurturing feelings of connectedness and belonging, prioritising social and emotional learning and making mental health support more accessible (Brock and Reeves, 2014). These methods of contributing to psychological and emotional safety should be undertaken alongside any necessary security measures in order to ensure safety in schools. A consideration of human rights is often a good place to start.

Rights

While it is easy to see school security measures as elements of peace-keeping, it is equally important to recognise the upholding of human rights as fundamental to protecting the safety of the individual. Schools are bound by law to uphold fundamental rights, including those laid down in the UN Declaration on the Rights of the Child. Technical security measures are of course important, but it is imperative equally to acknowledge that security and safety go beyond the physical and refer also to psychological and emotional safety. Sometimes these two are in tension with each other.

Article 19 of the UN Declaration on the Rights of the Child requires that "Governments must do all they can to ensure that children are protected from all forms of violence, abuse, neglect and bad treatment by their parents or anyone else who looks after them" (UNICEF, 2012). Article 28 requires that "Discipline in schools must respect children's dignity". Both these articles have direct implications not only for what schools do, but also *how* they do it.

Peace-keeping in schools requires a tricky combination of protection and respect, and there can be conflict between the rights of the individual and the needs of the institution. It may be necessary, for example, to limit certain freedoms, such as free access to toilets, in order to protect the safety and wellbeing of the student community as a whole. Decisions about the nature of the trade-off between freedom and safety will be on-going in any school, but this becomes problematic when peace-keeping measures dominate to the detriment of peace-building. A situation where students are not able to go to the toilet when they need to should not be a final resting place; solutions need to be found. Important questions could be asked about trust, responsibility and engagement. The student body could be involved in developing practical strategies to ensure that proper access to toilets is restored. Not only does this protect physical safety, it also protects emotional and psychological safety. In this way, young people are not made to suffer indignity or discomfort – they have become part of the solution instead of part of the problem.

As the Australian educationalist Bill Rogers makes clear, "The most fundamental rights of a classroom member are those of emotional and physical safety, mutual respect and fair treatment" (2012: xxiv). These rights are not automatic, however; they need to be upheld through the creation and maintenance of fair rules, agreed by all. The question of how to uphold rights while giving due regard to people's responsibilities is complex. Rogers provides a useful philosophical and practical perspective on these matters, helping to clarify this question in the school context by identifying three non-negotiable rights: the right to feel safe; the right to be treated with dignity; and the right to learn (and therefore to teach) (2012: 122). With these non-negotiable rights established, the school is then able to build systems, rules and processes to protect them. It is the establishment of this context of safety, dignity and learning that enables peace-keeping to move away from the expedient end of the spectrum and towards the educational end.

Making and enforcing the rules

Making and enforcing commonly agreed rules are thus fundamental to peace-keeping. As Michael Marland makes clear in his 1975 book, *The Craft of the Classroom: a survival guide*, which became a handbook for generations of teachers:

> Every kind of room, from a pub bar to a railway compartment, from a cinema to a snack bar, has to have its own conventions of control if the central activity is to take place at all, and if the people in it are to manage not to offend or interfere with one another.
>
> (1975: 45)

He makes the point that in all social life 'conventions' or rules are required. Within education, even the most libertarian anti-schooling institutions, such as A. S. Neil's Summerhill or Rudolf Steiner schools, have rules and conventions that apply to everyone. In these institutions people are held to account if they break the rules that everyone has agreed.

All schools are required, both legally and morally, to make and enforce rules, but there are many different ways of doing this. At one end of the spectrum, there is authoritarian behaviour management and at the other more collaborative, student-centred, developmental and democratic styles. Somewhere in the middle are behaviourist methods, designed to give young people an element of "choice" and to use sanctions and rewards to shape behaviour towards desired outcomes. These are not, however, without their issues, as will be discussed shortly.

Diana Baumrind's seminal work on parenting (1966) contrasts permissive, authoritarian and authoritative parenting styles and provides a useful distinction between the different stances that can be adopted by those in authority. A permissive approach is typically non-punitive, accepting and affirming, and involves high levels of consultation and low levels of demand and control; an authoritarian approach is typically highly controlling, restricts autonomy, demands obedience and uses punishment to ensure compliance; an authoritative approach values both autonomy and disciplined conformity and involves reciprocity, structure and support. Applying this model to schools raises challenging questions about power and control.

Looking specifically at the establishment and enforcement of rules as part of behaviour management in schools, a more authoritarian position might involve the senior management team writing school rules that students are simply expected to keep (and are punished if they do not). A more authoritative approach would be characterised by dialogue with all involved, in order to use reasoning and fairness to develop rules and sanctions collaboratively. Authoritative methods balance the responsibilities and rights of adults and young people and the need for both flexibility and consistency. It will be of no surprise that we advocate the latter, although we caution that authoritative discipline needs time and commitment to be done well. It also needs to be linked with a curriculum to develop the pro-social skills (speaking, listening, resilience, cooperation, problem-solving) that are necessary for successful outcomes. We expand on this in Part IV of this book.

We go on now to explore in more detail what an authoritative method of establishing school rules would look like. We argue that these approaches present a perfect opportunity to engage children and young people in thinking and discussion about why rules are needed, what behaviours are helpful and unhelpful in community life, and how behaviour is regulated. This is an intrinsically democratising process – it is meaningful, takes place in a real-life context and has immediate implications: the ideal conditions for learning to occur. The expectations or norms that are articulated through the rules that are agreed using this process are co-created and grounded in the needs of every member of the school community. The Spanish language has a wonderful concept, 'convivencia', which literally translates as 'living togetherness'. It is a concept that forms the bedrock of the school climate in Spanish-speaking countries; it expresses the needs and expectations of all members of the community to live together in harmony.

Thinking critically about rules and behaviour in schools can bring to light otherwise unchallenged assumptions and norms. For example, adults in schools often identify the playground as a site for poor behaviour. Young people may think differently about it. For them, it may be a heterotopic space (see Chapter 4) in which they disrupt adult norms and renegotiate space, power, identity and control. If schools have been successful in developing a sense of moral duty to others through authoritative discipline, then self-regulation will carry through to the playground. If discipline is based on an authoritarian system of control that seeks to enforce compliance through external regulation, then opportunities for learning will be lost and the playground may feel unsafe for some.

Rewards and sanctions

Many schools rely on rewards and sanctions for supporting and enforcing rules and for operationalising their discipline policy. We argue that this should be kept to a minimum, and we include systems of reward in this. These methods have grown out of behaviourist psychology and experiments on animals, most famously Pavlov's dogs (classical conditioning) and Skinner's rats (operant conditioning). Fixed consequences operate as if all students were the same, with identical needs and intentions. They do not enable the student to try to repair what has been done. Additionally, fixed consequences can reduce teachers' autonomy, preventing them from applying their professional judgement. In our experience most schools feel the tension between having a consistent approach to rewards and sanctions and allowing individual staff to be responsive (as opposed to inconsistent) in dealing with behaviour and relationships in their classroom. These conditions are not ideal.

Rewards are the flip side of the sanctions coin. They may be positive rather than negative, but they rely on the same behaviourist philosophy. Just like sanctions, they are based on extrinsic rather than intrinsic motivation. Students behave in particular ways because they want the sticker, the extra playtime or increasingly the Vivo Miles, not because they value positive behaviour for its own sake. Rewards keep the responsibility for promoting positive behaviour with the teacher – they give out a powerful message that students need to be coerced into behaving well.

Rewards and sanctions should be used mindfully. While there may be some value in using these methods as a step in the 'training' of children, it would be inappropriate to use rewards and sanctions as the main method of influence on young people's behaviour beyond this initial stage. There surely comes a time when it is not only philosophically desirable but also instrumentally important to make use of less deterministic and more developmental methods. Rewards and sanctions are imposed from the outside and do not lead to self-discipline, despite what is often claimed. They deny students opportunities to develop an internalised set of moral and behavioural norms. Self-discipline requires a learning environment that provides opportunities to learn from one's experiences – including mistakes – and to reflect on those experiences.

Beyond the philosophical objections to rewards and sanctions expounded above, there is also research evidence that reveals some of the difficulties involved at a practical level. For example, there is often a mismatch between what staff consider to be effective and what students give weight to. As Miller et al. (1998: 56) point out, "pupils consider information sent to their homes commending good work or complaining about unsatisfactory performance to be the most, or one of the most, effective rewards and punishments respectively", while "studies have shown that positive information sent home is not considered by teachers to be a particularly potent reward or to be used frequently, although a complaint home is relatively common" (Miller, 2003: 151). Therefore, at a very basic level there is a discrepancy in the efficacy attributed to different rewards between teachers and pupils. An Australian study revealed a similarly problematic picture (Mansfield, 2007). This study showed that rewards and sanctions can help already motivated and self-regulating pupils to correct their behaviour infringements and increase their sense of belonging to the school but that they can prove to be disaffecting for those students who are already struggling to regulate their behaviour. This can have the effect of further alienating them from the school.

If rewards and sanctions are to be used, schools might wish to consider the need for:

- consistency among teachers in their use of sanctions and rewards – this means a lot of time spent in discussion about shared values, setting up the system and negotiating reductions in teachers' autonomy;
- regular monitoring of how the system is working, looking at patterns of positive and negative referrals, investigating variation amongst departments or stages and taking steps to ensure consistency;
- avoiding rewards which have a monetary value or which signal that school work is not valued – for example being allowed to arrive late or being excused homework;
- ensuring that praise is genuine and deserved, not routine and trite;
- considering how the everyday good behaviour of the majority of students is taken into account;
- ensuring that sanctions are effective in deterring the undesired behaviour of those who receive them the most;
- ensuring that staff do not use sanctions as a way of avoiding teaching disruptive students;
- keeping the system fresh and meaningful – each year with the arrival of a new set of pupils it needs to be reintroduced.

In light of the above theoretical, philosophical and practical problems with systems of reward and sanctions, there is clearly a need to adopt a more sophisticated and nuanced understanding and application of rewards and sanctions (at the very least) if peace-keeping is to be effective and ethical. There are, however, more developmental ways of responding to different kinds of behaviour in schools, and we outline these in the next section.

Behaviour management policy

All schools are required to have a behaviour management policy. This is to ensure both consistency and transparency. Developing a behaviour management strategy, however, can be more than a statutory obligation, or a paper exercise. It can be grounded in values and dialogue, and it can provide a framework for staff and student development. We here offer a way of thinking about how schools exercise authority that fits with the notion of positive peace. It moves from away from management and towards development. Table 6.1 presents this useful distinction. The premise is that behaviour management is a necessary, but not sufficient, focus for schools; beyond behaviour management, schools would do well to pay attention to the behaviour development of their pupils.

The common phrase 'behaviour for learning' is here supplemented with the phrase, 'behaviour for living'. Our contention is that engaging pupils in processes of reflection, dialogue and problem-solving about their behaviour supports them in understanding how it affects others and making appropriate changes. This helps to develop an internal moral compass, thereby increasing the likelihood that they will become more self-regulating. We do not advocate, here or anywhere, adults abdicating responsibility for protecting the human right of every child to learn and grow in safety. We do suggest, however, that this can be done in ways that encourage development, rather than in ways that merely manage and control.

Table 6.1 Behaviour management and behaviour development

	Behaviour management	Behaviour development
Misbehaviour is . . .	An obstacle to learning	An opportunity for learning
Main theoretical basis	Behaviourism	Humanistic psychology
Aim	Pupils to comply with the rules	Pupils to learn appropriate behaviour
Methods	Rewards and sanctions	Explicit teaching of behaviours
	Hierarchical sanctions system	Modelling
	Punishment	Dialogue
	Zero-tolerance	Collaborative problem-solving
Outcomes	External locus of control	Internal locus of control
	Extrinsic motivation	Intrinsic motivation
	Behaviour for learning	Behaviour for living

We give some examples below of what this might look like in practice. Later in the book we will give examples of more developmental peace-building activities that support this work. For now, we focus on peace-keeping and the need to maintain order and safety. This list, alongside Table 6.1, could be used as part of a professional development exercise for staff in schools (and even adapted for parents).

Attack the problem and not the student

    X   You are a pain.
    √   What you just did is a pain.

Focus on the positive

    X   You haven't tidied away yet.
    √   Well done, you have tidied most of your things, now what about the rest?

Affirm positive behaviour

    X   How many times do I have to tell you, Sean, stop tapping that pencil . . . .
    √   Well done, Ben, you are ready to listen and not fiddling with anything . . . Oh well done, Sean, you too . . . .

Use neutral language

    X   You are behaving very badly today.
    √   You are choosing to behave badly today. How about you make some different choices?
    X   Put that gum in the bin, now!
    √   Pop that in the bin, thank you.
    X   You'd better tell me what you are going to do about this.
    √   I wonder what you could do to make things right again.

Catch them red handed being good

    X   (Silence).
    √   Do you know, I was so proud of you all today when I came back into the room and you were all working quietly . . . .

Bring yourself into the equation

- X   You can't go out to play until you have finished your writing.
- √   I don't want you to go out to play until you have finished your writing.
- X   For goodness sake, stop shouting.
- √   I don't like it when you shout like that.

Explain why you are asking a student to do something

- X   Get out of the mud now.
- √   Michelle, get out of the mud. When your shoes get dirty you bring mud in the classroom.

Rewards/sanctions do not have to be complex

- X   If you carry on using scissors dangerously you will lose your break for a week.
- √   If you carry on using scissors dangerously, you will be the last in the line to go to break.

Acknowledge powerful feelings

- X   For goodness sake, stop sulking.
- √   I can see that you are really upset about that. It must have been quite hard for you.

Discuss the consequences of the student's behaviour

- X   Get out! (Why?) Because I say so.
- √   Stop kicking Arif now! It hurts him, and we have agreed to keep hands and feet to ourselves . . . .

Using this language might feel alien for some teachers, but it is useful to reflect on how the alternative language here frames discipline as a contractual arrangement that is based on fairness, reason, clarity and cooperation. When language reverts to being authoritarian, it can reflect structural and cultural violence and it takes responsibility away from young people.

Furthermore, authoritarian language is no longer fit for purpose. The exigencies of the world in which young people are growing up place ever-greater importance on developing responsibility, a moral compass and self-regulation. Young people of school age, for example, are natives of the virtual world; most adults working in schools are tourists. Young people have the edge over adults in their mastery of the virtual world and social media. It is simply not feasible for adults to set the rules for young people's behaviour on social media and in the virtual world; young people know better than the adults how the new technologies work and they are always many steps ahead. A recent Australian review of the literature reporting on young people and their use of social media makes the recommendation to "foster 'digital age literacies' among children and young people which span media, internet and social–emotional literacies that consider not only the safe use of social media, but the moral and ethical repercussions of their everyday practices" (Swist *et al.*, 2015). It is therefore essential, now more than ever, that schools work with students to help them to develop their individual and collective ethical literacy and to encourage them to navigate their increasingly complex worlds in ways that keep them safe, as well as limit the harm they do to others.

If the ultimate aim of the behaviour policy in a school is to achieve compliance with the agreed norms, then it is important to address the question of how the school can most effectively enable pupils to regulate their behaviour. One of the common assumptions in society (which has been internalised into the logic of schools) is that punishment is an effective form of creating compliance. At this point, we therefore turn to the question of punishment.

Discipline and punishment

It can be useful to contrast punishment with discipline. Both seek to achieve the same outcome – that is, compliance with the agreed rules. However, as Dyson (2014) points out,

> the word "discipline" comes from the Latin "discipuli", which means student or disciple, suggesting a teacher–pupil relationship. Punishment comes from the Greek word "poine" and its Latin derivative "poena", which means revenge, and forms the root words of pain, penalty and penitentiary.

This distinction is clear when self-discipline is contrasted with self-punishment. Self-discipline is a positive aspect of learning, whereas self-punishment carries more negative associations. We will return to the concept of self-discipline in the peace-building chapter.

It is useful to ask why schools use punishment so consistently, especially when the evidence suggests not only its undesirability but also its ineffectiveness. In many ways, it would seem that schools are simply continuing to do what they have always done; punishment is an intrinsic part of the repertoire of schools' thinking and acting and replicates the military, religious and judiciary origins of state education. Alfie Kohn (2006) suggests some of the reasons why schools punish so willingly. These include: the fact that it seems like a quick fix; people expect it (often especially parents); it asserts the authority of the school; it satisfies the need for a primitive form of justice based on revenge and shame; it avoids chaos reigning; and it gives the impression that something is being done.

There are, however, many reasons why punishment should be avoided where possible. Punishment aims to stop, rather than change, a behaviour; it does not encourage the wrongdoer to reflect on what they have done, or take responsibility for putting things right. It also encourages deceit – the most important thing becomes not getting caught. Punishment can create feelings of resentment and victimisation on the part of the wrongdoer; they can focus more on the harm done to them through punishment than on the harm that they may have caused. Finally, punishment models behaviours that adults claim to disapprove of: that inflicting pain and unpleasantness onto others is justifiable if people believe they are in the right. This is a dangerous thing to 'teach'. Perhaps Nietzsche says it best: "Speaking generally, punishment hardens and numbs, it produces concentration, it sharpens the consciousness of alienation, it strengthens the power of resistance" (1887: 73).

In our discussion of structural and cultural violence in schools in Part I, we cited research evidence that rote learning and teaching to the test led to increasing numbers of students developing negative attitudes towards learning. Should these students be punished? Should they be labelled as having behavioural difficulties or even special educational needs if the learning environment is neither engaging nor inclusive? How should teachers value those students who want different things or who think in different ways? The new *Code of Practice for Special Educational Needs and Disabilities in England* (DfE, 2014) has helpfully removed behaviour as a special need and instead requires school to "consider whether continuing disruptive behaviour might be a result of unmet educational or other needs" (DfE, 2016: 4). Already, we have witnessed the start of a shift in how schools think about and work with behaviour difficulties. One inner-London local authority has produced a strategy to support schools to work with students displaying disruptive behaviour through assessment of needs and appropriate social and emotional wellbeing interventions (Hackney Learning Trust, 2015). This helps to shift the focus from direct to structural and cultural violence and bears out the fact that the student alone does not create conflict and indiscipline, even though he or she may be the one enacting it.

This is not to say that punishment is never useful or appropriate. A review of research evidence on whether punishment works concludes that, for punishment to be effective as a deterrent, it must be administered for the right misdemeanour, by the right person, at the right time, for the right reason (Sanson *et al.*, 1996). As we identified with rewards and sanctions, punishment may play a limited part in the maintenance of safety and order in schools. As Kathy Bickmore argues,

> [w]here standards for nonviolent behavior are communicated clearly and upheld in an equitable manner, as part of a broad repertoire of conflict management and restorative practices, strict punishment (reserved for only the most serious violent behaviors) may form a defensible part of a comprehensive anti-violence system.
>
> (2011: 650)

In this way, punishment is not excluded from the spectrum of approaches that a school may adopt, but rather it occupies a very clearly defined place within a broader context of peace-keeping, peace-making and peace-building.

If punishment is to be used, it is useful to begin to unpick some of the erroneous assumptions that underpin its over-use. To this end we have devised a survey (presented in Table 6.2) that can be administered to both adults and young people in order to establish whether or not a particular protocol, in this instance, detention, is delivering the outcomes a school staff might believe it does. Our survey is based on an original survey first presented in Thorsborne and Blood (2013). Other protocol reviews can be developed along similar lines, and we suggest that simple online tools (e.g. Survey Monkey) are used so that collating responses is very easy. It might even be helpful to include parents in the survey. Clearly, it is important that the survey is administered anonymously, and that students understand that there are no right or wrong responses. They won't get in trouble for honest answers.

Once data have been gathered, comparisons can be made between both sets of results to see whether or not adults and young people share the same views about the purpose and outcomes of the detention protocol. When both sets of results have been fed back to staff (and students), discussion can follow about their meaning and implications. Such an exercise might finish with a question: does detention have a place in our school, and, if it does, how might we improve it in line with our positive peace-building activities?

Table 6.2 Detention survey

Detention survey	Please tick a box			
	Strongly agree	Agree	Disagree	Strongly disagree
1. Detentions tell students that teachers take bad behaviour seriously.				
2. Detentions help students think about the things they did wrong.				
3. Detentions are good for helping students improve their behaviour.				
4. Pupils deserve the detentions they are given.				
5. Pupils don't mind doing a detention if they deserve it.				
6. Pupils skip detentions where they can.				
7. Detentions remind students that adults are in charge.				
8. Some teachers give lots of detentions and others give out very few.				
9. When students have done a detention, there are no bad feelings towards the teacher who gave it.				
10. Students are better behaved for teachers that give out lots of detentions.				
11. Detentions are a good way to make sure our school is a safe school.				
12. What suggestions do you have that might improve the effectiveness of detention as an intervention to develop better behaviours for learning?				

Safeguarding and child protection

A final area to be discussed here in relation to peace-keeping is safeguarding and child protection. In the UK, child protection has a high profile and a focus on safeguarding has become embedded as one of the functions of schooling and children's services. The most recent addition to the list of risks that schools have a duty to protect children and young people from is radicalisation. Section 26 of the Counter-Terrorism and Security Act 2015 requires that schools have "due regard to the need to prevent people from being drawn into terrorism". This is particularly relevant to our discussion of peace-keeping in schools.

Placing statutory duties onto teachers through counter-terrorism law is an act that surely requires interrogation. Criticism has come from those on both the Left and the Right of politics. *The Telegraph* newspaper in an article in March 2016 reported that "teachers and legal experts have expressed concerns over wrong referrals to the police and also the danger of closing down spaces for debate in school, which may lead to radicalisation". The teaching unions have strongly criticised the so-called Prevent strategy, which aligns safeguarding children from extremism with the promotion of identified 'British' values.

Two of the principal criticisms levelled at the Prevent strategy are that it creates relationships of suspicion between teachers and pupils and that it is likely to be counter-productive by further marginalising those members of society who are most at risk of radicalisation.

This is perhaps the most recent iteration of the structural and cultural violence in schools that we identified in Part I of this book. Distrust, fear and suspicion of otherness lie at the core of the Prevent strategy. The teaching unions report overly simplistic training on the Prevent strategy, leading to confusion and anxiety among teachers. Teachers are, in the eyes of some, increasingly used as the soft police of the State.

In her 2008 book *Educating against Extremism*, Professor Lynn Davies provides an insightful analysis of the complexities of extremism, fundamentalism and radicalisation, as well as a constructive alternative framework to the Prevent agenda. Davies calls for a stronger and more active political education of pupils alongside critical media education and active citizenship education, as well as critical and comparative religious education. All of this, she argues, needs to be undertaken from a universal value position around human rights. Davies' approach to the threat to young people posed by fundamentalism is strongly aligned with our own approach to peace-building: one which is founded on promoting critical awareness of the world in which young people live, and which builds active critical citizenship.

Conclusion

In this chapter, we have attempted to navigate the tricky area of peace-keeping within an educational context. It is clear that, if schools can avoid militaristic, authoritarian and pseudo-judiciary processes, they will have reduced need for peace-keeping. In such circumstances peace-making and peace-building can thrive and contribute towards a culture of positive peace. While many peace educators have argued against some of the measures that we have outlined here, we choose to acknowledge that rules, rewards, sanctions, behaviour policies and security measures do have their place within contemporary systems of schooling. In this, we continue to attempt to maintain a balance between idealism and realism and to acknowledge that direct, structural and cultural violence in schools need robust and expedient (as well as more proactive long-term and creative) responses.

References

Baumrind, D. (1966). Effects of authoritative parental control on child behavior. *Child Development*, 37(4), 887–907.

Bickmore, K. (2011). Policies and programming for safer schools: are 'anti-bullying' approaches impeding education for peacebuilding? *Educational Policy*, 25, 648–687.

Biesta, G. (2014). *The Beautiful Risk of Education*. Boulder, CO: Paradigm Publishers.

Brock, S. and Reeves, M. (2014). *Psychological Safety: moving beyond the basics to make our schools safer*. [Blog] SafeandSoundSchools. [online] Retrieved 5 August 2016 from www.safeandsoundschools.org/2014/07/23/psychological-safety-moving-beyond-the-basics-to-make-our-schools-safer

Cremin, H. (2012). *The Impact of Intergenerational Conflict on the Civic Action and Volunteering of Disadvantaged Youth in the UK*. Paper presented at the American Educational Research Association Conference, Vancouver, April 2012.

Cremin, H., Mason, C. and Busher, H. (2011). Problematising pupil voice using visual methods: findings from a study of engaged and disaffected pupils in an urban secondary school. *British Educational Research Journal*, 37, 585–603.

Davies, L. (2008). *Educating Against Extremism*. Stoke-on-Trent: Trentham Books.

Department for Education (DfE). (2015). *Special Educational Needs and Disability Code of Practice.* London: DfE.

Department for Education (DfE). (2016). *Behaviour and Discipline in Schools: advice for headteachers and school staff.* [online] Retrieved 18 September 2016 from www.gov.uk/government/uploads/system/uploads/attachment_data/file/488034/Behaviour_and_Discipline_in_Schools_-_A_guide_for_headteachers_and_School_Staff.pdf

Dyson, M. (2014). Punishment or child abuse? *The New York Times.* [online] Retrieved 18 September 2016 from www.nytimes.com/2014/09/18/opinion/punishment-or-child-abuse.html?_r=2

Hackney Learning Trust. (2015). *No Need to Exclude.* [online] Retrieved 18 September 2016 from www.learningtrust.co.uk/TPG/PFS/Pages/NoNeedtoExclude.aspx

Kohn, A. (2006). *Beyond Discipline: from compliance to community.* Alexandria, VA: Association for Supervision and Curriculum Development.

Mansfield, C. (2007). *Responding to Rewards and Sanctions: the impact on students' sense of belonging and school affect.* Paper presented at the annual meeting of the Australian Association for Research in Education, Fremantle. [online] Retrieved 18 September 2016 from www.core.ac.uk/download/pdf/11232163.pdf?repositoryId=342

Marland, M. (1975). *The Craft of the Classroom: a survival guide to classroom management in the secondary school.* London: Heinemann Educational.

Miller, A. (2003). *Teachers, Parents and Classroom Behaviour: a psychosocial approach.* Glasgow: Open University Press.

Miller, A., Ferguson, E. and Simpson, R. (1998). The perceived effectiveness of rewards and sanctions in primary schools: adding in the parental perspective. *Educational Psychology,* 18(1), 55–64.

Nietzsche, F. (1887). *The Genealogy of Morals.* New York: Boni and Liveright.

Rogers, B. (2012). *You Know the Fair Rule* (3rd edn). London: Pearson Publications.

Sanson, A., Montgomery, B., Gault, U., Gridley, H. and Thomson, D. (1996). Punishment and behaviour change: an Australian Psychological Society position paper. *Australian Psychologist,* 31(3), 157–165.

Swist, T., Collin, P., McCormack, J. and Third, A. (2015). *Social Media and the Wellbeing of Children and Young People: a literature review.* Prepared for the Commissioner for Children and Young People, Perth. [online] Retrieved 14 July 2016 from www.uws.edu.au/__data/assets/pdf_file/0019/930502/Social_media_and_children_and_young_people.pdf

Thorsborne, M. and Blood, P. (2013). *Implementing Restorative Practices in Schools: a practical guide to transforming school communities.* London: Jessica Kingsley Publishers.

UNICEF. (2012). *A Summary of the UN Convention on the Rights of the Child.* [online] Retrieved 5 August 2016 from www.unicef.org.uk/Documents/Publication-pdfs/betterlifeleaflet2012_press.pdf

Chapter 7

Education for peace-making

Introduction

Where peace-keeping refers to the ways in which peace is created around the person and around the school in the form of systems of security and discipline, peace-making refers to making peace between people in the aftermath of incidents of conflict. This is of course not limited to schools in settings affected by armed conflict. While peace education is increasingly associated with societies "recovering from high-level conflicts such as war" (Ashton, 2007: 40), it is worth reasserting at this point the need for peace education in apparently stable, democratic states such as the UK. Young people everywhere need to learn how to respond non-violently to conflict and how to work towards the reduction of destructive conflict and violence. The fundamental fact that the purpose of school is to educate is the main philosophical reason why peace-making is central for addressing conflict and violence in schools. Peace-making is an essentially educative approach to conflict resolution. The role of school staff and of schools is not the same as that of police officers or other professionals in the legal or criminal justice sector. The role of schools is to teach, and peace-making provides the ideal mechanisms for teaching young people many lessons from those moments when they get it wrong.

The reader will by now be familiar with the conceptualisations of violence, peace and conflict promoted in this book. We argue here and elsewhere that conflict is neither inherently good nor bad, constructive nor destructive; it just depends on how it is engaged with. Acknowledging that conflict is inevitable is not to underplay the harm that can be wrought in a school setting by incidents of conflict that occur. Peace-making approaches offer much-needed structure and calm at times of disruption, disturbance and distress. Essentially, peace-making activities have the aim of resolving flare-ups of conflict to restore harmony, but also of reducing the threat of escalation or recurrence. Returning to Johan Galtung's conceptualisation of positive and negative peace, positive peace requires the absence of violence in all of its forms. A peace-making response seeks to engage those involved in conflict in constructive processes of reflection, dialogue and resolution.

This chapter presents a rationale for peace-making in schools, setting out the philosophical and pragmatic reasons why a constructive approach to conflict is both important and useful. We begin with a review of conflict theory.

Conflict resolution

Theories originating in the field of conflict studies underpin many of the approaches to peace-making presented here. The work of the social psychologist Morton Deutsch has been particularly influential in developing what is now referred to as conflict resolution. The aim of Morton Deutsch's work was to distinguish between destructive and constructive conflict, and for Deutsch "the point is not how to eliminate or prevent conflict but rather how to make it productive" (1973: 17). On the basis of Deutsch's theories, brothers David and Roger Johnson have explored the importance of cooperation in school settings and have conceptualised conflict resolution as an opportunity for profound learning (Johnson and Johnson, 1996). This is not merely a technical process, however, despite the fact that conflict theory can sometimes make it appear so.

Deutsch's *Handbook of Conflict Resolution: theory and practice* (with Coleman and Marcus, 3rd edn, 2011) is widely used and is a good example of the kind of thinking that underlies the theory and practice of conflict resolution. Even the title is revealing: 'handbook', creating an image of someone in a workshop fixing something with a book containing practical guidance close at hand. The basic idea in the book is that destructive conflict (conflicting parties compete to determine who wins and who loses) can be transformed into constructive conflict (conflicting parties cooperate to resolve a mutual problem). The handbook deals with conflict at interpersonal, intergroup and international levels. Thus, the (2011) introduction begins with a series of conflict vignettes that aim to show that the principles of conflict and conflict resolution are universal, whether these apply to the interpersonal realm of family and friends, or to conflict between states. It is simply a matter of scaling up. The vignettes cover disputes between a husband and a wife, an intergroup conflict at a school and the conflict in Northern Ireland. The same universal laws of conflict resolution are seen to apply in all settings. The introduction goes on to list a series of questions that apply "to conflicts of all sorts" (2011: xxiv). We reject this rather mechanistic way of thinking about conflict, arguing that it is too firmly grounded in harmful discourses of modernity.

The field of conflict resolution in general tends to be built around modernist assumptions. It focuses on the intervention, rather than on the ground in which the intervention finds itself. There is an attempt to systematise and universalise through a plethora of theories, models, categories, levels, stages, tools, etc. The world is understood and manipulated through metaphors of the machine and agriculture. As Gur-Ze'ev points out,

> [i]t is . . . important to question the unproblematic introduction of conflict resolution skills and knowledge. From the postmodern perspective, these strategies are revealed as one of the many conflicting voices fighting over the position of silencing their Others, in context of constant semiotic bombardment. Peace education is unveiled as a position situated in the narrativisation of the individual and collective "self". As such, it is part and parcel of the conflicting violences competing over hegemony.
>
> (2001: 333)

In other words, this way of viewing conflict, violence and peace certainly has an elegant simplicity, but it lacks the messiness and unpredictability of conflict on the ground. While our own positive peace framework and iPEACE model contain some of these elements, we have tried to stress the importance of integrating both responsive and proactive peace-making and peace-building. This integration is key – it ensures that structural and cultural violence are addressed alongside presenting issues and that conflict resolution and peace-making embrace complexity and cannot degenerate into pacification and suppression. We hope that our readers will be encouraged to engage with all of the ideas presented here in holistic and creative ways.

Conflict resolution education, therefore, often works well when it is part of a wider peace education programme. For example, Kathy Bickmore includes "conflict dialogue pedagogies" within her citizenship learning and student voice programme (Bickmore and Parker, 2014). Others have gone so far as to claim that conflict resolution should not be included as part of peace education at all (Salomon and Cairns, 2009). Danesh (2006) has an interesting take on this, suggesting that peace education work should be grounded in a unity-based worldview, rather than in a conflict-based worldview. He takes a developmental stance to both individuals and societies. Conflict comes from survival-based stages of development during infancy and childhood (and from agrarian and pre-industrial periods of societal development) and from identity-based stages of development during the coming of age of both the individual and society. The unity-based worldview comes from maturity and is based on an understanding of the oneness of humanity. In this worldview, "society operates according to the principle of unity in diversity and holds as its ultimate objective the creation of a civilization of peace – equal, just, progressive, moral, diverse and united" (2006: 67–68). Thus, the focus of peace education should be on unity and not on conflict. We do not share this view, arguing here and elsewhere that peace-making and conflict resolution strategies more specifically have an important part to play in achieving positive peace in schools.

The three pillars of peace-making

The peace-making approaches that we have chosen to focus on here are restorative approaches (RA), peer mediation and peace-making circles. These three practices can all be defined as peace-making, because they share the common purpose of engaging people involved in incidents of conflict and harm in a process of reflection and dialogue, with the aim of achieving a resolution that addresses the needs of all parties. These three pillars are compared and contrasted in Chapter 5 as part of the iPEACE model.

The fundamentals of these practices and how they might be used are presented in more detail here. The three approaches are all founded on the principles of humanistic psychology and humanistic education "which are grounded in the idea that individuals will self-actualise given the right conditions of unconditional positive regard, empathy and genuineness on the part of a skilled helper" (Cowie, 2010: 5). They are all essentially postmodern in that they do not assume one "Truth" grounded in rationality and reason, working instead to enable multiple perspectives to be heard and solutions to be found that are right for the individuals concerned at any one moment in time. We begin with restorative approaches.

Restorative approaches

There is something of a difficulty when it comes to defining restorative approaches. As Johnson and Van Ness (2011) have remarked, restorative justice (from which RA have evolved) is an essentially contested concept. That is, like art and indeed peace itself, people assume there is a generally shared understanding of its meaning, despite a multiplicity of different ways of thinking about it. While on the one hand this can be frustrating, it can also be invigorating. The fact that it is essentially contested allows the concept to remain dynamic and subject to debate and renewal.

Given that RA in schools have evolved from restorative justice (RJ), it is important to trace the history of RJ in order to understand what RA are and how they have come to be adopted so widely in schools across the world in a relatively short space of time.

There are fuller accounts of the history of RJ elsewhere (e.g. Liebmann, 2007), but here we present an overview of the evolution of RJ with the aim of bringing clarity rather than comprehensiveness.

RJ has been called an ancient practice with a modern name, which refers to the fact that current restorative practice has its roots in the justice perspectives and practices of indigenous communities across the planet. These indigenous roots are one of three prime antecedents of what is today known as RJ, the other two being the foundational theoretical work of Nils Christie and Howard Zehr and the ground-level activities of practitioners such as Yantzi and Thorsborne.

The first of these, the indigenous roots of RJ, is fairly well established, although various authors argue about whether or not the indigenous roots of RJ are evidence of its essential universality or a romanticisation of human history (e.g. Braithwaite, 1993; Weitekamp, 1999). What is fairly uncontested is that RJ is influenced by rites and traditions that trace back to ancient ways of engaging with wrongdoing and justice, such as those of the Māori people and the First Nations communities (Pranis et al., 2003). David Carruthers (2013) provides an interesting insight into some of the constructs within the Māori worldview that can be seen to be fundamental within restorative practice. For example, the Māori concept of mana contains the idea of the prestige or agency of an individual, which is what needs to be restored following an incident of harm. The First Nation Navajo conceptualisation of justice is founded on the restoration of harmony, so that, rather than seeking to blame and punish those who have caused harm, the prime aim is to meet the needs of the victim and restore their wellbeing and at the same time restore and reintegrate the wrongdoer into the community (Sia, 2013). These indigenous roots have informed the foundations and principles of RJ.

The second important antecedent to RJ is the writings of Howard Zehr and Nils Christie. Norwegian criminologist Nils Christie's 1977 paper Conflicts as Property has come to be seen as highly influential in the evolution of RJ. In this paper he makes the argument that "conflicts . . . ought to be used, and become useful, for those originally involved in the conflict" (p. 1) rather than appropriated by "professional thieves" such as lawyers (p. 3). Howard Zehr, writing from a Mennonite perspective, drew on Christie's contributions in formulating the restorative justice paradigm, which he set in contrast to the retributive justice paradigm (1985). He later articulated three foundational principles of restorative justice in his now seminal work Changing Lenses. These are that "Crime is a violation of people and relationships"; that "it creates obligations to make things right"; and that "justice involves the victim, the offender, and the community in a search for solutions which promote repair, reconciliation and reassurance" (1990: 183). Christie and Zehr are two of the most widely acknowledged and cited informers of contemporary RJ. They helped to establish the theoretical perspectives on which the field is based. It was the activities of practitioners on the ground in different parts of the world, however, that played a crucial role in bringing RJ into action.

In 1974, in Ontario, Canada, the first application of RJ was documented. After two young offenders vandalised 22 properties in a small Ontario town, the assigned probation officer Mark Yantzi and a Mennonite prison support worker Dave Worth asked the judge for permission to arrange for the two offenders to meet the victims of the vandalism in order to see if reparations could be made. In 1994 in Queensland, Australia, school guidance counsellor Margaret Thorsborne collaborated with police officers to deal with an incident where three pupils from Maroochydore State High School assaulted another student following a school dance in a gang-related incident. The restorative conference that Marg Thorsborne facilitated under advice from the local police officers paved the way for the now burgeoning restorative approaches in schools movement (O'Connell, 1998).

RA in schools can be understood as "a philosophy, in action, that places the relationship at the heart of the educational experience" (Corrigan, 2012). Philosophically, RA represent a way of thinking about human behaviour (and misbehaviour) as an expression of needs. RA posit that, when wrongdoing occurs, as it inevitably will, then repairing the harm done is more important than dispensing punishment; it places the person harmed at the centre of its thinking. It further suggests that the needs of the person who has been harmed will be most effectively met by being an active participant in the ensuing process of resolution. Furthermore, RA involve identifying and meeting the needs of the person who has caused the harm, as well as the person who has been harmed. This is novel in two respects. First, schools traditionally have focused all of their attention on the wrongdoer and have ignored the plight of the person who has been wronged. Second, schools have traditionally framed the wrong-doer as bad and therefore not deserving of understanding or support. Working restoratively seeks to attend to the needs of all parties, including the needs of the community.

This alternative perspective on wrongdoing requires that different questions be asked of the person who has caused harm, the person who has been harmed and the community to which those people belong. Instead of focusing primarily, or even exclusively, on the person who has done wrong through a process of blaming, shaming and punishing, RA require teachers and others to invite the person who has been harmed into a process of inquiry and dialogue. RA offer tools that facilitate processes of inquiry, reflection and dialogue with both parties individually and potentially together. The aims of this way of thinking about and working with conflict are to meet the needs of the person harmed, to hold the person who has caused the harm to account and give them a supported opportunity to put things right. This enables both parties to move on from the incident with their respective sense of dignity and agency (*mana*) restored.

Practically, RA incorporate a number of specific interventions that can be employed to deal with negative behaviours and conflicts and to promote positive behaviour and relationships among members of the school community. All manifestations of RA have at their core a set of questions that put into practice the philosophy described above:

- What harm has been done?
- What needs has this harm created?
- Whose responsibility is it to address these needs, and how can they be enabled to do this?

Schools employ RA in the whole spectrum of contexts: staff may engage individual pupils in a 'restorative chat' in class, in the corridor or on the playground for low-level incidents of harm; students may be sent to a 'reflection room' when they are not able or willing to meet the expectations of the classroom; a 'classroom conference' may be convened to address harmful behaviours or relationships within the group; a 'community conference' may be convened for serious incidents of harm. In this way, schools and school staff can adapt the practice to suit their context. What underpins all restorative work are the values and principles that are expressed through the questions asked and through the attitude to wrongdoing and relationships that is adopted.

RA can be applied as part of our behaviour development framework (see Chapter 6). As a behaviour development intervention, RA seek to enable and encourage people who are responsible for causing the harm to come to a fuller understanding of what they did and how people were affected by their actions, with the aim of building their capacity to better manage their feelings, their behaviour and their relationships in the future. This aim is one aspect of the additional claim of RA to promote people's personal, social and emotional capabilities. The rationale for this is that actively engaging parties involved in an incident of conflict in a process of reflection, dialogue and resolution develops specific personal, social and emotional competencies, such as awareness of one's own feelings and understanding of how they link to one's behaviour, perspective-taking, empathy, problem-solving and moral reasoning.

Beyond being a peace-making process and a behaviour development process, RA have also been identified as having the potential to transform a whole-school ethos and culture to one with a strong focus on care and positive relations. Kane *et al.* reported in their evaluation of RA across 18 Scottish schools that they could serve as "a vehicle by which schools could develop a more positive ethos . . . a means of giving coherence and identity to established good practices and of further enhancing those practices" (2009: 248). In this way, RA can serve as a means for school change or even as a catalyst to generate a more relational school culture. It is in this way that RA can cross the boundary from peace-making (in terms of the mechanisms and activities it enables) to peace-building. In this, it is a vehicle for proactively creating a school culture that privileges collaborative problem-solving, care and compassion.

Recently, some authors have gone further with their claims for the potential of RA in schools. As restorative practice in schools matures, so some are beginning to call for a "radical, holistic version of RP" (McCluskey, 2013: 133). They see the opportunity for this values-based practice to bring to light, and to challenge, structural and cultural violence in schools. Dorothy Vaandering claims a critical role for RA in schools in confronting inequitable and unjust school cultures and practices. As she reports from her own research with school staff,

> [w]hat began as a strategy that they anticipated would respect students who had been harmed and caused harm, turned into a reflective practice that challenged educators to examine how the institutional structure itself, all its policies and practices, the curriculum and pedagogy, sent messages that honored or measured school participants.
>
> (2011: 323–324)

Vaandering draws a broad distinction between a focus on *measuring* pupils and staff (through testing and inspecting) and *honouring* pupils and staff through a more relational focus. The task of transforming structural and culturally violent systems of schooling can feel overwhelming (and we do not suggest here that hard-pressed, put-upon school staff should be expected to remedy the ills of society), but we do seek to raise questions about the wider potential of RA and new possibilities for creating transformative moments in schools. New spaces are indeed opening up as people engage with restorative practice in schools in increasingly creative and critical ways.

The evidence base for RA in schools provides useful information about the implementation of the practice (in terms of the conditions that are required to put this into practice effectively) and also about its impact (about the outcomes of implementing RA in schools). Implementation evidence reports that there are certain indicators of readiness for a school to adopt a restorative approach. These include: the full and informed commitment of the senior leadership team; a vision that is aligned with restorative values and principles; high quality training tailored to the needs of the school; and engagement with all members of the school community in order to understand what restorative approaches will mean in any particular context (Thorsborne and Blood, 2013).

Table 7.1 Research evidence on impact of restorative approaches in schools

Reduced	Increased	Improved
• Incidents of misbehaviour • Violence and bullying • Exclusions	• Teaching time • Safety • Connectedness to school	• Climate for learning • Social and emotional skills • Relationships among all members of the school

Sources: McCluskey *et al.*, 2008; Skinns *et al.*, 2009; Bevington, 2015

Evidence on the more readily measurable impacts of restorative practice in school settings is summarised in Table 7.1.

In summary, the various ways of applying RA to school practice, from conflict resolution to behaviour development to transforming school culture, can be aligned with the levels of violence articulated by Galtung. As a conflict resolution strategy, RA can serve to address and resolve incidents of direct violence. As behaviour development, they can address some aspects of structural violence in schools by providing experiences for pupils (and staff) to develop skills and characteristics that can help them to better achieve their potential. The higher level of application of RA to transform school culture provides intriguing possibilities for responding creatively to cultural violence. When a school refocuses its attention onto the quality and functioning of relationships, it can enable a mind-shift in individuals and a culture-shift in the institution.

Peer mediation

Mediation, like restorative justice, is a method of dispute resolution that rejects notions of universal truth and state-based justice. Its general thrust is towards a system of conflict resolution that empowers disputants at a local level to find their own solution to their own problems. Mediation is extensively used within the legal profession, where it is part of a wider system of alternative dispute resolution, but its usage has also extended into a range of other areas. These include community mediation, victim–offender mediation, environmental mediation, commercial mediation, family mediation, workplace mediation and inter-group conflict mediation, as well as peer mediation in schools.

Within a legal framework, mediation has been defined as "a voluntary process where a neutral mediator attempts to help the disputing parties to reach an agreement that is acceptable to both sides and that will bring the dispute to an early conclusion without having to go to court" (Genn, 2000). Mediators working in legal settings are usually contrasted with arbitrators or judges, who, unlike mediators, have the authority to make judgements or to force the parties to take a particular course of action.

Community mediation in the UK came from the United States in the 1980s. In the 1970s, the administration of President Jimmy Carter encouraged the creation of the first Neighbourhood Justice Centres. The goal of these centres, which became known as community mediation programmes, was to provide an alternative to court proceedings where local people could meet to resolve their disputes. Some of the most active of these centres were in New York, Los Angeles and Philadelphia. In the typical community mediation programme, a cross-section of neighbourhood volunteers was trained to mediate the disputes that arose in their community, including disputes between neighbours, family members, tenants and land-lords/landladies, consumers and salespeople, friends and small businesses. Some disputes were referred directly to the centre by local residents; others came through an affiliation with local courthouses and social service agencies. These centres typically worked with schools in order to avoid conflict arising in the first place. Since then community mediation (including schools work) has extended into Australia, Canada and many parts of Europe. Exponents in the field (for example Beer *et al.*, 1987) are often motivated by strong personal convictions. For many, a philosophy of non-violence underpins mediation, and the attraction for working preventatively in schools is very strong.

Drawing on her own work and Cornelius and Faire (1989), Liebmann (2000) lists a set of principles that is implicit in community mediation work:

- listening to others, for feelings as well as facts;
- cooperation with others, valuing their contributions;
- looking for common ground rather than differences;
- affirmation of self and others as a necessary basis for resolving conflict;
- speaking for oneself rather than accusing others;
- separating the problem from the people;
- trying to understand other people's points of view;
- using a creative problem-solving approach to work on conflicts;
- looking at what people want for the future rather than allocating blame for the past;
- looking at all the options before selecting one to try; and
- looking for a 'win–win' solution, where everyone's interests are satisfied, rather than the adversarial 'win–lose' approach where one person wins and the other person loses.

Clearly, these principles are ideally suited to schools, hence their early adoption as a promising form of peer education.

From a technical point of view, in both schools and communities face-to-face mediation usually involves four or five stages. There may be several meetings with each person to prepare and then a face-to-face mediation meeting would normally follow. The following instructions for mediators set out these stages:

Stages in mediation
Stage One: Introductions
Welcome everyone and remind them that:

 o You are impartial.
 o What is discussed is confidential.
 o Your role is to facilitate, not to offer solutions.

You need agreement from the people involved that they will:

 o speak respectfully;
 o listen without interrupting; and
 o focus on how they have been affected by the problem, not on blame.

Stage Two: What has happened?

o Each person has uninterrupted time to talk about the problem from their own point of view.

o Ask about feelings if not forthcoming.

o Summarise what has been said.

Stage Three: Acknowledging feelings and perspectives

o Ask each person if they can acknowledge the feelings of the other person (even if they do not agree) and then communicate this to the other person.

Stage Four: Creating options

o Ask each in turn to say what they would like to happen next.

o Ask for offers rather than requests at first.

Stage Five: Agreement

o Get them to agree a course of action based in the possible solutions they have generated.

o What do they need to formalise the agreement? Do they need to meet again to discuss progress?

These stages provide a framework for mediation, even though in reality the process is often cyclical and does not follow straight lines. Older peer mediators in schools tend to use all of these stages, whereas younger students will often skip the acknowledgement of feelings and the generation of more than one option for an agreement. They are usually happy with an agreement to make friends!

There are multiple benefits that a well-implemented peer mediation scheme can bring to a school. A meta-analysis of 18 empirical research studies into the effectiveness and impact of peer mediation in schools (Burrell *et al.*, 2003) reported the following findings:

- for mediators: "a substantial increase in academic performance after becoming a mediator" (p. 121); improved self-esteem; use of mediation skills outside the school setting, in the home and community;
- for those mediated: high degrees of satisfaction with the mediation process;
- for staff: high degrees of satisfaction with the scheme; a reduction in staff disciplinary actions; and
- for the school: improved school climate reported by pupils and adults.

The benefits of peer mediation can thus be summarised as: actively and purposefully developing young people's communication and problem-solving skills; reducing levels of conflict; freeing up adults' time to teach; and contributing to a more calm, positive school climate (NSPCC, 2004; Childline, 2005).

The many benefits of peer mediation in a school will only be achieved if the scheme is well implemented. There is ample evidence showing when and why peer mediation schemes fail: not enough or too many mediators; no lead member of staff; profile not maintained; mediators not sufficiently supervised and developed (Cremin, 2007). A thorough, thoughtful and sustained approach will help to avoid the common pitfalls. We therefore set out in Table 7.2 one model for developing and implementing a peer mediation scheme based on our experience of working with hundreds of schools.

Table 7.2 Scheme for introducing peer mediation into a school

Phase	Main actions	Notes
Peace-building scheme of work	Plan and deliver 4/6 week peace-building programme to the entire cohort of pupils who will be eligible to become peer mediators.	Can be delivered as part of the citizenship or personal and social education curriculum. Can also be delivered to students who will use the scheme in an age-appropriate way.
Application and appointment of peer mediators	Invite and encourage pupils to apply for a post as a peer mediator. Receive applications. Hold interviews. Appoint mediators.	Pupils complete application form, obtain references and undergo interview. When the scheme is established, this can be done each year by the previous year's mediators.
Peer mediators' training	2/3 days of training of the peer mediators.	Purposes: team building, proper rehearsal of mediation skills, pupils to develop their own guidelines for effective practice. If this is done by an outside agency, this also needs to be attended by the adults who will help to support the scheme.
Design the peer mediation scheme	Develop the scheme that fits best with the school context, and avoids common pitfalls.	Decisions need to be made about: what sorts of problems are appropriate for peer mediation; what number of mediators is required; rota; staff lead; venue for mediation; support and supervision for mediators, etc.
Launch the scheme	High-profile launch of the scheme with pupils, staff and parents.	Clarify and specify everyone's role in relation to the scheme.
Maintain the scheme	On-going support and development of mediators. Annually publicise the scheme.	Initially a weekly team session to debrief, share experiences and keep up a regular programme of review and development.

Students can be trained to become peer mediators as early as age 7 right through to adulthood. One concern about peer mediation and peer support schemes in general is that it is placing too high a responsibility on the shoulders of young people. Our response to this concern is that, if pupils are to be expected to take responsibility, they must be given responsibility. Notwithstanding this, one essential element of any peer mediation scheme is safeguarding the mediators and those pupils in conflict. For this reason, it is crucial to specify the conflicts to be mediated and also to conduct regular support and supervision with the mediators.

Peace-making circles

Circles are a leitmotif of restorative practice, peer mediation and peace-making more broadly. Circles represent interconnectedness, equality and flow. Peace-making circles have a centre, which is a space that anyone can put things into (stories, concerns, hopes) for them to be shared, looked at afresh and engaged with. There are rituals associated with peace-making circle work concerning the role of the facilitator (or the keeper of the circle), the use of a talking object and the process to be followed. Some peace-making circles involve parties experiencing conflict sitting with others who are also affected; others involve someone experiencing a difficulty being supported by a group to come to some kind of resolution, even if the other party is not in the circle.

Peace-making circles, like restorative justice, are found in the First Nation cultures of North America. Some find this to be a healthy reminder of the sacredness of human connection and interaction, while others are more dismissive of this fact. The authors' experience is that young people value the rituals of peace-making circles. These rituals provide a safe and boundaried space in which young people can express themselves and hear others in new and different ways. This often creates feelings of wonder and curiosity, as well as resolution and peace.

Peace-making circles can provide a structured format for dealing with difficulties that have arisen within a class, either a one-off incident or an on-going negative dynamic that is causing harm. These circles usefully adopt a no-blame approach. Where there are identified wrongdoers and a need to repair the harm done to individuals, then a restorative conference may be more appropriate. Bringing conflicting people together in a circle can be challenging. It can take people out of their comfort zone, as they face each other with no tables between them and no books or pens to distract them. It can feel exposing to have everybody's eyes and ears on you as you speak. This is where the ritual aspects of the circle are useful in denoting this as a different type of space requiring a different type of engagement. To do this, it is important to give attention to the specific details of working in the circle, such as the ritual aspect of opening and closing the circle, the guidelines for how people will act or behave in the circle, the use of a talking object and the role of the keeper or facilitator of the circle. This is discussed in more detail in the next chapter.

For younger children, it can be beneficial to use puppets, toys or masks. These can be used to create a short scenario to present a conflict that will be familiar to one or more of the children. Puppets create distance and allow children to think about the issues without singling anybody out. The process might proceed as follows:

- Puppets, toys or masks are used to introduce a conflict that members of the class are experiencing.
- Having watched the short scenario and listened to the teacher explaining a bit more about it, the children say what they imagine the puppet is feeling in a 'go-round' (see next chapter).
- The children suggest in another go-round what the puppet could do or what we could offer to do, to help her or him.
- Finally the teacher summarises what has been said and, where appropriate, asks the members of the class to make links to what happens in real life.

For adults and older students, a more direct approach can be used. The following four-step process is extremely useful. The main issue here is to ensure that group members own the advice that they give, and do not resort to telling the person experiencing the conflict what to do. This is achieved by giving feedback in the first person (If I were in this situation, I might . . .) rather than in the second person (you could . . .).

The teacher explains the five steps. These are:

- The person experiencing conflict sets out the parameters of the conflict and talks about it until they feel that they have covered all aspects.
- Students have a chance to ask questions for clarification.
- Next, in a go-round, each student says what they feel the conflict is about (in essence).
- In the final go-round, students say either " . . . name . . . , what I think I might do in your situation is . . . " or "What I could offer to do to help is . . . ". The student with the problem listens but does not need to respond.
- After time for reflection, the student with the problem feeds back to the group about which suggestions and/or support she or he wishes to act on.

Before they use the process, students need to remind themselves and each other of the ground rules of the circle. In particular, for this activity they need to avoid: mentioning by name other students who may be involved in some way; gossiping about what is said; and giving people advice or trying to persuade them to take a particular action. If a conflict appears to be straying into areas that are inappropriate for school life, the teacher needs to take timely and sensitive action, which may well include bringing the process to an end and continuing with the student on an individual basis.

Peace-making circles can also be used to promote more child-centred and collaborative processes of behaviour management, as discussed in Chapter 6. When a problem-solving approach is used rather than a punitive approach, discipline becomes developmental rather than merely expedient. As already discussed, it enables behaviours that affect others in negative ways to be discussed in ways that educate and inform.

The following example of a peace-making circle in a school is taken from the experience of one of the authors.

Collaborative discipline using a peace-making circle

There have been reports from a number of pupils and parents that pupils within a class are being unkind to one another and that this is affecting how the pupils feel and is interfering with their ability to work at their best. The school decides to convene a peace-making circle to engage all members of the class in addressing the difficulties and finding a way forward.

A preparation session is held with the class to explain the purpose and the process of the circle, and make agreement on the guidelines for working in the circle. The guidelines are typically that one person speaks at a time (facilitated by using a talking object), that everybody is there to make things better and that there are no put downs. It is made clear that this is a no-blame approach focused on hearing from each other what it is like to be in this class and to agree how the class wants things to be in the future. Part of the preparation involves all pupils (and staff where appropriate) completing an anonymous simple survey writing their answers to the following questions. What is the best thing about being in this class? What is the worst thing about being in this class? How do you want this class to be in the future? These anonymous responses are collated by the member of staff who will facilitate the circle.

The following day, the class brings chairs into a circle and the facilitator thanks the class for their cooperation and their willingness to sort out what has been going wrong. The facilitator asks each person in turn to use the talking object to say what they like about the class, based on what they wrote before, or what they have thought about since. Staff members then take the talking object and say what it is that they value about the class. This first phase of affirmation and validation is important in acknowledging the well-functioning aspects of the group and to build good foundations for exploring the more difficult aspects of the way the group is functioning.

The second phase involves the facilitator reading some of the responses to the second question, identifying what people do not like about being in this class (focusing on behaviours not people, and not using any names). At this stage the emotion of the circle shifts into a more subdued mood. Pupils and staff are then invited to say for themselves to the group what it is that they do not like about being in the class, again avoiding the use of names and focusing on feelings. This phase provides an opportunity for people to express their concerns and frustrations and to be heard by everybody. In this way, the difficulties in the group are made real, communicating the actual effects on the people present. This phase concludes with the facilitator asking whether anyone in the group has anything they want to say, having heard how people in the class are being affected. At this stage, pupils can take the opportunity to apologise for their part in the difficulties if they so wish. They may even want to apologise to individuals for harm they have caused. The facilitator thanks people for taking responsibility for their actions and behaviour, and marks a symbolic line between what has been happening up to this point and what will happen from this point forward.

The focus then shifts towards the future and the facilitator reads aloud the suggestions offered for how the class members want things to be from now on. Again, people are invited to say for themselves how they want things to be. Based on the suggestions, a class agreement is written, which all members of the class are invited to sign. Two members of the class are then elected by the group to report to an appropriate member of staff on how the class is sticking to the agreement. The circle is then closed by the facilitator with recognition of the goodwill, maturity and responsibility shown. The class then engages in some fun activities in the circle to celebrate and change the mood.

In our experience, such peace-making circles are extremely powerful spaces that mark a significant moment in the life of a class. As well as the clarity and resolution brought about from the circle itself, they also offer a model of working together as a group to connect, understand each other better and resolve difficulties as they arise. The example involves a whole class, but the same structure can of course be employed with smaller groups, where there has been a falling out among a group of students. We have also used the peace-making circle structure to successfully address problematic dynamics within staff groups. Again, it is the intentionally different space and structure of the circle that is so powerful in engaging people in a different type of dialogue that is capable of addressing difficulties constructively, rather than defensively and destructively.

Conclusion

It will be clear that there is close alignment, and at times overlap, between the three pillars of peace-making presented in this chapter, despite the fact that they lend themselves to rather different kinds of conflict. The approaches and practices are mutually reinforcing and provide sufficient diversity for schools to select the elements of peace-making that they are ready, willing and able to engage with. It will also be clear that some aspects of peace-making work have the potential to challenge robustly some of the structural and cultural violence in force in schools and schooling. In this way, some of the pillars presented here may start to build towards peace, to which we turn in the next chapter.

References

Ashton, C. (2007). Using theory of change to enhance peace education evaluation. *Conflict Resolution Quarterly*, 25, 39–53.

Beer, J., Steif, E. and Walker, C. (1987). *Peacemaking in Your Neighbourhood: mediator's handbook*. Concordville, PA: Friends Suburban Project.

Bevington, T. (2015). Appreciative evaluation of restorative approaches in schools. *Pastoral Care in Education*, 33(2), 105–115.

Bickmore, K. and Parker, C. (2014). Constructive conflict talk in classrooms: divergent approaches to addressing divergent perspectives. *Theory & Research in Social Education*, 42(3), 291–335.

Braithwaite, J. (1993). Shame and modernity. *British Journal of Criminology*, 33, 1–18.

Burrell, N., Zirbel, C. and Allen, M. (2003). Evaluating peer mediation: outcomes in educational settings – a meta-analytic review. *Conflict Resolution Quarterly*, 21, 7–26.

Carruthers, D. (2013). The journey from criminal justice to education: utilising restorative justice practices in schools in New Zealand. In E. Sellman, H. Cremin and G. McCluskey (Eds), *Restorative Approaches to Conflict in Schools: international perspectives on whole school approaches to managing relationships*, 23–31. London: Routledge.

Childline. (2005). *Every School Should Have One: how peer support schemes make schools better*. London: Childline.

Christie, N. (1977). Conflicts as property. *The British Journal of Criminology*, 17(1), 1–15.

Cornelius, C. and Faire, S. (1989). *Everyone Can Win*. Sydney: Simon and Schuster.

Corrigan, M. (2012). *Restorative Practices in NZ: the evidence base*. [online] Retrieved 18 September 2016 from www.dsc.z2systems.com/np/viewDocument?orgId=dsc&id=4028e4e55 2ab49ae0152c7a5d37800b3

Cowie, H. (2010). *Restorative Practice in School: a psychological perspective*. Paper presented at the ESRC-funded seminar series: Restorative Approaches in Schools. Seminar Three, Nottingham, 14 September 2010. [online] Retrieved 18 September 2016 from www.nottingham.ac.uk/education researchprojects/documents/restorativeapproaches/septrepairingthedamagehcowie.docx

Cremin, H. (2007). *Peer Mediation: citizenship and social inclusion revisited*. Buckingham: Open University Press.

Danesh, H. (2006). Towards an integrative theory of peace education. *Journal of Peace Education*, 3(1), 55–78.

Deutsch, M. (1973). *The Resolution of Conflict: constructive and destructive processes*. New Haven, CT: Yale University Press.

Deutsch, M., Coleman, P. and Marcus, E. (2011). *The Handbook of Conflict Resolution: theory and practice* (3rd edn). San Francisco: Jossey-Bass.

Genn, H. (2000). *Mediation in Action: resolving court disputes without trial*. London: Calouste Gulbenkian Foundation.

Gur-Ze'ev, I. (2001). Philosophy of peace education in a postmodern era. *Educational Theory*, 51(3), 315–336.

Johnson, D. and Johnson, R. (1996). Conflict resolution and peer mediation programs in elementary and secondary schools: a review of the research. *Review of Educational Research*, 66, 459–506.

Johnstone, G. and Van Ness, D. (2011). *Handbook of Restorative Justice*. London: Routledge.

Kane, J., Lloyd, G., McCluskey, G., Riddell, S., Stead, J. and Weedon, E. (2008). Collaborative evaluation: balancing rigour and relevance in a research study of restorative approaches in schools in Scotland. *International Journal of Research & Method in Education*, 31(2), 99–111.

Liebmann, M. (2007). *Restorative Justice: how it works*. London: Jessica Kingsley Publishers.

Liebmann, M. (2000). *Mediation in Context*. London: Jessica Kingsley Publishers.

McCluskey, G. (2013). Challenges to education: restorative approaches as a radical demand on conservative structures of schooling. In E. Sellman, H. Cremin and G. McCluskey (Eds), *Restorative Approaches to Conflict in Schools: interdisciplinary perspectives on whole school approaches to managing relationships*, 132–141. London: Routledge.

McCluskey, G., Lloyd, G., Kane, J., Riddell, S., Stead, J. and Weedon, E. (2008). Can restorative practices in schools make a difference? *Educational Review*, 60(4), 405–417.

NSPCC. (2004). *Peer Mediation in the UK: a guide for schools*. London: NSPCC.

O'Connell, T. (1998). *From Wagga Wagga to Minnesota*. IIRP. [online] Retrieved 18 September 2016 from www.iirp.edu/article_detail.php?article_id=NDg5

Pranis, K., Stuart, B. and Wedge, M. (2003). *Peacemaking Circles: from crime to community*. St. Paul, MN: Living Justice Press.

Salomon, G. and Cairns, E. (2009). *Handbook on Peace Education*. London: Routledge.

Sia, L. (2013). Restorative justice: an international perspective. In E. Sellman, H. Cremin and G. McCluskey (Eds), *Restorative Approaches to Conflict in Schools: international perspectives on whole school approaches to managing relationships*, 11–22. London: Routledge.

Skinns, L., Du Rose, N. and Hough, M. (2009). *An Evaluation of Bristol RAiS*. London: Institute for Criminal Policy Research, King's College London.

Thorsborne, M. and Blood, P. (2013). *Implementing Restorative Practices in Schools: a practical guide to transforming school communities*. London: Jessica Kingsley Publishers.

Vaandering, D. (2011). A faithful compass: rethinking the term restorative justice to find clarity. *Contemporary Justice Review: Issues in Criminal, Social, and Restorative Justice*, 14(3), 307–328.

Weitekamp, E. (1999). The history of restorative justice. In G. Bazemore and L. Walgrave (Eds), *Restorative Juvenile Justice: repairing the harm of youth crime*, 75–102. Monsey, NY: Criminal Justice Press.

Zehr, H. (1985). *Retributive Justice, Restorative Justice*. Elkhart, IN: MCC US Office of Criminal Justice.

Zehr, H. (1990). *Changing Lenses: a new focus on crime and justice*. Scottsdale, AZ: Herald Press.

Chapter 8

Education for peace-building

Introduction

Moving on from the dimensions of peace-keeping, which is about keeping the peace by securing safety, and peace-making, which is about making peace in the aftermath of conflict, we now turn to the forward-looking, preventative dimension of peace-building. Peace-building is about engaging in thinking, doing and being in ways that sustain positive peace. In the field of international relations and conflict resolution, peace-building is the phase that follows on from the peace-keeping and the peace-making; it is the work that is done to address the underlying causes of violent conflict, which are inequity, exclusion and intolerance (structural and cultural violence).

Just as in international relations, peace-building in schools is a long-term endeavour that touches on diverse aspects of people's internal and external worlds. It requires imagining how things could be and working towards that vision. We have found it useful to conceptualise peace-building in schools through three pillars: inclusion, citizenship and wellbeing. It is these three areas, in our view, that most closely support a school to articulate its values, purpose and vision. We set out in this chapter how engaging with these three pillars in a maximal, rather than a reductionist, way can provide schools with a holistic understanding as well as practical ways of working towards creating a culture of positive peace.

We caution, however, that while peace-building work in organisations such as the United Nations and the World Bank typically follows a modernist agenda (as explored in Chapter 4 of this book), a more integrated, postmodern, holistic agenda is needed. Our conceptualisation of peace-building in schools thus brings together the inner with the outer, and the personal with the structural. The rationale for selecting the areas of inclusion, citizenship and wellbeing is that all three do just that, as well as addressing foundational concepts of equity, agency and harmony. In brief, inclusion practices go to the very heart of addressing questions of equity; citizenship education addresses questions of agency and personhood; and wellbeing addresses the question of harmony and inner peace. Equity, agency and harmony are, we argue, requisites of a socially just, positively peaceful school. We begin by addressing inclusion as one of the pillars of peace-building.

Inclusion

Inclusion contributes to peace-building work in schools by: reducing barriers to learning and participation for all students; addressing questions of equity; promoting understanding and valuing of difference; and thereby building a more cohesive community within and beyond the school. Inclusion can be thought of as the value that a school gives to educating all young people within its locality and the ways that it goes about this. As discussed in the first part of this book, however, this seemingly simple idea has become enormously complex and contested within contemporary systems of schooling. Questions emerge, such as what is meant by a locality and when does parental choice degenerate into schools choosing students? With a plethora of different ways of organising schools, there is a danger of them becoming more segregated than the rest of society. Social and educational inclusion is difficult to achieve in settings where young people rarely engage with those whose identities, life-chances and perspectives are significantly different from their own.

Another important question concerns the ways in which inclusion and social justice may be in tension with each other. There are many 'inclusive' practices in schools that are in fact forms of exclusion. The inclusion room, for example, began to emerge in schools around 15 years ago. In the main, they were an attempt to provide appropriate additional support for students who were 'struggling to cope' in mainstream classes. While there are many examples of this space being used in a productive and short-term way to enable students to reintegrate into the mainstream, all too often these spaces became the notorious 'sin-bins' of old. One of the authors recalls accompanying a student on a visit to a new secondary school and hearing the student declare that he 'didn't want to be included' after being shown the inclusion room!

Sheila Riddell (2009) provides a useful discussion of these issues. Drawing on theorists such as Nancy Fraser, Amaryta Sen and Iris Marion Young, she frames her critique around redistribution and recognition. Riddell unpicks the apparent contradiction of addressing questions of both redistribution and of recognition, where the former seeks to redress the differences between people, and the latter to celebrate them. When seeking to build positive peace in schools, therefore, there may be a certain tension between the need to address inequality and the need to value individual difference. This is a tension that many teachers, in our experience, regularly struggle with. Having reviewed the research evidence, Riddell concludes that, "categories such as learning disabilities and social, emotional and behavioural difficulties are applied disproportionately to children from socially disadvantaged backgrounds, cementing rather than challenging their marginalisation" (2009: 283). Inclusion work thus needs to be grounded in our second pillar of citizenship in order to ensure that it is critical and dynamic. Conceived in this way, inclusion can be one of the most powerful tools at a school's disposal to challenge and counter cultural and structural violence, disadvantage and marginalisation.

Inclusion work that takes account of structural and cultural violence generates feelings of belonging and community. The 'I' becomes a 'we'. Educational thinkers who have written about inclusion and the 'we', in times of postmodernity, include Gert Biesta and Betty Reardon. In his book *Beyond Learning: democratic education for a human future*, Gert Biesta (2006) draws on thinkers such as Levinas, Butler, Arendt, Foucault and Peters to suggest that education enables learners to 'come into the world' through interaction with other people. Thus, the subjectivity of the learner involves responding to, and being responsible for, the 'other'. Learning is always a social and experimental process, in which the learner encounters different ways of being human. There is no pre-existing notion of human essence, so that learners must re-discover anew with every encounter the ways in which they can express their own humanity. The key question is not what is present, but who is present. In a similar vein, Betty Reardon frames peace educators as edu-learners who engage in a life-long process of learning, collaboration and growth alongside their students. This process is both global and local and takes account of the inner and outer dimensions of self, community and planetary system (Reardon, 1998).

Inclusive practice

Schools communicate powerful messages about inclusion and 'otherness' through their practice. Good inclusive practice will enable students, and staff, to develop a strong sense of their own identity, as well as a positive attitude towards difference. Poor inclusive practice contributes to individuals viewing difference as pathological, and seeing others as competitors or threats. Despite the fact that most people find it difficult to be confronted with their own privilege (whether, for example, as a white person, a neurotypical person or a straight person), schools must create spaces for exploration, dialogue and reflection on issues of dominant power relations and how these play out in schools and society. It is equally important that schools adapt their policy and practice as a result.

One resource that provides an excellent way for schools to do this and to think more broadly and deeply about questions of inclusion is the *Index for Inclusion* (Booth and Ainscow, 2011). The *Index for Inclusion* covers themes such as environmental sustainability, global citizenship, community building, health promotion, values, rights and non-violence. Here, we align ourselves with the extended understanding of inclusion presented in that resource: that inclusion is not just about those students who require additional support due to an identified special educational need or disability. Rather, inclusion is about the wellbeing and engagement of all members of the school community.

We would encourage readers to engage with the *Index for Inclusion* as a useful and practical tool for reviewing and developing school policies and practices to build towards a more broadly and deeply inclusive school culture. Given the long-standing and thorough work that has gone into its development and review, we would recommend that schools use it to structure their peace-building efforts.

Another form of inclusive practice in schools that we would urge our readers to embrace is circle learning. Circle time, as developed by people such as Jenny Moseley, is already established in many schools, but this is not the only way of learning in circles. Kay Pranis gives examples of the ways that circles can be used, such as: check-in/check-out circles, resolution circles, support circles, talking circles, community-building circles, celebration circles and reintegration circles (2005). There are now well-developed resources to support a wide array of circles work in schools (e.g. Boyes-Watson and Pranis, 2015). We include more ideas about working with peace-building circles in Chapter 11.

The culture and expectations that are set up in circle learning can extend to activities outside the circle, although the circle remains at the core. In circle learning, as in circle time, the students sit in a circle (on chairs or on the floor) in order to engage in activities that build inclusion, citizenship and wellbeing. It focuses on speaking, listening and the social and emotional aspects of learning. There are two fundamental ground rules for the circle: one person speaking at a time; and equal respect for all contributions.

One of the main circle activities is the go-round. This involves one student at a time around the circle making a short verbal contribution about the topic of the go-round. A talking object can be passed around to identify whose turn it is to speak. Anyone who does not wish to speak can simply pass the object on without saying anything. The advantage of this is that the students learn to speak one at a time, and those students who find it hard to make the space to be heard have an automatic opportunity to contribute or else to pass and still be included in the activity. The students know that only the person holding the object can speak and so it avoids interruptions. It is important that adults also respect this convention as much as is practical and possible. In this way, inclusiveness, acceptance and an atmosphere of trust are developed.

The starting points for circle activities will depend on the group. As a guiding principle, these should build on success and work in the zone where the group is capable, without being over-stretched. This can take a while to work out and so it is safest to keep initial activities simple, especially with a group who are not used to this way of working. Go-rounds should be short and unproblematic (e.g. my favourite meal), with games used to energise, motivate and reward. Success is defined as the whole group performing well; problems displayed by one or more individuals can be discussed together as a problem-solving exercise (without naming names). Breaking activities into achievable pieces is a strategy that often works, as well as setting clear targets (e.g. pass a smile around the circle in 20 seconds) and naming desirable behaviours clearly. It does not work well if students are berated for what they are not doing, or if activities are extended for longer than the class is able to focus, or if the teacher reverts to authoritarian discipline during the circle learning, or if the teacher is disengaged and distant. As an example of this, one of the authors remembers observing a circle learning session that involved a cooperative activity with a parachute. The teacher (a physical education specialist of the old school) was very proud of what his class had achieved and wanted to show how quickly and effectively they could throw a ball up and catch it in the parachute ten times. Unfortunately, this involved him barking instructions and blowing a whistle to indicate what they should do next. The task was performed to perfection – but the learning was zero. In other classes known to the authors, progress in parachute games is slow. At least one person wants to grab attention and turn the activity towards their own ends or else will not engage; cliques and subgroups become highly visible. This is the very stuff of circle learning; it is the beginning of a conversation, not the end. If the teacher avoids all of this by taking control, behaviour is managed rather than developed, and students are denied opportunities to learn self-discipline as part of a collaborative process.

Disruptive or uncooperative behaviour during circle learning needs to be handled with care. There is a real tension here. Often, those students who exhibit this behaviour have the most to gain from the activities, and the class have much to gain from learning how to manage the challenging behaviour of an individual who risks disrupting their learning. This behaviour must not be allowed to sabotage the efforts of the class, however. It is particularly important that no one is harmed during circle learning by the ridicule or disrespect of others, especially if the topic of the go-round is sensitive. Both timing and the language used by the teacher or facilitator in these situations is key. The early stages of circle learning with a group need to be more directive in order to establish a safe and conducive atmosphere for the circle work. As time goes on, the class can increasingly take responsibility for maintaining this ethos. As described in Chapter 5, language needs to attack the problem and not the individual. Thus, a useful way of finding the right words is to focus on the behaviour, its effect and the needs and agreement of the group. In this way, "Sahida and Jo, stop that whispering – you're spoiling it for everyone else and you've broken the rules" becomes, "Whispering (the behaviour) stops us from hearing what each person is saying (the effect) and we have agreed to listen with respect to each person (the agreement). Let's try it again."

A more intractable difficulty with an individual student would use this same formula. Thus, a teacher might say:

> James, we like you and we want you in our circle/group but we don't like insults (the behaviour) because they are very hurtful and stop people from feeling that they can speak in the circle (the effect). In this group we have no disrespectful language (the agreement).

If there is more than one appeal or reminder of this sort, it may be necessary to ask James to leave the circle. He will need to negotiate his re-entry with the teacher and the group outside the circle learning session, but this needs to remain possible.

Above all, however, circle learning should be about learning by having fun together, sharing and valuing each other's insights and moving forward as a class or community. For the teacher or facilitator, creating an affirming atmosphere is very important. Thanking students for contributions and warm eye contact help build up good feelings. Focusing on the positive and giving frequent praise help students feel more able to speak. The detail of what happens in the circle is decided through an iterative process of observation. This can be observation of what happens during circle learning, or of what happens outside it. Difficulties in areas such as respecting the ground rules, cooperating as a group or girls and boys mixing are all potential starting points.

One final point: it is worth taking the time to set up a circle of chairs with space in the middle, if at all possible (and working out how this can be done quickly and efficiently as a cooperative activity) as this enables a wider range of games. When students sit on the floor, there is always a risk of fidgeting and students creeping forwards or backwards so that the circle gets out of shape. In addition, adults sitting on chairs are forced to look down on children sitting on the floor, so that some of the equalising power of the circle is lost.

We now turn to our second pillar of peace-building – citizenship.

Citizenship

Returning to Galtung's interpretation of positive peace as an absence of structural and cultural violence, it is clear that citizenship education sits at the heart of the endeavour to prepare young people for life in an increasingly globalised, postmodern and inequitable society. Citizenship enables schools to engage students in thinking critically and acting with integrity in the world in which they live, and for which they will ultimately be responsible.

Citizenship education in schools, however, is sometimes conceived and enacted in ways that diminish its potential. Self-evidently, citizenship education will vary according to how the 'ideal citizen' is framed. In the English national curriculum, for example, a rather modernist, conservative and state-centric view of the citizen is presented:

> Citizenship Education helps to provide pupils with knowledge, skills and understanding to prepare them to play a full and active part in society. In particular, citizenship education should foster pupils' keen awareness and understanding of democracy, government and how laws are made and upheld. Teaching should equip pupils with the skills and knowledge to explore political and social issues critically, to weigh evidence, debate and make reasoned arguments. It should also prepare pupils to take their place in society as responsible citizens, manage their money well and make sound financial decisions.
>
> (DfE, 2013)

While there are some elements of this definition that are helpful in considering the place of citizenship education in promoting positive peace and social justice, it is not difficult to detect the strongly utilitarian model of citizenship that underlies it. Other agencies, such as the Citizenship Foundation, adopt a broader perspective on what citizenship education is. Importantly, the Citizenship Foundation calls for schools not just to teach citizenship but to **"demonstrate citizenship** through the way they operate" (2016). This call for education *through* citizenship and not just *about* citizenship lies at the heart of good peace-building prac-tice. We use the term congruence here to describe this essential element of peace-building: that is, the authentic and truthful connection between the inner and the outer, between what is believed and what is practised.

Taking a more global perspective on the ideal citizen, UNESCO have outlined their vision of what *Global Citizenship for the 21st Century* might entail:

- an attitude supported by an understanding of multiple levels of identity, and the potential for a 'collective identity' which transcends individual cultural, religious, ethnic or other differences;
- a deep knowledge of global issues and universal values such as justice, equality, dignity and respect;
- cognitive skills to think critically, systemically and creatively, including adopting a multi-perspective approach that recognizes the different dimensions, perspectives and angles of issues;
- non-cognitive skills including social skills such as empathy and conflict resolution, com-munication skills and aptitudes for networking and interacting with people of different backgrounds, origins, cultures and perspectives; and
- behavioural capacities to act collaboratively and responsibly to find global solutions for global challenges, and to strive for the collective good.

(UNESCO, 2014)

Its programme aims to find new ways for young people to participate and engage in the civic life of schools and communities. It also aims to develop these capacities within young people formally and informally, implicitly and explicitly. As the UNESCO programme makes clear, "holistic approaches to GCE [Global Citizenship Education] demand formal and informal approaches, curricular and extracurricular interventions and conventional and unconven-tional pathways to participation" (2014: 10). These pathways to participation might take place in cyber-space. Indeed, civic engagement in postmodern times is likely to include an online element. Dr Tom Harrison has coined the term 'cyber-phronesis' (2016: 8) (based on the ancient concept of practical wisdom discussed in Part II), as a way to help young people to develop their social and moral awareness in the virtual world. Harrison presents cyber-phronesis as an educative, preventative way to address the problem of cyber-bullying, as well as a framework for extending citizenship education into the online world.

More is required of citizenship education, however, if it is to be part of peace-building in times of postmodernity. The congruence that we allude to above needs more than global or web-based perspectives. It also needs robust responses to structural and cultural violence and an integration of inner and outer peace. This might draw on feminised perspectives of what it means to be a citizen, as well as critical theory and pedagogy. Vanessa Andreotti, for exam-ple, contrasts soft versus critical citizenship education in ways that mirror our own distinction between modern and postmodern perspectives. She argues that "a complex web of cultural and material local/global processes and contexts needs to be examined and unpacked" if young people are to gain a deep understanding of the global issues. Andreotti challenges schools to consider whether they are delivering 'soft' or 'critical' global citizenship education and provides a useful summary (shown in Table 8.1) for schools to use to interrogate their policy and practice (2006: 46–48).

Table 8.1 Soft versus critical citizenship education

	Soft *global citizenship education*	Critical *global citizenship education*
Problem	Poverty, helplessness.	Inequality, injustice.
Nature of the problem	Lack of 'development', education, resources, skills, culture, technology, etc.	Complex structures, systems, assumptions, power relations and attitudes that create and maintain exploitation and enforced disempowerment, which aim to eliminate difference.
Basis for caring	Common humanity/being good/sharing and caring. Responsibility *FOR* the other (or *to teach* the other).	Justice/complicity in harm. Responsibility *TOWARDS* the other (or to *learn with* the other) – accountability.
Grounds for acting	Humanitarian/moral (based on normative principles for thought and action).	Political/ethical (based on valuing of relationships).
What needs to change	Structures, institutions and individuals that are a barrier to development.	Structures, (belief) systems, institutions, assumptions, cultures, individuals, relationships.
What for	So that everyone achieves development, harmony, tolerance and equality.	So that injustices are addressed, more equal grounds for dialogue are created and people can have more autonomy to define their own 'development'.
Basic principle for change	Universalism (non-negotiable vision of how everyone should live, what everyone should want or should be).	Reflexivity, dialogue, contingency and an ethical relation to difference (radical alterity).
Goal of global citizenship education	Empower individuals to act (or become active citizens) according to what has been defined for them as a good life or ideal world.	Empower individuals to reflect critically on the legacies and processes of their cultures, to imagine different futures and to take responsibility for decisions and actions.
Strategies for global citizenship education	Raising awareness of global issues and promoting campaigns.	Promoting engagement with global issues and perspectives and an ethical relationship to difference, which addresses complexity and power relations.
Potential benefits of global citizenship education	Greater awareness of some of the problems, support for campaigns, greater motivation to help/do something, feel-good factor.	Independent/critical thinking and more informed, responsible and ethical action.
Potential problems	Feeling of self-importance and self-righteousness and/or cultural supremacy, reinforcement of colonial assumptions and relations, reinforcement of privilege, partial alienation, uncritical action.	Guilt, internal conflict and paralysis, critical disengagement, feelings of helplessness.

The adoption of a more critical approach to citizenship education will enable a school to actively and proactively engage with education for positive peace. Our assertion is that critical citizenship education, allied with an inclusive school culture that values wellbeing and excellence, provides constructive steps towards positive peace, not only within the school, but also beyond its boundaries.

Finally, we argue here that citizenship education for peace-building in schools in postmodern times needs to draw on feminised perspectives, affect and care, and an integration of inner and outer peace. As various feminist theorists have pointed out (e.g. Lister, 1997; Arnot, 2009), gender continues to play a role in popular notions of what it means to be a citizen and in the kind of citizenship that is promoted in schools. These theorists suggest that the public/private divide (outer and inner peace) within traditional concepts of citizenship has resulted in the marginalisation of women from the public sphere and the exclusion of the private sphere from education about rights, duties, justice and freedom.

Plummer's (2003) concept of intimate citizenship is useful for countering the traditional 'masculinist' view of citizenship and citizenship education. It holds that citizens need to be bound together by a sense of interdependence and care, rather than by social, political or economic contracts. Intimate citizenship repositions issues that have traditionally been seen as a matter of private choice or personal morality as directly relevant to the political world. Likewise, Barbalet (2001), in developing a systematic approach to the sociology of emotion, has developed new ways of thinking about citizenship. This work "is not an argument against reason, only against the inflation of reason at the expense of emotion" (Barbalet, 2001: 2).

An understanding of the emotional basis of political beliefs and prejudices is vital for integrating inner and outer peace. Citizenship education should aim to be part of this process, improving communication across ideological, ethnic and class boundaries in ways that take account of emotion as well as reason. One of the key education theorists in this area is Nel Noddings. She has written specifically about peace education (Noddings, 2011), but her earlier work *Caring: a feminine approach to ethics and moral education* (1986) is also highly relevant to citizenship education. This book makes a strong argument for education to be based on natural processes of caring. Refreshingly, Noddings is not interested in how moral reasoning develops in children, nor in teaching about morality through rational argument. She prefers instead to examine what it means to care and be cared for, and how caring functions in an educational context.

Noddings is interested in the linguistic, cultural, gendered and socio-political structures that maintain a culture of conflict, violence and war. While not suggesting that feminised ways of being are the sole preserve of women, she maintains that feminised and masculinised identities operate very differently. With respect to conflict, crime and justice, for example, masculinised perspectives might be centred on principles, fairness and precedent. Feminised perspectives might be centred on feelings, needs and personal impressions; there might be more interest in the needs of the victim, or the motives of the offender.

Due to the historic marginalisation of women in public spaces, feminised perspectives on conflict and caring are often seen as 'odd' or relegated to the private realm. Noddings wishes to change this and to challenge the dominance of standardised rules, debate and rational–cognitive approaches in education. This has implications for her own teaching in higher education. She writes that whatever she teaches (fascinating or boring, significant or trivial, challenging or tedious), it should not affect her relationship with her students: "the student is infinitely more important than the subject" (1986: 20). It is in the quality of the relationship – the commitment to care – that the student is set free to receive an education that is worth its name. In this, she points towards the integration of inner and outer peace.

In her later book, specifically about peace education, Noddings (2011) brings the ethics of care into the field of peace studies. Drawing on the work of thinkers such as Elise Boulding (2000), she argues that schools have a role to play in moderating the psychological factors that promote violence. She calls for peace educators to help young people become more aware of the forces that seek to manipulate them; to imagine new ways of educating children for a more peaceful future; and to enable feminised perspectives on care, love, home and community to flourish in their classrooms. She reflects:

> It might rightly be said that genuine education begins with feeling (the twinge we call interest) and moves toward wisdom as we think openly and clearly about what we feel. To that end, schools must move beyond the weary, highly unrealistic organization of knowledge into narrowly defined disciplines and begin to address great universal aims such as happiness, existential meaning, what it means to be a moral person, and our role as individuals and members of various groups in promoting peace. The pursuit of any of these aims requires not only that we speak freely but also that we listen openly and lovingly.
>
> (Noddings, 2011: 154)

Within international settings affected by armed conflict, there has also been an affective turn in peace-building work. For example, the PBEA (Peacebuilding Education and Advocacy) programme – a 200-million-dollar four-year partnership (2012–2016) between UNICEF, the government of the Netherlands and the national governments of 14 participating countries – has developed the theme of reconciliation as a core concept (Novelli et al., 2015). The programme uses reconciliation as the fourth 'R' in Nancy Fraser's foundational framework for justice, grounded in recognition, redistribution and representation (1995, 2005).

These authors all call for more attention to be paid to the relational and affective aspects of peace-building in and through education. They suggest that the current global education agenda (focused on education for all and sustainable development goals) is too strongly influenced by economic concerns, and they argue for "a much greater focus on education's potential to . . . prioritise interventions that favour the promotion of social cohesion and reconciliation" (Novelli et al., 2015: 7). A focus on structural inequalities without this relational and affective element is surely set to fail, and there is an increasing awareness of this in the international development research community.

These perspectives, which value the affective, relational, contemplative and feminised dimensions of experience, run counter to a view of citizenship education as a sort of humanities curriculum based on curricular content. In this, citizenship education links with our other two pillars of peace-building – inclusion and wellbeing. We turn now to wellbeing.

Wellbeing

Wellbeing is one of those terms that can mean everything and nothing! It is therefore important to have a working definition that can enable, rather than disable, thinking and action in this arena. To this end, we have drawn on the definitions provided by the UK's National Institute for Health and Care Excellence (NICE, 2013) to articulate our own view, and we add a fourth dimension of spiritual wellbeing. We hope that this satisfactorily resolves the tension between an inclusive, extended sense of the term and a more restricted sense of how it can be operationalised in schools. We recognise, of course, that these dimensions are interrelated and mutually reinforcing:

- emotional wellbeing – this includes being confident, happy and secure;
- psychological wellbeing – this includes the ability to be autonomous, to manage emotions and be resilient;
- social wellbeing – this includes the capacity to have good interpersonal relationships, and to avoid disruptive, aggressive or bullying behaviour;
- spiritual wellbeing – this includes aspects of inner life through which students are able to grasp a non-material dimension to life and intimations of an enduring reality.

It should be clear by now why we believe that wellbeing is such an important part of peace-building. All of the above dimensions have an important part to play, although we do not have the space to review them in detail here. Other books treat all but the final dimension in more depth, and most of the other dimensions have already featured in our earlier discussions. In this section, we will focus primarily on spiritual wellbeing. Briefly, emotional wellbeing can be regarded as the presence of harmony or inner peace within individuals. Psychological wellbeing pertains to the domain of resilience and the capacity to regulate thoughts and actions. Given that conflict is inevitable, psychological wellbeing plays an important part in enabling young people to engage with conflict in positive ways; this involves taking appropriate responsibility for harm, as well as avoiding being overwhelmed by conflict. Social wellbeing describes that aspect of wellbeing that is about being in relation and in community. Spiritual wellbeing is connected with feelings of awe, wonder, purpose and meaning; this returns us to harmony and inner peace.

Mindfulness

Schools are increasingly addressing wellbeing through the practice of mindfulness, which draws on Eastern spirituality and philosophy and creates the conditions of inner peace. In the UK, a mindfulness all-party parliamentary group (MAPPG) has been established to review the evidence on mindfulness and to develop recommendations for government (not just in education). MAPPG defines mindfulness as "paying attention to what's happening in the present moment in the mind, body and external environment, with an attitude of curiosity and kindness" (2015: 13). Its comprehensive review found that mindfulness programmes in schools have had an impact on students' executive control, emotional regulation, learning and academic attainment. The authors therefore recommend government-funded programmes for the future.

Mindfulness programmes in schools do not only benefit students, however; they also benefit staff. Katherine Weare, one of the leading academic voices in the field of mindfulness and wellbeing, has conducted a meta-analysis of research into mindfulness in schools (2014). Based on the 13 studies published in peer reviewed journals that she reviewed, she reports the following outcomes for staff in schools:

- reductions in stress, burnout and anxiety, including a reduction in days off work and feelings of task and time pressure;
- improved ability to manage thoughts and behaviour, an increase in coping skills, motivation, planning, relaxation and problem-solving;
- better mental health including less distress, negative emotion, depression and anxiety;
- greater wellbeing, including life satisfaction, self-confidence, self-efficacy, self-compassion and personal growth;

- increased kindness and compassion to others, including greater empathy, tolerance, forgiveness and patience, and less anger and hostility;
- better physical health, including lower blood pressure, declines in cortisol (a stress hormone) and fewer reported physical health problems;
- increased cognitive performance, including the ability to pay attention and focus, make decisions and respond flexibly to challenges;
- enhanced job performance, including better classroom management and organisation, greater ability to prioritise, to see the whole picture, and to be self-motivated;
- greater attunement to students' needs, and more supportive relationships with them.

(Weare, 2014: 2)

These outcomes go a long way towards addressing the cultural violence that we identified in the GERM phenomenon earlier in the book. Positive peace in schools will only ever be achieved if the wellbeing of teachers and other adults in school is valued as much as that of students. Peace education will fail if it only targets young people. Teachers also need to be treated with dignity, respect and trust. Without this, they will not have the capacity to carry out their roles with care, dynamism and compassion.

Spiritual wellbeing and inner peace

Turning to the well-known sentiment of Black Elk that there can never be peace between nations until there is first peace within the souls of men and women, we now explore spiritual wellbeing more fully, and the connections between peace within and peace without. Tenzin Gyatso, the 14th Dalai Lama, summarises the nature of this relationship beautifully:

> The question of real, lasting world peace concerns human beings, so basic human feelings are also at its roots. Through inner peace, genuine world peace can be achieved. In this the importance of individual responsibility is quite clear; an atmosphere of peace must first be created within ourselves, then gradually expanded to include our families, our communities, and ultimately the whole planet.

(cited in Mayton II, 2009: 61)

Inner peace is part of spiritual wellbeing. It is characterised by presence, calmness and connection with self, as well as freedom from inner conflicts. It "refers to a state of well-being that is not contingent on the presence of external or internal pleasurable stimuli" (Mitchell, 2001). Spiritual wellbeing also involves outer peace. In fact, spiritual wellbeing can be characterised as a synthesis between inner and outer peace. As Edward Brantmeier makes clear, "the cultivation of inner peace can contribute to knowledge paradigms that are supportive of peace, and can provide a foundation for social action toward supporting peaceful attitudes, dispositions, values, action-orientations, behaviors and social structures" (2007: 120).

In promoting a spiritual foundation for wellbeing, we are making a distinction here between 'spiritual' and 'religious', and we are including moral and humanistic perspectives. This fits with recent census data, which suggests that most people believe in God but do not participate in organised religion. For example, the World Values Survey, a research project conducted internationally over decades and based in the University of Michigan, suggests that, in societies that are educated and democratic, up to 70 per cent of the population has moved on from traditional faith to a more "generalised spirituality". In these societies there is often a belief in something that gives life purpose and meaning, but this does not necessarily involve the supernatural, an after-life or institutionalised religion. Peace-building grounded in spiritual wellbeing takes account of this. It contains at its heart notions of the sacredness of life, the interconnectedness of all things at the local and global level, and the wonder of creation.

This more generalised spirituality is characteristic of postmodern times. Religion has been (and continues to be) at the heart of some of the world's most intractable conflicts, and many reject it for this reason. It has been co-opted by kings, nations and clerics as part of state-building; and it has been used in schools to generate hatred and violence, as much as it has been used to generate love and peace (Trifonas and Wright, 2012). It has also tended to rely on hegemonic ideas of peace. Alongside peace scholars such as Betty Reardon and Dale Snauwaert (2015), Wolfgang Dietrich (2012), for example, points out that education for world peace, grounded in spirituality, needs to draw on the global East and South, and not only on Western traditions.

Eastern and Southern traditions are often built on aesthetics, beauty and harmony, rather than on the idea of one creator-God. Dietrich uses the word 'Tantra' as an umbrella term for practices, rites and techniques, such as mindfulness, that aim to free the mind from the games of the intellect and the illusion of separateness. Tantrism uses a human being's physical, psychic, intellectual and spiritual capacities to experience connection between the inner and the outer world of the body and the cosmos. Tantric metaphysics, whether in the Hindu, Buddhist or Taoist versions, unites all dualities or polarities. It is assumed that the universe is formed by the polarity of active and passive, female and male, Shakti and Shiva. The energy that flows between them is life.

Dietrich suggests that peace educators should integrate these philosophies into their peace work. They should not restrict themselves to conflict resolution, aiming instead for conflict transformation and peace-building, based on spiritual traditions. Dietrich uses the term 'transrational' peace to signify an approach that is similar to Gandhi's Satyagraha and Johan Galtung's positive peace. According to Dietrich (drawing on Fromm, 1970), transrational peace begins with an inward gaze. It integrates spirituality and rationality, but is not limited to either. Transrationality "does not deny rationality. It also does not overcome it, but crosses through it and adds the aesthetic component that is always inherent in interpersonal relations but that has not been observed that attentively by modernity" (2012: 266). Transrationality can be seen, not as a denial of enlightenment ideals, nor as a rejection of postmodern critique, but as a completion of all of them in a mature global ethics that is free from universalised norms.

We find the work of Martin Buber (1928) inspirational in this regard. He based his philosophy on the fact that human beings are constantly in relation to each other and the world. They can either relate to others as I–It (as objects) or as I–Thou (as fellow subjects). God occupies the space between (the hyphen) when I–Thou relations are established. God does not exist outside of that, as a separate entity. Buber argued that the I–Thou relation lacks structure and content because infinity and universality are at the basis of the relation. He understood that human existence consists of an oscillation between I–Thou and I–It relations, and that I–Thou experiences are rather few and far between. Following Buber, Cremin and Guilherme (2015) suggest that an 'epistemological shift' needs to take place in peace education in order to create the conditions where I–Thou relations become more likely, that is, where human beings cease seeing the Other as an It. It is only when this 'shift' occurs that Galtung's positive peace can be achieved.

We hope that our readers are still with us! These concepts may be unfamiliar to many in the West, but it should be borne in mind that they are not dissimilar to many of the discoveries of recent science, especially in quantum physics. In quantum physics, "peace is the stability of the dynamic equilibrium within the pulsating world system, and it is thus a constantly chang-ing phenomenon, dependent on observation, a reflection of consciousness" (Dietrich, 2012: 180). This is a significant departure from a Newtonian worldview, in which an unobserved observer can manipulate a clockwork universe. Thinkers from the fields of psychology and psychotherapy, such as Carl Jung and Roberto Assagioli, have also attempted to bridge the gap between East and West; Jung adopted the concept of the self from Taoism. Humanistic psychology, through therapists such as Rogers and Maslow, placed empathy, unconditional love and authenticity at the heart of the therapeutic process, and Gestalt psychotherapy further developed notions of interconnectedness. (This even entered into Paulo Freire's *Pedagogy of the Oppressed.*) Although there appears to be a contradiction between the autonomous subject of Western modernity on the one hand, and the yogic self as part of a collective mind on the other, we hope that we have been able to demonstrate that inner peace can be achieved through a contemplative tradition and that outer peace achieved through rational processes and Western, liberal, securitised notions of peace is only part of the story.

Returning briefly to education, it is worth noting that, perhaps somewhat polemically, a new concept of 'spiritual intelligence' has emerged. Spiritual intelligence is emerging as the focus of interest of researchers from a range of disciplines (transpersonal psychology, neuroscience, psychoanalysis, etc.), and it has been posited that spiritual intelligence (measured by SQ) rep-resents the third type of intelligence alongside intellectual intelligence (measured by IQ) and emotional intelligence (measured by EQ) (Emmons, 2000; Mark 2010). While we regret that spirituality has been reduced in this way to that which is measurable, we nevertheless assert that this aspect of human lives should be taken seriously in schools. Danah Zohar, a physicist and philosopher at the Massachusetts Institute of Technology, is one of the principal thought-leaders in this emerging field of inquiry. She describes SQ as

> the intelligence that makes us whole, that gives us our integrity. It is the soul's intel-ligence, the intelligence of the deep self. It is the intelligence with which we ask fundamental questions and with which we reframe our answers. It is our transformative intelligence.
>
> (Zohar, 2015)

Conclusion

Lubelska (2012) defines peace as the practical outcome of spirituality. We find this an inspiring idea. In this chapter we have argued that peace-building needs to be grounded in a dynamic interplay between the three pillars of inclusion, citizenship and wellbeing and that all three need to be re-conceived to take account of the conditions of postmodernity. The truisms of the past, from both religion and science, no longer hold true for all times and all places. Education in general, and peace education in particular, need to embrace a more mature, complex and inclusive idea of what it means to build peace in the twenty-first century. There is a need for transformation: transformation of knowledge about peace and conflict; transformation of perspectives (epistemology); and transformation of relationships, with the self, with other people and with the cosmos.

References

Andreotti, V. (2006). Soft versus critical global citizenship education. *Policy & Practice: A Development Education Review*, 3, Autumn, 40–51.

Arnot, M. (2009). *Educating the Gendered Citizen: sociological engagements with national and global agendas.* London: Routledge.

Barbelet, J. (2001). *Emotion, Social Theory and Social Structure: a macrosociological approach.* Cambridge: Cambridge University Press.

Biesta, G. (2006). *Beyond Learning: democratic education for a human future.* London: Routledge.

Booth, T. and Ainscow, M. (2011). *The Index for Inclusion: developing learning and participation in schools.* Bristol: Centre for Studies on Inclusive Education.

Boulding, E. (2000). *Cultures of Peace: the hidden side of history.* Syracuse, NY: Syracuse University Press.

Boyes-Watson, C. and Pranis, K. (2015). *Circle Forward: building a restorative school community.* St. Paul, MN: Living Justice Press.

Brantmeier, E. (2007). Connecting inner and outer peace: Buddhist meditation integrated with peace education. *Journal of Peace Education and Social Justice*, 1(1), 120–157.

Buber, M. (1928 [2004]). *I and Thou*. London: Continuum.

Citizenship Foundation. (2016). *What Is Citizenship?* [online] Retrieved 19 September 2016 from www.citizenshipfoundation.org.uk/main/page.php?286

Cremin, H. and Guilherme, A. (2015). Violence in schools: perspectives (and hope) from Galtung and Buber. *Educational Philosophy and Theory*, 48(11), 1123–1137.

Department for Education (DfE). (2013). *Citizenship Programmes of Study.* [online] Retrieved 19 September 2016 from www.gov.uk/government/uploads/system/uploads/attachment_data/file/239 060/SECONDARY_national_curriculum_-_Citizenship.pdf

Dietrich, W. (2012). *Many Peaces: interpretations of peace in history and culture.* New York: Palgrave Macmillan.

Emmons, R. (2000). Is spirituality an intelligence? Motivation, cognition and the psychology of ultimate concern. *International Journal for the Psychology of Religion*, 10(3), 26.

Fraser, N. (1995). From redistribution to recognition? Dilemmas of justice in a 'post-socialist' age. *New Left Review*, I(212), 68–93.

Fraser, N. (2005). Reframing justice in a globalized world. *New Left Review*, 36, 79–88.

Fromm, E. (1970). *The Crisis of Psychoanalysis: essays on Freud, Marx and social psychology.* London: Penguin.

Harrison, T. (2016). Cultivating cyber-phronesis: a new educational approach to tackle cyberbullying. *Pastoral Care in Education*, 34(2), 65–66.

Lister, R. (1997). *Citizenship: feminist perspectives.* Basingstoke: Macmillan.

Lubelska, A. (2012). Peaceful schools. *International Journal of Children's Spirituality*, doi:10.1080/1 364436X.2012.727501.

MAPPG. (2015). *Mindful Nation UK: report by the mindfulness all party parliamentary group.* [online] Retrieved 19 September 2016 from www.themindfulnessinitiative.org.uk/images/reports/ Mindfulness-APPG-Report_Mindful-Nation-UK_Oct2015.pdf

Mark, C. (2010). *Spiritual Intelligence and the Neuroplastic Brain: a contextual interpretation of modern history.* Bloomington, IN: Authorhouse.

Mayton II, D. (2009). *Nonviolence and Peace Psychology.* New York: Springer.

Mitchell, D. (2001). *The Way of Buddhism: introducing the Buddhist experience.* New York: Oxford University Press.

NICE. (2013). *Social and Emotional Wellbeing for Children and Young People.* [online] Retrieved 19 September 2016 from www.nice.org.uk/advice/lgb12/chapter/introduction

Noddings, N. (1986). *Caring: a feminine approach to ethics and moral education.* Berkeley, CA: University of California.

Noddings, N. (2011). *Peace Education: how we come to love and hate war.* Cambridge: Cambridge University Press.

Novelli, M., Lopes Cardozo, M. and Smith, A. (2015). *A Theoretical Framework for Analysing the Contribution of Education to Sustainable Peacebuilding: 4Rs in conflict-affected contexts.* [online] Retrieved 19 September 2016 from www.learningforpeace.unicef.org/partners/researchconsortium/research-outputs

Plummer, K. (2003). *Intimate Citizenship: private decisions and public dialogues.* Washington, DC: University of Washington Press.

Pranis, K. (2005). *The Little Book of Circle Processes.* Intercourse, PA: Good Books.

Reardon, B. (Ed.) (1998). *Educating for Global Responsibility: teacher designed curricula for peace education.* New York: Teachers College Press.

Reardon, B. and Snauwaert, D. (2015). *Betty A. Reardon: a pioneer in education for peace and human rights.* Basel: Springer International Publishing.

Riddell, S. (2009). Social justice, equality and inclusion in Scottish education. *Discourse: Studies in the Cultural Politics of Education*, 30(3), 283–296.

Trifonas, P. and Wright, B. (Eds) (2012). *Critical Issues in Peace and Education.* New York: Routledge.

UNESCO. (2014). *Global Citizenship Education: preparing learners for the challenges of the 21st century.* [online] Retrieved 19 September 2016 from www.unesco.ch/fileadmin/user_upload/3_Wie/bildung/Global_Citizenship_Education.pdf

Weare, K. (2014). *Evidence for Mindfulness: impacts on the wellbeing and performance of school staff.* [online] Retrieved 19 September 2016 from www.mindfulnessinschools.org/wp-content/uploads/2014/10/Evidence-for-Mindfulness-Impact-on-school-staff.pdf

Zohar, D. (2015). *What Is SQ?* [online] Retrieved 19 September 2016 from www.danahzohar.com/www2/?p=53

Part IV

The praxis of positive peace

Introduction

The three chapters that make up the final part of this book focus on the detail of how the principles and theories introduced thus far can be implemented and enacted in practice within schools. Paulo Freire reminds us of the importance of praxis: "reflection and action upon the world in order to transform it".[1] It is of course not enough to know of these themes and to discuss these questions; it is essential to act in the world to transform it. The first chapter of this part presents an overview of the ways in which schools can engage in and with research to support the building of a culture of positive peace. The next chapter contains a number of case study examples of schools that have engaged with various aspects of positive peace education. The final chapter of this part presents a compendium of practical activities that can be used with staff and with students to promote and develop the attitudes, knowledge and skills required for a school culture of positive peace.

Note

1 Freire, P. (1996). *Pedagogy of the Oppressed*. London: Penguin.

Chapter 9

Considering research

Introduction

This chapter takes the ideas developed up to this point in the book and presents the different ways in which professionals working in and with schools can engage with research in order to support the creation of a culture of positive peace. Throughout the preceding chapters, we have made reference to relevant research that helps explain and explore why and how the various approaches and practices work. We have also drawn attention in Chapter 3 to the potential of the evidence-based practice movement to constitute a form of cultural violence. In this chapter, we seek to develop and extend these lines of inquiry by presenting a rationale for engaging with research evidence and research processes as well as identifying specific approaches and tools that satisfy the requirement to be useful and are philosophically congruent with the peace practices we seek to promote.

On behalf of the Department for Education, Scott and McNeish (2013) have published a clear guiding document for school leaders on the ways in which schools can usefully and meaningfully engage with research. They distinguish two ways for schools to do this: to know about and apply existing research-based evidence; and to engage in their own practice-based research.

Engaging *with* research

There is an increasingly strong call from both policy makers (DfE, 2013) and academics (Coe, 2013) for teachers to engage with and develop evidence-based practice. The field of evidence-based practice in education is one that is marked by contentious dissension, and it is not possible to engage here sufficiently with the deep and important questions that mark this field.[1] Instead, we raise some of the questions that are important to consider when looking to engage with research to inform the development of a positively peaceful school culture.

There now exists a number of important initiatives and bodies that support, promote and develop the use of research in education, such as the Centre for the Use of Research Evidence in Education and the Education Endowment Foundation. Such initiatives are tangible manifestations of the new culture of creating and using evidence and research in schools. Understanding of how to engage with research evidence in ways that are both meaningful and useful is thankfully becoming more refined and nuanced. Researchers, policy makers and practitioners are increasingly engaging with research in less definitive vertical ways and in more tentative horizontal ways.

The field of evidence-based practice in education can be crudely characterised as a spectrum with, at the one end, a model of evidence-based practice originating in the medical world, one which is largely positivistic in its aims and claims and is seeking to establish generalisable truths about the world out there through experimentation (typically through randomised control trials). At the other end of this spectrum sits a more pluralistic and interpretivist way of thinking about and working with evidence in practice, one which eschews the possibility of grand truths about the social world and which gives at least equal status to local evidence and personal/professional judgement. The argument lies not in whether evidence matters, but rather in what evidence matters and how professionals can engage with the different forms of evidence in ways that are meaningful, useful and congruent with their purpose.

In the spirit of positive peace, it is important to interrogate some of the apparently irrefutable arguments presented in the field of evidence-based practice, which, as we exposed in Chapter 3, is one of the new orthodoxies of the education world. We therefore take the position as academics that the findings from empirical research studies and meta-analyses are one form of evidence that a school should consider, with practice experience, locally gathered knowledge and professional judgement being other equally important forms of evidence.

Both Robert Coe (1999) and Martyn Hammersley (2001) raise important questions about evidence in education which continue to be pertinent. The first question is what counts as evidence? Scott and McNeish highlight the point that "too great an emphasis on research evidence can exclude valuable insights derived from other sources, such as practice experience and underestimate the importance of professional judgement" (2013: 7). This supports the view presented by Sue Clegg that "evidence-based practice is currently being used to undermine professional autonomy and to valorise the 'gold-standard' of randomised control trials" (2005: 415). This latter point raises the question of the methods employed (and valued) in gathering evidence. Drawing on John Dewey's transactional theory of knowing, Gert Biesta (2007) provides a searing critique of the more definitive positivistic take on evidence-based practice. Biesta incisively interrogates the epistemological assumptions underlying and reproducing an evidence-based form of teaching and schooling. Again, these debates are deep and wide, and so we raise the questions and introduce a perspective on them that is consistent with the philosophy of positive peace.

With these caveats and considerations in mind, there are multiple research studies that can help to inform schools in the development of policies and practice to create a culture of positive peace. Relevant studies have been referenced throughout the three chapters on peace-keeping, peace-making and peace-building.

Engaging *in* research

The second way identified by Scott and McNeish in which school staff can engage with research is to engage in their own practice-based research. It is our contention that the aspects of school life touched on through this book offer a rich opportunity for individual staff and for the school community as a whole to engage in meaningful and useful research. Engaging in a research process in the development of peace work will not only ensure the most considered and appropriate form of implementation but also maximise opportunities for reflection and learning. Further, we would argue that engaging in the development of a culture of positive peace as a research process or project requires and at the same time develops many of the aptitudes and attitudes to be developed through the peace work: they are mutually reinforcing. For example, engaging in research requires an inquisitiveness about learning about other ways of seeing, thinking and doing. Engaging in peace work requires a welcoming of the perspective of the other, a curiosity about how things could be.

As discussed in Part II, the *how* of peace education is at least as important as the *what*. It is therefore essential to employ methods and methodologies that are aligned with the values and aims of peace education. Susy Lee Deck (2010) has identified five characteristics of peace education that can be useful in assessing the appropriate methods and manners with which to engage in building a culture of positive peace. They are: transformative, process-centred, participatory, relational and sustainable. It would therefore be desirable for the methods employed in the research process to be strongly and intentionally aligned with these characteristics.

We return here to the four-phase sequence of conceptualisation, formulation, implementation and evaluation of peace-building work introduced in Chapter 5 as the proactive iPEACE peace-building model. The purpose of re-presenting this sequence here is to provide a structure for the process of building a culture of positive peace in a school. As discussed earlier, the sequence is not intended to be a prescriptive model that schools should follow devotedly. Rather, it is presented as a stimulus for schools to consider the appropriate questions and factors at different phases of the process of building a culture of positive peace. In the context of research, one very obvious way in which a school can engage in research in developing its peace profile would be to conduct the phases as a piece of action research managed within the school, or in partnership with an academic institution.

Suggested methods

We here suggest some research methodologies and methods with which we have worked. These are methods that have established validity, reliability and importantly congruence with the philosophical premises of peace-building. The first phases of the sequence presented above involve great opportunities for eliciting the voices, perspectives and knowledge of the various members of the school community.

Surveys

A simple and time-efficient method for gathering a broad picture of people's experiences and perceptions is to use a survey. A good one to use for peace-building is adapted from the life in schools checklist (Arora, 1994). The survey includes 20 positive statements and 20 negative statements about what students or adults might have experienced in the previous week. The participants tick those that apply and thus produce a snapshot of their week in school. Table 9.1 reproduces the items in this survey.

There are several advantages with this survey: first, it gives a well-defined and recent timescale to aid recall; second, it captures both student and related staff experiences; third, it includes both positive and negative experiences; and fourth, it can easily be administered using a resource such as Survey Monkey. It can then be repeated over time to see whether or not experiences in school for students and adults are getting more positive and less negative as peace-building work continues. It can also, of course, be used from the start to analyse differences in student and adult experiences or perceptions of conflict, cooperation, wellbeing, friendship and inclusion.

Table 9.1 Life in schools checklist

Last week someone....... (yes/no or likert scale)

Items for students	Items for staff
Called me names	Spoke disrespectfully to me
Said something nice to me	Complimented me
Teased me about my family	Was rude about my family
Was very nice to me	Was very nice to me
Teased me because I am different	Teased me and made me feel uncomfortable
Shared something with me	Shared something with me
Threatened to hurt me	Threatened me
Chose me to be in their group	Chose to work with me
Lent me something	Lent me something
Fell out with me	Fell out with me
Told me a joke	Told me a joke
Told me a lie	Told me a lie
Helped me to make friends with someone	Helped me sort out a conflict
Tried to make me hurt other people	Tried to involve me in unpleasantness
Smiled at me	Smiled at me
Tried to get me into trouble	Tried to get me to break the rules
Made me fall out with them	Made things difficult for me
Helped me with my classwork	Helped me with my work
Made me do something I didn't want to	Coerced me into something I didn't want
Took something off me	Took something from me
Shouted at me	Shouted at me
Played a game with me	Involved me in social activities
Tried to trip me up	Intimidated me physically
Laughed at me	Laughed at me
Threatened to tell on me	Threatened to discredit me
Told a lie about me	Told a lie about me
Made me feel good about myself	Made me feel good about myself
Left me out of a game	Left me out of something that is my role
Noticed that I was unhappy	Noticed that I was unhappy
Chatted about things that matter to them	Chatted about things that matter to them
Made me feel special	Made me feel special
Listened to me	Listened to me
Told me off	Told me off
Said sorry to me	Said sorry to me
Made me feel lonely	Made me feel lonely
Played with me	Included me
Helped me when I needed it	Helped me when I needed it
Ignored me	Ignored me
Had fun with me	Involved me in fun activities
Helped me sort out an argument	Helped me sort out an argument

The number of experiences that are common to adults and children, such as being told a lie, or being spoken to with respect, are striking and serve to reinforce the point that adults and young people in any school community essentially want and need the same things in order to thrive. Sometimes in schools adults are expected to bracket their own wellbeing in order to prioritise the needs of children, and sometimes children are expected to downplay their needs in favour of adults. No school can be a healthy peace-building school unless these things are in balance, however, and this survey begins to provide the information that will enable the right kinds of action to be taken.

This survey will create a snapshot of school life at any one moment in time, but it is also useful to reflect on the different kinds of existing school data that might help to inform a project such as this. School inspection reports and development plans might be useful, as well as existing survey data, such as data from bullying or wellbeing questionnaires or student and parent satisfaction surveys. Clearly, data about temporary and permanent exclusions will be useful as well as data about critical incidents, behaviour referrals, rewards and sanctions.

Interviews

In order to deepen understanding of how adults and young people in school experience conflict and peace, interviews with various groups and members of the school community may be useful. If a school chooses to carry out interviews or focus groups, it can either carry these out directly, or involve other adults or young people. Questions to think about would be how power imbalances and confidentiality will be managed, how the data will be analysed to find out what is meaningful and useful and how to report back on what is found. All of these questions will need to be considered in advance in order to make the interviews serve a real and practical purpose. Interviews and, in particular, focus groups with small groups of individuals can be facilitated in creative and engaging ways.

Photo-voice

Following on from the examination of the importance of creativity in Chapter 5, it is highly desirable to seek out the opportunities for creative engagement within this work. Photo-voice is one methodology that can be enormously interesting and useful in researching how students and staff feel about violence, conflict and peace in schools. Photo-voice involves participants taking photographs to express something about their everyday lives or concerns. It is a method of eliciting the student voice. It can also be used to elicit the teacher voice.

Participants are usually asked to represent their school or point of view by taking photographs, discussing them together and writing captions and words to annotate the photos. It can be useful to give a focus; in this context, for example, people could be asked to capture where there is peace in the school and/or where there is violence. For the purposes of research, a sample of participants can be interviewed talking about the photographs and their annotations. These can then be analysed thematically alongside the photos themselves. While the process of this method of gathering data for research is highly participatory and creative, it is also capable of producing engaging and provocative products. The annotated photos can be displayed and used in various ways to stimulate discussion and raise awareness of topics that are of importance to members of the school community.

Appreciative inquiry

Appreciative inquiry is one methodology that has been successfully applied both to the formulation and the evaluation of peace programmes. Appreciative inquiry provides a highly congruent, deeply meaningful and strongly validated framework which a school could employ either to conceptualise, formulate and implement its work in this area, or alternatively as a methodology to evaluate the implementation, impact and influence of the work over time. Appreciative inquiry focuses on assets rather than deficits and has been shown to be capable of capturing rich and sometimes unexpected data. The simple premise of appreciative inquiry is that

> every organization has something that works right – things that give it life when it is most alive, effective, successful, and connected in healthy ways to its stakeholders and communities. Appreciative inquiry begins by identifying what is positive and connecting to it in ways that heighten energy and vision for change.
>
> (Cooperrider *et al.*, 2003: xvii)

Participants engage in a four-stage process of Inquire: discussing peak moments in their work, their values and wishes for their work; Imagine: creating a vision of the school at its best in the area under focus; Innovate: translating the vision into actionable statements; and Implement: putting the plan into action. Appreciative inquiry provides the school with a participatory and creative process of reflection, dialogue and change.

Evaluation

In the context of research, it is worth taking a moment to consider the question of evaluation. Given the contested and complex interpretations and understandings of peace, it is not surprising that evaluation of peace education has proven particularly slippery: "evaluation is often considered elusive for peace education, given the ephemeral nature of transformation: is it enough for a participant to undergo the process and 'transform', or must one transform to a predetermined endpoint?" (Del Felice *et al.*, 2015: xvii). Nevertheless, it is important to assess the value of what we are doing in schools, and it is not sufficient to justify working on peace education for purely philosophical reasons, because it is the right thing to do. It is essential to understand what can realistically and meaningfully be achieved through a focus on creating a culture of positive peace. Lack of a body of evidence on peace practice in schools can lead on the one hand to well-intentioned but ultimately ineffective practices, and on the other hand to disillusionment with the work because the hoped for outcomes were unrealistic. It is essential to build a body of evidence of what can be done in schools, what the aims and claims of this work are, what are the conditions required for it to succeed and how we know what effects it has had.

Conclusion

This chapter has sought to present the importance of engaging with and in research in ways that are congruent with the philosophy of building a culture of positive peace. Again, we find ourselves in the tension between peace as a philosophy and peace as a practice. In engaging with research evidence, a focus on peace provides a rationale and an opportunity to consider more critically some of the contentious questions within the field of evidence-based practice. Viewing research and evidence from a positively peaceful perspective privileges aspects such as the significance and importance of local, even personal, knowledge and experience. Equally, engaging in processes of research in the conceptualisation, formulation, implementation and evaluation of peace work in schools creates a forum and space within which to explore both the philosophical and the practical aspects of peace openly and systematically.

Note

1 For a fuller exposition of some of the key debates in the field of evidence-based practice in education, see, for example:
Biesta, G. (2010). Why 'what works' still won't work: from evidence-based education to value-based education. *Studies in Philosophy and Education*, 29, 491–503.
Hammersley, M. (2005). The myth of research-based practice: the critical case of educational inquiry. *International Journal of Social Research Methodology*, 8(4), 317–330.
Hargreaves, D. (1996). *Teaching as a Research-Based Profession: possibilities and prospects.* Paper presented at the Teacher Training Agency annual lecture. [online] Retrieved 10 September 2016 from www.eppi.ioe.ac.uk/cms/Portals/0/PDF%20 reviews%20and%20summaries/TTA%20 Hargreaves%20 lecture.pdf

References

Arora, C. (1994). Measuring bullying with the life in school checklist. *Pastoral Care in Education*, 12(3), 11–16.

Biesta, G. (2007). Bridging the gap between educational research and educational practice: the need for critical distance. *Educational Research and Evaluation*, 13(3), 295–301.

Clegg, S. (2005). Evidence-based practice in educational research: a critical realist critique of systematic review. *British Journal of Sociology of Education*, 26(3), 415–428.

Coe, R. (1999). *Manifesto for Evidence-Based Education.* [online] Retrieved 19 September 2016 from www.cem.org/attachments/ebe/manifesto-for-ebe.pdf

Coe, R. (2013). *Improving Education: a triumph of hope over experience.* [online] Retrieved 19 September 2016 from www.cem.org/attachments/publications/ImprovingEducation2013.pdf

Cooperrider, D., Whitney, D. and Stavros, J. (2003). *Appreciative Inquiry Handbook.* Bedford Heights, OH: Lakeshore Publishers.

Deck, S. (2010). *Transforming High School Students into Peacebuilders: a rationale for the youth peace initiative model of peace education.* [online] Retrieved 19 September 2016 from www. sydney.edu.au/arts/peace_conflict/docs/working_papers/Transforming_high_school_students_ into_peacebuilders.pdf

Del Felice, C., Karako, A. and Wisler, A. (2015). *Peace Education Evaluation: learning from experience and exploring prospects.* Charlotte, NC: Information Age Publishing.

Department for Education (DfE). (2013). *Building Evidence into Education.* [online] Retrieved 19 September 2016 from www.gov.uk/government/uploads/system/uploads/attachment_data/file/ 193913/Building_evidence_into_education.pdf

Hammersley, M. (2001). Some questions about evidence-based practice in education. [online] Retrieved 16 September 2016 from www.leeds.ac.uk/educol/documents/00001819.htm

Scott, S. and McNeish, D. (2013). *School Leadership Evidence Review: using research evidence to support school improvement.* [online] Retrieved 19 September 2016 from www.bristol.ac.uk/ media-library/sites/cubec/migrated/documents/evidencereview3.pdf

Chapter 10

Case studies

Introduction

Throughout this book, we have sought to keep in mind the reality of schools. While recognising that most schools will be already engaged in some of the practices presented in the peace-keeping, peace-making and peace-building chapters, it is our contention that the framework we have presented can provide a useful way for schools to draw this work together into a coherent whole.

This chapter contains five case studies, where three primary schools, one secondary school and one further education college share their stories of how they have engaged with building a culture of positive peace. The aim of this chapter is to share the learning from their experiences and to illustrate from real-life examples how this work can be developed in creative and highly beneficial ways. We present here the words of the school staff reporting on their experiences in their own voices.

The first case study reports the aims, experiences and reflections of Holte Secondary School in Birmingham. We prioritise Holte School's story because this is the first school to have engaged in a holistic way with the iPEACE model presented in this book. In this way, it is hoped that the iPEACE model can be brought to life for the reader. The subsequent case studies report on schools across England that have engaged with different aspects of peace-keeping, peace-making and peace-building work.

Holte Secondary School, Birmingham

What was the motivation for engaging in peace education work at your school?

The motivation to engage in peace education work was based on previous experiences of successful practice in a similar secondary context. Restorative approaches can transform a school's culture of behaviour management and positively impact upon incidents of low disruption, fixed and internal exclusions and bullying and discrimination. Peace education is also a key strategy for facilitating school improvement and has been at the forefront of outreach work undertaken by Holte School in terms of personal development, behaviour and wellbeing. Holte School is in the Lozells area of Birmingham, one of the most deprived areas of the country and a community significantly affected by a drug culture and high levels of violent crime, including gun crime. Peace education provides an opportunity to engage students, parents and the local community with strategies for resolving conflict, in all its guises, and as such helps improve our community as a whole.

With respect to our school, peace education was not introduced to address an explicit issue such as bullying or discrimination, although it is clear that it could do so. In an outstanding school setting, peace education provided an opportunity for the school to develop further and to be innovative in the way in which it managed behaviour. More explicitly we sought to reduce the number of incidents of all forms of exclusions (internal and external) including repeat incidents and to develop greater consistency in the way in which behaviour is managed at the school. Above all we sought to engage all stakeholders within our community with a range of strategies for managing conflict with the aim of ensuring that our students can access 'iPEACE' at school, home and in the local community.

How did you go about implementing your peace practice?

We went through a series of phases, stages and interventions, which was carried out in collaboration with Dr Hilary Cremin, Cambridge University, on iPEACE and alternative resolution of conflict. Within this work, we sought to include restorative approaches within all aspects of the pastoral team's practice. Some of the stages were as follows.

- An action plan was developed for establishing iPEACE and this plan (including an application for funding) was presented to the headteacher and senior leadership team (SLT).
- A commitment was made by the SLT to invest financially in training for staff and students in iPEACE, including peer mediation. This training was included in the school's CPD plan.
- All staff received some training on restorative approaches. Intensive training was delivered to year coordinators, mentors and teaching assistants,
- An audit of existing practice was completed, with the feedback being used to further develop the action plan and the strategic development plan.
- An iPEACE 'action group' was established including teachers (both newly qualified and experienced staff), middle and senior leaders, governor and support staff. This group also includes staff from our main feeder primary school. The special educational needs coordinator and teaching assistant led restorative practice for special educational needs students and families.
- The iPEACE 'action group' completed training in iPEACE and mediation.
- iPEACE has been included within the school's strategic development plan for Inclusion for 2015/16 and 2016/17. Departments have been encouraged to include 'iPEACE' within department development plans and to work with the iPEACE action group.
- Twelve peer mediators were trained. The course has since been accredited by the College of Mediators. Peer mediation is offered to all students via self-referral or referral from the pastoral team. Holte peer mediators mediate at a local primary school for two days a week.
- Peer mediation training is offered annually to all students. Students are required to apply for the position and are interviewed by senior peer mediators. Peer mediation is promoted amongst students through assemblies and school noticeboards.
- The iPEACE 'action group' and peer mediators led staff training at the school on restorative approaches in the classroom and mediation.
- iPEACE was presented to the governing body. The behaviour policy was updated to include the school's commitment to iPEACE and restorative practice.
- iPEACE parenting programme was offered to parents. However, sessions were poorly attended and the school is looking to develop this further next year.

- Collaborative work took place with a local community youth group. Peer mediators and the iPEACE action group provided training on mediation. Mediation is used to resolve conflict in the community. A member of the iPEACE group works as a link between the school and the local youth group providing support as required.
- The induction programme for new staff includes a twilight session on iPEACE training led by the iPEACE action group.
- A member of the iPEACE action group assumes responsibility for staff mediation, and a member of iPEACE assumes responsibility for peer mediation. All incidents of mediation are recorded and the impact is evaluated as part of the school's evaluation process.
- All exclusions and internal exclusions are followed by restorative intervention that may include mediation led by mentors from the school's learning support centre.
- The school has led restorative conferences with families and groups of students supported by West Midlands Police where appropriate.
- Restorative behaviour panels have been led by the school's junior leadership team. Governing body behaviour panels now use restorative questions.
- A personal, social and health education, citizenship and spiritual, moral, social and cultural (SMSC) programme of study has been developed by the iPEACE action group to include lessons on restorative approaches and mediation. Resources will be developed further in the coming year.

What have been the impacts of this work?

The impact of peace education on behaviour at the school has been significant. There has been a reduction in fixed term exclusions, so that they are below the national average, and a marked reduction in the number of repeat incidents of exclusion. Peer mediation has not only led to a reduction in the incidents of conflict, including bullying and physical aggression, but has ensured that most incidents of conflict are successfully resolved. All staff at Holte School regard restorative approaches and mediation as an integral part of the school's processes and procedures for managing behaviour. Most importantly, iPEACE has placed relationships at the heart of everything we do at the school, which has had a significant impact on both behaviour and teaching and learning. There has been a transformation in culture from a position of 'them and us' and a dichotomy of power to one where we are all part of a community where behaviour is taught as much as the subjects of science, maths and English. Where there is conflict in the classroom, staff are more aware of the antecedents of student behaviour and their roles and responsibilities with respect to conflict and the restoration of peace.

At times students have felt that they are subject to an arbitrary system of behaviour management that is inherently unjust and founded on a relationship of power between teacher and student. Particularly within our local context our students have an acute sense of justice/injustice, and our vulnerable students especially have a certain disdain and mistrust for the authority that the school sometimes tries to impose. iPEACE ensures that both students and staff understand that they attend school in order to learn how to develop socially, morally, spiritually and culturally as much as they attend to learn about maths and English. Sometimes there is a false expectation from adults that students should simply comply and behave and respect the authority of adults. iPEACE has allowed all members of our community to participate equally and justly within a process of learning and teaching about behaviour. Importantly for students, this is a process that they control and have ownership of, and one that is fundamentally just. It provides students with a voice that is so often sub-verted by individuals and school procedures. Students simply feel valued by a school that promotes peace education.

With respect to peer mediation, this has provided an incredible opportunity to develop our students as leaders. As students are required to apply for the position of peer mediators we ensure that we have a commitment to both iPEACE and the process of mediation. Students volunteer their time in order to improve their community and they have grown in confidence, developing a range of skills and qualities, modelling our school's core values of collabora-tion, aspiration, responsibility, respect and equality. It is clear that conflict is more effectively resolved by students rather than staff, perhaps due to the fact that there is greater trust for peers than staff and greater confidence that there is equity within the process of peer media-tion. The impact of peer mediation has meant that adults have a greater appreciation of how effective student-led activities can be and that students can make a difference.

Peace education has allowed our school community to actively promote our core values and to provide genuine opportunities for our students to develop socially, culturally, spiritu-ally and morally. In fact, peace education is perhaps the most tangible embodiment of SMSC and character education that you will find within a school.

The school started to monitor the effectiveness of mediation during the summer term 2016. During this time there were 35 mediations (peer and staff led) with only three examples of mediation not being effective (e.g. conflict was not resolved). The school will monitor and evaluate the effectiveness of mediation as part of its pastoral report to the senior leadership team and governing body.

The creation of an 'action group' has been pivotal in embedding iPEACE at Holte School. All members of our school community are represented within this group, enabling us to win hearts and minds across our community. The willingness of staff to participate within the process of mediation demonstrates their commitment to the principles of iPEACE. Whilst staff do, at times, require more guidance and support when participating in mediation, they readily acknowledge its value. The biggest challenge for everyone involved with schools is time, and there must be the time and resources available to promote iPEACE. There still remains, at times, an obsession with punitive responses to conflict, which are at times appro-priate. It is important that restorative approaches and mediation are seen within the context of a wide range of interventions that should be determined by those involved within conflict. Unfortunately, staff do at times want the 'pound of flesh' that punitive interventions provide.

It is very rare that staff don't want to participate in mediation or apply restorative approaches in the classroom. With respect to mediation, staff are almost unequivocal in their desire to have time to discuss conflict with students, and respond positively even when stu-dents are brutally honest with staff. There has been an overwhelmingly positive response from staff regarding iPEACE, because it highlights that outstanding behaviour, teaching and learning and outstanding outcomes are founded on outstanding relationships between adults and students. iPEACE has ensured that all relationships are valued within our school and regarded as the key to success.

The school has not yet formally elicited the views of our students on their views regarding restorative approaches and mediation. However, the willingness of students to participate in mediation and the impact of mediation is evidence of their positive attitude towards it. Indeed, students frequently refer themselves for mediation both with their peers and staff.

Our peer mediators are extremely positive about the work they have undertaken and the impact it has on improving relationships within the school community and on their own personal development. The school recently recruited its next batch of peer mediators and received 65 applications for 12 positions, from Year 7–12 students. The fact that the training is provided by an external agency and is accredited by the College of Mediators has helped recruitment from Key Stages 4 and 5, as students see both the training and the role of mediator as evidence of them demonstrating a wide range of skills and qualities.

In terms of mediation, students who are reluctant to participate often recognise a relationship based on an imbalance of power between the student and teacher. Mediation allows students to overcome this feeling of injustice and gives them a sense of belonging within the school community.

The school has not yet formally elicited the views of our parents on their views regarding restorative approaches and mediation, nor has the school effectively promoted their work with parents beyond the iPEACE parenting programme. It is a focus for the school to promote our work with parents during the next academic year and to fully engage with our local community.

The school is due an inspection from Ofsted during the academic year 2016/17. In June 2016 the school was awarded the Inclusion Quality Mark (IQM) Flagship Award and is one of only 20 schools in the UK to have received the award. iPEACE was one of 8 targets achieved as part of the award. IQM noted that

> [t]he important thing, however, is that iPEACE involves not just pupils, but teachers, parents and community workers and develops a better understanding of conflict in the school, including low level disruption in the classroom and uses appropriate conflict resolution strategies that can be used in the classroom, working towards more peaceful and productive learning environments, homes and communities while promoting an authoritative approach to behaviour management that is based on education, relationships and actively promotes social skills. As such the school will continue to organise fully accredited mediation training for peers and staff to ensure that iPEACE is sustainable. **This is a fantastic programme that should be rolled out across the UK and delivered in more school settings.** It will be interesting to see the impact of iPEACE at next year's review point and to see the school become a hub to disseminate this exceptional programme.

The school has support from West Midlands Police in the form of a school link officer. The officer regularly attends the school to lead mediation and conferences between students, and in some cases between families. Our link officer has received training in restorative justice and complements provision within the school. Where appropriate the school will lead mediation in response to incidents of anti-social behaviour in the local community and vice versa. As such, West Midlands Police have demonstrated a commitment to such approaches to responding to conflict.

What have you learned from your engagement with peace work?

Peace education provides an invaluable opportunity to transform behaviour in schools, enabling and empowering all stakeholders to become agents of change by placing relationships at the heart of the school community. It can engender greater consistency in schools by promoting greater ownership of behaviour from all stakeholders. Above all peace education ensures that behaviour is not managed and improved as a result of a system or process but by relationships that are based on mutual respect and fairness.

Peace education also provides a genuine opportunity for the effective promotion of students' SMSC development, character education and the demonstration of a school's core values.

The most significant changes that have been seen as a result of the work include the following:

- Peace education has helped reduce fixed-term exclusions and repeat incidents of internal and external exclusions and incidents of low-level disruption in the classroom. Most notably over the course of the academic year the number of incidents where students have been removed from lessons has reduced significantly, indicating that there is greater ownership of student behaviour.
- Incidents of physical aggression, bullying and discrimination have reduced as a result of mediation.
- There is an appreciation from staff and students alike that behaviour must be taught at school and that relationships are paramount in its management. Behaviour management is reflective rather than overly punitive. It is less likely that staff will use a system to manage behaviour, and there is greater ownership from them.
- Peer mediation provides an excellent opportunity for students to make a difference in their community as leaders and to develop socially morally, spiritually and culturally.

In terms of the future, the school is seeking to develop the principles of Carol Dweck's growth mindset in all areas of the school. It is clear to me that 'peace education' is a clear example of a growth mindset approach to pastoral issues and we will be developing this as such. It is anticipated that our work on establishing a growth mindset at Holte School will further vindicate and promote our work on peace education.

A further focus for the school is to develop restorative approaches and mediation within the school community, including local youth groups and with parents. The school has worked successfully with the local community youth group and our students can access mediation both in school and the local community. It is our aim to extend this further to other youth groups in the local community.

Kings Norton Primary School, Birmingham

What was the motivation for engaging in peace education work at your school?

As a school we were often saying that the children didn't have a vocabulary to express their emotions, other than happy or sad, and that when discussing issues, we felt that they didn't seem able to see any perspective other than their own. We were also seeing the same children being brought to us, as senior leaders, as they were 'repeat offenders' when there were behaviour incidents to deal with. This made us realise that we were not developing the children's skills in managing difficult situations or helping them to be empathetic and understanding of the needs of others.

We wanted the children to develop the ability to make good relationships, have the skills and ability to address difficult issues when they occurred and understand that they weren't the only ones 'injured' when these situations happened.

We also needed a common language and structure that all the adults interacting with the children would use, and a common approach to provide consistency.

How did you go about implementing your peace practice?

Initially we worked with West Midlands Quaker Peace Education Project (WMQPEP) to create a peer mediation scheme, but then it became clear that we needed all the children to be involved. This led to us developing a whole-school Peacemakers approach. This involved intensive training and input, which led on to us establishing and maintaining the restorative approach day to day through circle time and a consistent restorative approach to conflict.

What have been the impacts of this work?

There has been a reduction in the number of incidents being brought to the attention of the senior leaders. Traditional 'punishments' are rare as the children come to their own agreements about the resolution to their issues. All the children take part in weekly circle times and they ask for these to happen, more recently at a particularly difficult time of stress within the life of the school. There is an expectation among the children that we will listen to their points of view and allow them to resolve issues. Staff describe restorative approaches as 'the way we work', and not as a separate part of school life, as it runs through our ethos.

Children have expressed that they can work with others in the class that previously they would have avoided. The children are more able to express their feelings with confidence and using a more accurate vocabulary. This has enabled them to understand the feelings words that others use too, so that there is a more accurate picture of the effect that incidents have on people.

We have run circle time workshops with children and their parents. These are some of the children's comments following these workshops:

"Circle time makes you have good friends."

"People who don't know you can still have good team work."

"I learned that parents sometimes struggle with things."

"I learned that, to complete something with people, you have to cooperate."

This is what some of the parents said they learned from the workshops:

"I learned what circle time actually was, and how the school are trying to get the children to deal with emotions, problems and confidence problems."

"How important it is to encourage children to listen and empathise with each other."

"Seeing how children are building long-term relationships – rather than just fixing issues."

"Why my children want to have their say when they argue and fall out at home."

"How to solve problems without feeling like I am giving out punishments."

One of the most significant changes has only recently happened, a couple of years into the work. It became clear that the parents, while having been informed about Peacemakers, still expected us to deliver traditional punishments that they were familiar with. There was a clear need to involve the parents in the process more fully. Given that the role play experiences in the training for children had a great impact in helping them to understand the resolution process, we needed our parents to experience this as well. This has resulted in parent circle time workshops and a parents' forum where they can discuss and develop restorative approaches for use in the home. This completes the consistency aim which we had originally articulated and has also helped the parents to understand why issues were not being resolved in the way that they had expected. These comments were made after the parents' forum meeting:

> "After the workshop I went home and polished shoes. The slogan on the polish was 'shines, nourishes, protects'. I thought this perfectly summed up the partnership of Peacemakers and Kings Norton Primary School and how the children benefit from the programme. Peer mediation and circle time protects them as they become able communicators and listeners, nourishes them with the ability to sort out conflicts and be respected, and allows them to shine and thrive."
>
> "I learnt that it may be an effective idea to let children think of solutions to their own problems rather than always attempting to implement your own solutions to the situation."

What have you learned from your engagement with peace work?

This work does need to be a whole-school approach in order to transform the staff as well as the structures and systems within the school. The approach needs to have enthusiastic leadership and has to be modelled and encouraged at all opportunities to embed it within the school's practice. The two years allowed the staff to internalise restorative practice and support the children in developing good relationships. So my advice would be to remember to commit the time to the change process and to be patient for the outcomes.

To sustain this work we now need to train and employ a Peacemakers leader, so that new staff in any role can be quickly immersed in restorative approaches, enabling our way of working and our ethos to be constantly maintained.

Queensbridge Primary School, Hackney, London

What was the motivation for engaging in peace education work at your school?

We introduced restorative approaches as a whole-school approach to address some very challenging behaviour.

How did you go about implementing your peace practice?

Key members of staff were identified and attended a three-day training course. These staff members then delivered whole-staff training in how to use the restorative chat and all staff were given prompt cards to wear on their lanyards.

Incidents of behaviour were dealt with using the restorative language to encourage the children to reflect on their actions and to think about how their behaviour has affected other people. Children were given the chance to talk about what happened, whether they were the wrongdoer or the person who'd been harmed.

Lunchtimes were a particular focus as children were coming back to class angry or upset by something that had happened in the playground that had not been properly resolved. This was having a very negative effect on the class as a whole and on the individuals' ability to access the learning and contribute to the lesson. The learning mentor ran restorative sessions at the end of every lunch break to sort out issues so children could feel the problems had been resolved and they could go back to class calm and ready to learn. Class teachers reported fewer incidents of disruption and a much more focused class.

The headteacher and the senior management team were fully supportive and ensured that RA would be adopted as a whole-school approach and that it would continue to evolve and develop.

To ensure restorative approaches were used consistently across the school it was aligned with the 'stay on green' behaviour system already in place. Clear guidance was given whereby a child would be given a verbal warning for an incident of poor behaviour followed by a yellow card if it continued. At that point, the child on a yellow card would have a very restorative, positive chat about the importance of getting 'back to green' by making good choices. If after this the behaviour failed to improve, a red card would be given which meant the child was sent to a partner class with a restorative reflection sheet to be filled out. At a later point, the child would have a restorative chat asking the questions: What happened? What were you thinking and feeling? Who's been affected? What's needed to make things right? and, What can we do to make sure this doesn't happen again?

Restorative no-blame class conferences are carried out, which give children the chance to discuss issues in their class openly and honestly and to take responsibility for their behaviour.

Three years ago, peer mediation was introduced as a next step of the restorative journey. Older children are now trained as mediators and sort out conflict between younger children using a restorative script. One of the benefits of having a peer mediation scheme has been fewer incidents for staff members to deal with at playtime, freeing them up to engage in activities with the children. Peer mediation has also had a very positive impact on the mediators themselves, some of whom have been targeted for the scheme as they have faced conflict issues themselves. The mediators also learn a very important life skill in being able to listen, to be non-judgemental and to see both sides of the story.

What have been the impacts of this work?

Restorative approaches are now fully embedded in the school and this has created a culture where children are listened to and able to talk about their feelings and to think about others. Children report that they are able to be more honest and they feel that situations are dealt with fairly. This culture is evident in the way children and staff communicate with each and also in social and emotional interventions such as circle time.

The number of high-level incidents has dropped, as incidents are dealt with through restorative approaches as an early intervention, before things escalate. Staff and children report being happy and there is a consistently settled learning environment across the school.

A partner school with whom we worked to develop their restorative practice, received this recognition in their Ofsted report:

> Restorative justice, which encourages pupils to discuss issues where there have been disagreements or conflict, is a formidable tool for ensuring that there is no discrimination and that pupils make carefully considered moral choices and develop the range of social skills needed to move on to the next phase of their education.

What have you learned from your engagement with peace work?

Restorative practice and peer mediation have been really useful ways to bring our school values to life. By making explicit our values, we have been able to use these practices to help all members of our school to feel listened to, valued and cared for.

Raddlebarn Primary School, Birmingham

What was the motivation for engaging in peace education work at your school?

I had previous experience working with the Peacemakers project prior to joining this school regarding peer mediation. I was keen to introduce the approach, as I felt it was not only a positive way of dealing with conflict, but was also empowering for those involved and supported a positive school ethos.

We wanted a whole-school approach when dealing with behaviour and conflict. We also wanted to reduce the number of behavioural incidents while up-skilling pupils and staff in dealing with conflict and building positive relationships so that they could address areas of difficulty without leading to negativity or a sense of injustice.

How did you go about implementing your peace practice?

The headteacher and deputy head were extremely supportive of the whole approach and wanted our school to be a restorative one. They fully engaged with the process; we were then lucky enough to obtain the support and skills we needed from the Peacemakers project. We obtained funding to support it from our budget and had a bursary fund to cover the final amount.

What have been the impacts of this work?

We now have a more 'peaceful school' – not a quiet one or one that doesn't have issues or conflict, but one that has the skills to address issues and to build and maintain positive relationships.

Initially, staff were mixed with their responses to the approach. Some felt it was 'woolly', 'soft'. It was only through the training and total immersion that their attitudes changed. It is now seen as a strength of the school, underpinning our core values and ethos.

Our pupils value this approach. They perceive it as fair and consistent. Those who are involved in incidents value its fairness. In the early days, if a member of staff or even a visiting member of staff did not use this approach, the pupils felt unheard and unjust. Without check in and check out, they actively seek adults to report to them how they are feeling. As new pupils come into the school, they are soon inducted into the approach, by the pupils themselves. This is 'their approach'; through their actions it clearly demonstrates they respect and support this approach.

We have received letters of thanks and support from pupils' parents who have had incidents dealt with in this way. Additionally, those parents who we speak to accept issues are dealt with thoroughly. The parental feedback this year is the most positive it has ever been: 96 per cent of parents believe the children to be happy in our school, and we feel this is partly as a result of the restorative approaches used.

Ofsted said:

> The school actively promotes respect and tolerance, fosters good relations and ensures there is no discrimination. Good manners are promoted very strongly and successfully from when children start school in the early years foundation stage. Staff are also very positive about the behaviour of pupils and the consistent approach taken by all adults in the school has ensured that behaviour has improved over time. There has been a reduction in recorded behavioural incidents and a large reduction in the number of fixed term exclusions over the last two years.

What have you learned from your engagement with peace work?

Although at first it is tricky, the benefits of this work for the pupils and staff alike are immense. This is an approach that, hopefully, will help develop our pupils into adults who have social skills which foster, develop and maintain good relationships.

Although there has been a significant reduction in behaviour incidents, the biggest impact has been with the people involved, staff and pupils alike. No one feels it is 'soft' or 'woolly' anymore; everyone values the impact it has on every member of school. It is always our first resort; how can this be dealt with restoratively is our first thought. In addition, on a personal level, I know it has changed the way I deal and discuss things at home with my family: there are not many initiatives that do that!

Hackney Community College, London

What was the motivation for engaging in peace education work at your college?

We were concerned about the high numbers of learners who were being excluded and also about our disciplinary process that didn't in any way repair relationships with staff, students or other stakeholders. We were looking for ways to reduce exclusions, improve student behaviour and improve satisfaction with disciplinary processes. We also wanted students to develop conflict resolution skills they could take outside college, given that their lives are typically marked by high levels of personal and social conflict.

We have increasing numbers of high needs students for whom the formal student disciplinary approach was not appropriate because there was limited understanding of why the behaviour was unacceptable or of the impact of the behaviour on others. This meant that there was effectively very little impact on changing the behaviour of these students. We wanted all students to have an increased understanding of the impact and consequences of behaviour, which would in turn be supported by appropriate interventions.

How did you go about implementing your peace practice?

We decided to engage with restorative practices as a way to meet these identified needs. We started by sending key members of staff on restorative approaches training provided by the local authority. From this training we identified certain individuals within the college who became champions and rolled it out across the whole college. We started using it as an alternative way of handling conflict and gradually embedded it within our disciplinary policy.

The work has been embedded in all programmes and differentiated models have been developed in our provision for students with high needs and with our 14–16-year-old students.

Educational psychologists who were working with students contributed to the development of a new behaviour management policy for high needs students.

Performance is regularly monitored and fed back into the senior management team and across the wider college to staff and students.

What have been the impacts of this work?

We have seen a significant drop in exclusions and a significant reduction in staff complaining about behaviour. Staff have developed more solution-focused approaches to behaviour management and development with supportive follow-up strategies rather than opting for exclusion.

Senior managers are happy as exclusions have dropped. There are fewer behaviour incident referrals and teachers report better student behaviour.

Students have fed back that they feel "safe in college". In addition, some students have told us that they have learned wider conflict resolution skills that they have applied outside college and at home and in the community.

Response from parents has been more mixed. Some parents are happy with the process and others would prefer that harsher disciplinary action were taken. Where parents are involved in the restorative meetings, they see the value of the approach when they witness the impact on their son or daughter's reflective practice.

We received a good Ofsted Report in October 2015 and restorative practice was cited as a strength:

> Learners' behaviour at the college is exceptionally good. Staff at all levels are highly skilled in modelling and managing good behaviour and, as a result, learners demonstrate high levels of respect for staff and peers. The exceedingly effective 'restorative justice' approach to conflict resolution complements the college disciplinary process well. As a result, learners develop very good strategies for managing and dealing with conflict; they adopt and share these strategies within their own families and communities.

What have you learned from your engagement with peace work?

It's not a quick win and it does require time to implement, but it is worth it. It's also perfectly suited to education as it makes conflict a learning opportunity for the whole range of students and staff. There is no 'blueprint' for implementation as every organisation is different. At our college, there has been a cultural change. There is a less formalised/legal way of dealing with conflict issues and more of a human restorative/healing approach. It's not perfect and not suitable for every situation but does help to create a more cohesive and caring learning community.

Conclusion

We hope that the voices and journeys of these schools prove both hopeful and inspiring in showing how the various theories, practices and approaches advocated in this book can be put into action. As these case studies attest, the journey towards building a culture of positive peace has to be crafted and created according to the needs and opportunities of the specific school context. This journey has to involve and engage all members of the school community, and even the wider community. This journey has no fixed destination, if any destination at all. But it is a journey that affirms and enacts the highest hopes we have for our children and young people.

Chapter 11

Curricular activities

Introduction

This chapter now goes on to provide a practical curriculum for working towards a culture of positive peace in school. It contains up-to-date activities that build on an older and much-used text, *Let's Mediate*, which was co-written by one of the authors nearly 20 years ago (Stacey and Robinson, 1997). It also draws on new resources, such as *Learning for Peace: a guide to developing outstanding SMSC in your primary school*, developed by the West Midlands Quaker Peace Education Project (2016).

The activities included here are not a blueprint; teachers and others will need to adapt and plan, sometimes repeating, combining or shortening activities. There is now a plethora of books and websites that contain many more such activities so that an extended curriculum for the whole school can be planned, if desired. We have avoided specifying learning objectives, precise timings and links to national curriculum documents here, as the book is aimed at an international audience, and we feel that our readers are intelligent educators who will wish to work with us, not simply swallow lesson plans whole! The whole point of this work is that teachers actively engage with these ideas, with half an eye on the activities and theories behind them, and half an eye on how the class is doing.

Students can also be involved in observing and planning. The nature of this work is that students evaluate their own performance and develop strategies to ensure that everyone succeeds. There is no age restriction on this, provided they understand what they are setting out to achieve. You can ask students, 'Why are we doing this?', 'What is this helping us to do?' and 'What skills do we need to play this game well?' By involving the class in a process of reflection and evaluation, they are already working towards inclusion, citizenship, peace-making and wellbeing.

The rest of this chapter outlines some activities, many of them games, for developing positive peace in schools via peace-building activities though inclusion, wellbeing and citizenship. Games help reinforce teaching points, mix students up and energise or calm them down. They are central to processes of teaching and learning and are not to be dismissed as a Friday afternoon treat.

The activities that follow are aimed mainly at the 8–13 age range, but they can be extended upwards or simplified to take account of other age groups. They can also, of course, be adapted for children and young people with learning special educational needs and disabilities and students who have English as a second language. We rely here on the creativity and resourcefulness of the teaching profession!

Inclusion

These activities use people's names and non-verbal communication to build friendship, rapport and feelings of belonging. They aim to set the class up as a cohesive learning community, capable of working together in a variety of different configurations and tolerant of difference and personalities. The activities begin to break down cliques and gender divisions, among others, and enable young people to extend their friendship groups and honour each other, particularly at times of transition for the class or for individuals. The key message here is that they do not have to like everyone in the class, but they do have to be able to work with everyone. More positively, they need to keep an open mind and engage with people they have not yet had a chance to get to know in the class. This is how communities are built.

Name games

These games build trust and familiarity. They can be used at the start of a school year (or in the beginning phase of any new group) and can either accelerate the process of learning everyone's name, or else build group identity through re-acknowledging each other's names. They generate an atmosphere of fun, cooperation and inclusion.

Organisation and resources   circle of chairs and a ball

Time   3–5 minutes each game

(First) introductions

- Roll or throw the ball across the circle.
- Get a student to say their name when they catch it. They then roll/throw it on to someone who has not had it. Continue until everyone has been included.
- Repeat, but this time the thrower says the name of the person who is about to receive the ball.

This can be extended or varied by saying good morning/afternoon . . . (name) to the person who is about to receive the ball, and the recipient saying thank you . . . (name) to the person who threw/rolled it to them, before throwing/rolling it on in turn and saying good morning to the next person. This can be a good way of introducing a new language to the class, especially if there are people in the class who speak the language at home. They can teach the group how to say good morning and thank you in their language.

Introducing partners round the circle (1)

Say your own name, the name of the person on your right and the name of the person on your left (I am . . . this is . . . and this is . . .). Get the student sitting next to you to do likewise, continuing around the circle until everyone has had a go.

Introducing partners round the circle (2)

- Get students to work in pairs with the person sitting next to them in the circle. They each find out one piece of positive information about their partner (favourite game/colour/

food/season, something they like to do in their spare time, one thing they think is good about school, etc.).

- They then introduce their partner to the group and share the information (having checked that this is OK).

Ghost in the cupboard

- One student (the guesser) goes outside.
- One (or more) hides out of sight in the room – in a cupboard?
- Everyone else stands up and changes places.
- The person outside comes in and has to guess the name of the ghost in the cupboard (i.e. who is missing from the circle).
- They can ask for clues if they get stuck. Clues should always be positive and affirming to the person listening in the cupboard!

Non-verbal friendship games

These games involve passing round an action, touch or a smile. They are designed to build cohesion, rapport and wellbeing, and are particularly useful with very young children, or with young people who are developing second language skills. They are good for reinforcing eye contact and positive touch, although the usual caution over cultural sensitivity applies. These games can be used with young children to establish turn-taking, and the basic structures of circle time, and can support early language development.

Organisation and resources   students sitting in a circle, can be on the floor

Time   2–3 minutes each game

Passing a touch

- Ensure that students are quiet and attentive.
- Explain that a word, action, touch or smile will be handed round.
- Begin by touching the person next to you on the shoulder, for example, and encourage them to pass it on.
- Watch carefully, maintain the silence and affirm success.

You can also pass on a handshake, a greeting gesture from the culture of a person in the class, a smile (my favourite) or a frown (can they do this without giggling?). If the class is used to holding hands, they can pass on a squeeze. If you want to introduce simple language, you can use greeting words such as hello, or Namaste.

Games for mixing and including

These games energize the class and bring them together. They also mix students up in the circle and ensure that they are not sitting in their usual friendship groups. Mixing games are often carried out at the start of a circle time session and lead nicely into pair work, as pairs are more random than would otherwise have been the case. Mixing games can also be used to make 'silent statements' and to reinforce vocabulary.

Organisation and resources   students sitting in a circle of chairs, cards for the card activity

Time   3–5 minutes each game

Stand up and change places if...

The teacher (or a student) asks everyone to stand up and change places if... for example:

- ... you had toast for breakfast this morning
- ... you are wearing black shoes
- ... you like chocolate
- ... you have a brother.

This can be done purely as a mixing-up game or it can be extended to help students to get to know each other better by including categories of information about likes and dislikes, position in the family, where you were born, festivals you celebrate, languages you speak, pets, etc. With a well-established group, it can be used to make silent statements about levels of bullying, pressure over homework or engagement in lessons.

This activity can also be linked with other parts of the curriculum. For example, it can be used as part of a citizenship lesson to gauge people's opinions on certain topics and to see if they have changed their view by the end of a topic. With younger children it can be used to reinforce vocabulary so that, for example, students are given the name of one of three farm animals around the circle, and the caller indicates that all the "hens" should change places, or the "sheep". When "farmyard" is called, everyone changes places. This can also be used with older students in a modern foreign languages lesson.

I love all my friends especially those who...

This is similar to 'Stand up and changes place if...' but this time one student stands in the middle and their chair is taken away. They say: "I love all my friends, especially those who...", for example, are wearing black shoes. Anyone with black shoes changes places. The student in the middle tries to sit down also, leaving another in the middle at the end whose turn it is to begin the next go.

This activity can also be linked with other curriculum areas. For example, it can be used in a maths lesson by giving students a number around the circle. The student in the middle calls out "all odd numbers" or "all prime numbers" or "all numbers that can be divided by three", depending on the lesson.

Pairing up

- Students sit in a circle and are all given a card with, for example, the name or picture of an animal on it. There are two of each animal.
- They are asked to move into the middle of the circle and find their partner.
- When they have found their pair, they go and sit down together.

A variation is for them to look at their card but not show it to anyone, and then find their pair by using mime or animal noises. Another variation is for them to find others who share particular characteristics, such as a partner who lives in the same street, or has seen the same film, and to link arms with them before sitting down.

Games for extending friendships

These games develop students' ability to work in a random pair with anyone else in the class. This should be make an explicit aim and shared early on with students. The ultimate goal of ensuring that everyone in the class can work productively with anyone else, regardless of personal feelings (both in circle time and elsewhere in school life) can be celebrated when it is met. Individuals can be encouraged to self-evaluate around such targets as 'working well with a boy/girl (different gender)' or 'working well with someone I don't usually play with'.

It can be pointed out that it is hurtful when someone is less that than enthusiastic about working with you and that a nice smile is the best way to greet the news of who you have been paired with! This is an important skill for life and can begin in the primary school classroom. This is not to say that students should never pick their partner, but they should feel comfortable working outside their usual gender and friendship groups in an inclusive school that values positive peace.

These games focus on similarities and differences and encourage students to get to know a bit more about each other. Students might be surprised to learn how much they have in common with people they think are very different, and vice versa. They might find that their friend does not think in the same way that they do, or that their opinions differ. This is an equally important lesson for life, especially in learning to avoid the negative consequences of peer pressure.

Organisation and resources   students working in pairs while remaining in a circle, a talking object

Time   5–10 minutes

We both . . .

- Use a mixing game to jumble the group up around the circle; just number them one or two, and get all the number ones to change places.
- Pair the students off with the person sitting next to them around the circle.
- Ask them to give their partner a nice smile!
- Give the pairs a subject, for example, 'Find out one thing you didn't already know about your partner' or 'Find two things you both have in common' or 'Find two things that make you different', and then give them 2 minutes of discussion time. Ask them to be as creative as possible.
- Each pair reports back to the circle using a talking object, for example, 'Amy looks after her granddad's pigeons'. (Amy then takes the talking object and reports on her partner.)
- There should be loads of praise given to pairs who worked well together and general discussion of the process.

As an extension, the topics for discussion and sharing can be adapted to the time of year: (one thing that I want to achieve this year . . . one thing that I can do this year that I couldn't last year . . .); or to a topic (in this topic I have learnt . . .); or to wellbeing (my favourite place to be is . . .); or to problem-solving (we both think a way of stopping accidents in the playground would be . . .). The list is endless.

Welcoming and saying good-bye

In pressurised classrooms it is easy to forget that young people within them make up a small community with needs and perspectives of their own. It is particularly important to recognise the transition points, beginnings and endings that are significant for that community. While many of the games and activities in this section can be adapted to support beginnings and endings, it is worth pausing here to consider the effect on any group when members leave or arrive. These processes need to be given time. Sometimes groups will unconsciously 'punish' someone who is about to leave, or else project unrealistic expectations onto a newcomer. Part of the role of a teacher of positive peace is to notice and pre-empt such things. What might the class need to do in order to recognise and celebrate the contribution of someone who is about to leave? How might they express their sadness? What might they need to consider in the days before a newcomer arrives? How might a newcomer be given the space to ask for what they need? Some of the affirmation activities in the wellbeing section of this chapter would be useful here, or else the creative problem-solving activities.

Citizenship

These activities support young people to be comfortable with difference and to understand that there are multiple perspectives on most things. Through them, young people learn how to engage with others in ways that do not require everyone to agree and to work together to achieve common goals. The activities also teach the skills of active listening, and conflict resolution.

Remaining open to other people and learning from their perspectives is an important part of citizenship education. Citizenship education aims to prevent fearful responses to difference, and to enable young people to feel secure with diversity. The benefits of this for communities at all levels – from local to global – cannot be emphasised enough. The ability to bracket one's own perspectives and needs for long enough to engage with another person in a meaningful way is a significant part of citizenship. Active listening activities have therefore been included in this section on citizenship education, although they could equally have been placed in the sections on inclusion and wellbeing.

Many of these activities are games. In many schools, the time for play is being squeezed. This is tragic, especially for young children and for kinaesthetic learners who need to run around and walk through problem-solving. Play is often arranged, directed and supervised by adults – all too often creating a sterile and artificial environment that denies them opportunities to learn from peer interaction. Add to this the contemporary fear of litigation and children coming to harm, and a situation is created where young people are safe but unhappy. In reality, these conditions are toxic, even life-threatening. As young people succumb to obesity, inactive lifestyles, depression, ADHD and self-harm, adults continue to drive them everywhere and deny them participation in activities which are seen as too risky. Ironically, the risk of harm through passive lifestyles is far greater than the risk of harm through exceptional events. People are literally dying younger than they need to because they have never learned to engage in an active lifestyle, to play, to take risks, to learn and to grow. To use an old adage: adults need to give young people carpet slippers, not try to carpet the world. Resilience is a precious gift, and young people are not being allowed to develop it. Instead they are blamed for spending too much time staring at a screen. To turn this around, they need more freedom to do other things, and they need opportunities to learn how to play. The games and activities in this section provide young people with a context to practise their group-forming skills, to make mistakes and to learn how to be part of a team. These are valuable skills for family life and for most workplaces, quite apart from being central to wellbeing and to most processes of teaching and learning in primary and secondary schools.

Finally, the activities in this section support the training of peer mediators. You may wish to do this with the whole class, so that everyone knows how to mediate, or you might want to reserve the training for those young people who have been selected to be mediators. Either way, this is an invaluable part of learning to be a citizen.

Learning to be comfortable with difference

These activities demonstrate to young people that their perspectives and interpretations of events are not universal and that other people might see things differently. They aim to show that there is no right or wrong answer a lot of the time and that it is not always necessary to persuade others of your point of view. The age of 8–13 is all about learning about difference, belonging, identity and personality, and many young people struggle in these years. Levels of bullying peak, and peer pressure is very strong. These activities can begin to offer a counterpoint and orientate young people towards a more open worldview.

Organisation and resources   students sitting in a circle for some of the activities, at tables for others; any pictures, optical illusions, or adverts; the story of the people in the dark and the elephant: www.jainworld.com/literature/story25.htm

Time   5–15 minutes each activity

What is your perspective?

- Start by reading the story of the people in the dark and the elephant. This is a traditional tale that originated in the Indian subcontinent and is about people who cannot see, each reaching a different conclusion about what an elephant is, based on whether they can feel the leg, trunk, tail or tusk. It has made its way into many world religions; a link to the Jain version is given above.
- Discuss the moral of the tale.
- Stand in the middle of a circle of chairs and ask the students to describe you, but only on the basis of what they can actually see. You could use an object instead if it looks different from different angles.
- Discuss the fact that each person sees something different depending on where they are looking from.
- Discuss the ways that this might happen in everyday life.

Picture it

- With the students sitting at tables in silence, distribute a picture to each table. Ask them to write down in secret what is the most important or interesting thing about the picture. Pictures with a fair amount of detail are most suitable for this activity.

- When they have finished, get them to discuss what they wrote down, and any differences.
- Follow this up with a whole-class discussion about people seeing things differently, even when they are looking at the same thing.

This activity could also be based on optical illusions, the most famous being the old woman and the young girl, and the vase and the two faces. Ask them to say what they see and then discuss it with someone who sees something different. Why do people see things differently? Can they switch between the two perspectives?

On the bus

- Clear a space and create a 'bus' by using two ropes.
- Get the students to stand between the two ropes, and pretend to be on a bus.
- Tell them that, when you call out some bus stops, they have to decide whether to get out on the right side or the left side, depending on which they prefer. They should jump quickly and not think about it too much. Your bus stops calls need to set up a series of contrasting choices, for example:

  o   marmite – love it or hate it
  o   dog or cat
  o   chocolate biscuits or chocolate cake
  o   maths or reading
  o   wet play or normal play
  o   hot or cold
  o   morning or evening

- Discuss the differences in people's preferences and the fact that none of these are right or wrong. We need to value diversity in all its forms.

If this activity generates divisions, ridicule or competition, remind the class of the circle time rules and do a series of go-rounds as soon as possible to discuss how this made people feel and how to avoid this in future.

Active listening

The activities in this section set young people up with skills for active listening. At the heart of active listening is the idea that listening can benefit the speaker, not just the listener, and that the listener needs to play an active role if the speaker is to get the full effect. I sometimes explain this to young people as being like a switch in their head that they can flick to open up their ears and heart and to temporarily close down their own need to be listened to. I also explain that active listening is not the only kind of listening; it is just different and very powerful. It cannot happen all of the time, because we all need to listen and be heard. That is why it is important to be clear from the start who is listening to whom, and for how long – a kind of listening contract. The following activities set up a structure that is invaluable in any classroom, not only for opening up to other people, but also for a whole range of teaching and learning activities. They enable young people to: develop their speaking and listening skills more generally; benefit from high quality listening (there are many more pairs of ears in the classroom than there are available adults!); gain clarity and focus; reflect and summarise; and generate new ideas.

Organisation and resources   students sitting in a circle, sometimes in pairs or threes; a talking object; access to a whiteboard; exercise books

Time   5–20 minutes each activity.

Listening checks

- Use the circle time format to do a go-round (any).
- Afterwards, send the talking object round the circle again in silence. One person who has their eyes closed says, "Stop". The person holding the object at that moment stands up.
- The group are asked to remember the contribution made by the standing person.
- When they sit down, this is repeated so that three or four people in the circle get to stand up.
- Give loads of praise and reinforcement at the end for good listening.

This activity works best when people do not know what is coming. Students are reminded, after the event, that a go-round is about listening and not just waiting your turn to speak. An active listener remembers what people have said. It aims to demonstrate that certain types of listening are active and not passive, and to enable young people to feel heard and valued by the class.

Five questions

- Students are given five questions to ask their partner. The questions should be very simple, for example:

  o   What is your favourite food?
  o   How do you get to school?
  o   What do you do on a Saturday?
  o   What is your favourite game?
  o   What irritates you?

- The students ask the questions one after another and try to remember what their partner said without taking notes.
- When each student has given five responses, their partner tries to repeat back what they have heard. At the end the students give each other feedback about how accurately they were listening.
- Discuss as a class, in or out of the circle.

This activity gets students used to the idea that they need to both listen and remember in active listening. This is a skill that might need to be practised.

Thirty-second pair work

The teacher times the students to work in twos (preferably sitting in a circle) to listen to each other for 30 seconds as follows:

- The first time both students are set the challenge of talking simultaneously for 30 seconds without taking any notice of what the other is saying.

- The second time one of the students is told to speak (e.g. my happiest day . . .) whilst the other uses body language to suggest that they are bored or not interested in listening.
- The third time the same student who spoke last time repeats their story while their partner uses body language to show that they are listening very carefully. You can extend this a bit if you like.

The discussion afterwards can focus on what each situation felt like and on the body language for listening and not listening. You can explain that both talking at the same time is like when one person is talking and the other is having a conversation in their head about what they will say next. Active listening involves switching off this need to be heard for a while. At some point, the students can make a record of good and bad body language for listening in their books. This would include, for example, eye contact, facial expression, leaning in or turning away, fidgeting, arms folded or open, etc.

Listening: SARAH

- Brainstorm different things that people listen to (e.g. the TV, music, the teacher in assembly, birdsong, their friend telling secrets . . .).
- Discuss what is involved in each different situation. Who is the listening 'for' and what kind of listening is it? How focused does it need to be in different situations? Introduce the term 'active listening' and explain how it is different. In particular, point out that it is for the benefit of the speaker, and not just the listener. The 'contract' is different.
- Explain that SARAH can be used to as a reminder of what to do in active listening. SARAH stands for:

  - **S**top talking
  - **A**ctive listening
  - **R**epeat back what was said
  - **A**ccept feelings
  - **H**elp them to think about next steps

- Students can copy this into their books.

Triads

- In threes (not around a table if possible) students choose a speaker, a listener and an observer. The teacher or the speaker chooses a topic. The listener concentrates on using the SARAH technique. The observer watches the interaction ready to feed back what the listener did well and what they recommend might make it even better. The observer also keeps a check on the time limit of 3 minutes or whatever has been agreed.
- The triads swap roles until all three have had a chance to try listening.
- A final go-round focuses on what it felt like to be listened to so well and any other comments about how well the listener listened, observer feedback, etc.

This can be more structured by using the 3–2–1 technique: 3 minutes for uninterrupted speaking, 2 minutes to feed back, 1 minute for the observer to feed back. The teacher organises timings for the whole group together.

Questioning techniques

- Explain the difference between open and closed questions. Closed questions can usually be answered by a simple yes, no or a brief fact. They are often followed by silence. They are useful to illicit specific information and to verify when and where things happened, but they have the effect of closing down, rather than opening up, discussion. Open questions encourage people to talk more freely. They begin with words like 'what' and 'how' or phrases such as, 'tell me more about that . . . '. They leave the person free to answer in a variety of ways and to explore their thoughts and feelings more thoroughly.
- Ask them to phrase the following closed questions as open questions, or choose your own:

  o   Did the exam go well?
  o   Do you hate school?
  o   Are you getting on OK with your friends?
  o   Do you find your work difficult?
  o   Who started it?
  o   When did you find out about it?
  o   Are you feeling angry?
  o   Do you want to be friends?
  o   So, your teacher is annoyed about that?

- Next explain why it is important to avoid leading questions. Leading questions can be an undercover way of trying to influence people. Active listening is supposed to support the speaker to find their own ways forward, not suggest them in ways that imply that the listener is some kind of guide or expert.
- Ask them to rephrase the following questions as open questions:

  o   Have you tried . . .
  o   You would agree with me on that . . . , wouldn't you?
  o   Do you think that you did that because you were upset?
  o   Would it have been better if . . . do you think?

- Discuss how hard it is, and why closed and leading questions come so naturally to us.

Cooperative games

These activities build citizenship, wellbeing and inclusion through forming a sense of team. They enable the class to function effectively as a large group, a group that includes absolutely everyone. Often in schools young people are supported to work in pairs, or as part of a small group, but not so often as a whole class.

The parachute games included here are fun and provide an important lesson – you cannot achieve your goals on your own; you have to work together as a team. They also enable young people to take their cues from each other, as do some of the other cooperative activities described here. These games enable a sense of shared achievement and fun when they go well, and they provide plenty of material for circle time problem-solving when they do not. If a class cannot cooperate to make the sounds of a tropical rain forest, for example, they certainly will not be able to cooperate to perform a more serious task.

Organisation and resources   a large parachute (these are made especially for schools and are easily purchasable), a light football, a large space, perhaps outdoors

Time   30 minutes per session, plus debriefing time

Parachute games

- With the students sitting in a circle, get them to hold onto the edges of a parachute Explain why you are playing with the parachute.
- Get them to make it like the sea. Can they flap the parachute up and down to make a quiet and then a stormy sea? Can they make one wave go from one side of the parachute to the other? Can they make a wave circle around the edge of the parachute?
- Can one person walk across the parachute whilst the others make gentle waves?
- While most of the class continues to make waves, can one student be a cat and the other a mouse? The cat walks on top and tries to spot the mouse and touch them on the back to capture them. The mouse tries to get from one side of the parachute to the other by crawling underneath.
- Get them to stand up. Can they raise their arms above their heads quickly and then lower them slowly, making a dome with air trapped underneath?
- While the parachute is making a dome, can some children swap places before it falls again, while others hold onto the parachute? Criteria for changing places can be colours of clothes, pets, favourite food or simply having your name called.
- Place a ball on one side and ask the students to make the ball roll all the way round the edge.
- Place the ball in the middle; get them to use the parachute to toss it into the air and catch it again.
- Depending on the gap at the centre of your parachute and the size of ball used, ask students to roll the ball so that it goes down through the gap in the middle or so that it rolls to rest there.
- Make a tent out of the parachute by making a dome and then quickly sitting down and tucking the parachute behind them, under their bottoms as they sit down.

We have known classes spontaneously to burst into song when sitting in their 'tent'. It is a strange experience for the adult left standing outside!

These activities will often throw up problems that are perhaps covert at other times. This is a real benefit, and the importance of discussion and debriefing cannot be over-emphasised. Much of the value of the work likes in shared analysis of how the class worked as a team. Who went out of their way to help others? Is there a natural leader in the class, or several leaders? How should a leader lead? Was there a sabotage attempt? Did anyone try to dominate inappropriately? etc. As ever, discretion is advisable. There are no hard and fast rules – and there are times when hard messages need to be heard – but this should not descend into a shaming exercise for any one individual.

Rainforest

- Begin by passing a simple action or touch round the circle so that students can practise taking their cue from the person sitting next to them and not from across the circle or from the person leading the actions (this will probably be you).

- Explain that you are going to use the sounds made from the actions that you are passing round the circle to build up a sound picture of a tropical rainstorm building up and dying away.
- Remind them to copy the person next to them on their right (check they know right from left) and not to change what they are doing until that person changes. The effect is a bit like the ripple of a Mexican wave.
- Start by rubbing your hands together in a circular movement. The person on your right should do the same, followed by the person on their right and so on round the circle.
- Next tap two fingers on your palm slowly. The person on your right then changes from rubbing hands to tapping fingers and so on round the circle.
- When everyone is tapping their palm you start the next sound, which is clapping an uneven rhythm like rain falling.
- Thunder is next, made by stamping feet whilst still clapping.
- The thunder of feet stops but clapping continues.
- Clapping becomes palm tapping again.
- Palm tapping becomes rubbing hands.
- Rubbing hands then stops gradually round the circle as hands are placed on knees.
- There is silence.

This activity creates a lovely atmosphere. It is nice to enjoy the silence together for a while afterwards. The activity can be practised to get the sounds absolutely right. To do it really well, it is necessary both to act, and to be still enough to listen to the overall effect. This is a wonderful lesson in wellbeing.

Cooperative knots

- Get the students into small groups of six to ten standing in a circle.
- They close their eyes, put their hands in the middle and grasp the hands of two other people. They must not have the hand of anyone next to them or two hands of the same person.
- They then untangle themselves and end in a circle without letting go of the hands they are holding.
- This is possible! Some people may end up facing backwards.

Fives

- Students sit in a circle.
- Everyone begins by standing up. The purpose is to be the last one standing.
- Count round the circle up to five, with the first student saying one, the second two and so on. Student number five sits down. The next student starts again at one. The main interest of the game is that students can choose to say two numbers together (e.g. one and two, or two and three) in order to keep someone in or get someone out.
- Keep going round the circle until one person is left standing and is the winner
- Repeat, this time as a cooperative activity to ensure that the person who sat down first is the winner next time.

Our experience of this activity is that it is highly enjoyable for groups of all kinds, including adults, for some reason. Maybe it is because it involves eye contact and laughter, or because it creates its own simple and arbitrary rules, or because 'losing' is meaningless. We have often used it at the end of a long day, as a reward, or simply because we were begged!

Spontaneous counting

- Students sit in a circle, or are able to see each other.
- Students are asked to count to five as a group with individuals calling out one number in the sequence. If two or more students call the same number at the same time, the class has to start all over again. No discussion of tactics allowed during the game.

This game calls for observational skills, restraint and teamwork. It is quite good for developing intuition and eye contact. This game is harder the larger the group.

Fizz buzz

- Students sit in a circle.
- In this activity students count round the circle with each person calling out numbers in sequence. A number, for example five, is chosen and the group are told that when a multiple of five comes up then the whole class shout "fizz" (1, 2, 3, 4, fizz! 6, 7, 8, 9, fizz!).
- This activity can be made more difficult by having a fizz number and a buzz number. If the two numbers were five and three for example, five would be fizz, nine would be buzz and fifteen would be fizz-buzz. The aim is to keep counting around the circle for as long as possible.

This game, or course, has applications for numeracy.

Activities for comparing cooperation and competition

Both of the activities below are based on the notion of the prisoner's dilemma, in which two prisoners in adjacent cells need to decide whether to cooperate and confirm each other's story or else to compete and give information about the other in order to get away free. The risk is always that the other will choose to compete when you are choosing to cooperate, and there is no way of knowing in advance what they will do. In his version of this game, Robert Axelrod (1984) investigated which strategy would work best using a computer simulation game. He found that competition at the first move worked best when repeated interactions are unlikely, but that sustained cooperation works best over multiple occasions when there are long-term relationships. Sustained cooperation can only work when trust is established. This is underpinned by the fact that any one party will use a tit-for-tat strategy if their partner competes at any point. It is interesting to reflect on this in the context of schooling.

Organisation   a small table with two chairs, visible to the group, small treats, sweets or healthier alternative

Time   30 minutes or more

Cooperative prizes

- Two students sit on two chairs on either side of a small table. They put their elbows on the table and grasp each other's right hand. The activity looks like arm-wrestling but the teacher should take care that any reference to arm-wrestling comes only from the students and is not confirmed.
- The students are told that the person whose hand is on top will be given a small prize (e.g. a sweet), and that the main aim of the game is to get the maximum number of prizes to the maximum number of people in the shortest time.
- Students are left to devise their own ways of organising this, with the proviso that only the one table and two chairs can be used at a time and that only one prize is to be given for every hand that is on top.
- If students run it as a contest (which most do) the teacher should emphasise that the group as a whole is losing, with most of them having had no prizes and the whole thing taking too long.
- Eventually someone will suggest that they cooperate, which will mean that each pair take it in turns to have their hand on top once and then pass on to the next pair.
- The activity now shifts from being perceived as a competition to being a group challenge to get everyone as many prizes as possible in the time allocated.
- Debrief – why did they assume that this was a competitive activity? Where do these assumptions come from? What did it feel like to win, to lose and to cooperate? Be aware that some children will always prefer to compete and win. This is fine, but the downside needs to be pointed out. Most often in life, cooperation brings greater rewards for all.

Fist and palm

- Get the students into pairs. Tell them that the aim of the next activity is to get as many points as possible for yourself. The scoring is like in the prisoner's dilemma – they can get one point, two points or no points. There are multiple opportunities to score within a limited time.
- Points are scored when each pair brings their hand from behind their back to reveal whether it is showing a palm or a fist. Fist means 'compete'; palm means 'cooperate'.
- If two fists are showing, there are no points for anyone. If two palms are showing, each gets one point. If one person shows a fist and the other a palm, the person showing a fist gets two points, the person showing a palm gets no points.
- The activity is timed, giving them 30 seconds, for example, to get as many points as possible. They can go as fast as they like.
- At the end go round and ask each individual to say what he or she scored in total.
- Some of the students might have realised that cooperating every time is a quick and efficient way of scoring maximum points for each of them. Others will have tussled and cancelled each other and come away with low scores. They will be intrigued as to why some scores are so high. Repeat this activity until everyone uses the cooperation strategy.
- Discuss and debrief.

Cooperative small group work

Once basic cooperation skills are established though whole-class activities, there are endless ways of using them to support teaching and learning in smaller groups. Small groups can be more self-directing than larger groups. They enable students to take up different positions within the group and to evaluate their role. It is surprising how rarely self and peer evaluation takes place after group work, given how often students are required to work in groups. This is a particular issue in secondary schools where young people might have a range of different subjects in which group work expectations and practices vary.

According to Johnson and Johnson (1989), structuring teaching to ensure cooperation throughout the curriculum leads to a variety of positive learning opportunities for students. These include:

- providing each other with efficient and effective help and assistance;
- exchanging resources such as information and materials and processing information more efficiently and effectively;
- providing each other with feedback in order to improve the subsequent performance of their assigned tasks and responsibilities;
- challenging each other's conclusions and reasoning in order to promote higher quality decision-making and greater insight into problems being considered;
- influencing each other's efforts to achieve the group's goals;
- acting in trusting and trustworthy ways;
- being motivated to strive for mutual benefit;
- benefitting from peer pressure.

Johnson and Johnson have carried out research in schools over a number of decades and have pinpointed five core elements of effective cooperative learning. These are: positive interdependence; individual accountability; mutual aid; effective social skills, including decision-making, negotiation, leadership etc; positive evaluation of each member's role within the group, and of the group's success. Cooperative group work does not just happen automatically without consideration of these factors. Positive interdependence, for example, means that group members are linked to each other in such a way that that no one can succeed unless everyone succeeds. This takes more care and preparation than simply putting students into small groups and expecting them to get on with it.

Organisation   one wooden jigsaw for each table, with eight to ten pieces; one envelope or small container for each child, big enough to contain up to three jigsaw pieces; a whiteboard

Time   30 minutes or more for each activity

Cooperative jigsaws

- The aim of this activity is for each table to complete a jigsaw.
- Prepare beforehand by creating an envelope for each child with parts of his or her table's jigsaw in it. Distribute the pieces unevenly, so that one envelope contains three, for example, and another contains none. Also, place one or two pieces from another table's jigsaw into one of the envelopes for each table.
- Each table is asked to reconstruct a jigsaw following the rules:

  o   Do it in silence.
  o   Do not ask for pieces yourself, or signal that you need them.
  o   Do not take pieces from other people.

    o   You can accept pieces when offered.
    o   You can move around.

- The game is complete when each table has a completed picture.

This activity enables you to discuss the process of cooperating as part of a small group and the need for generosity. Did anyone give away some of their pieces to someone who did not have any or to a table that needed them? What did it feel like not being able to ask for something? What did it feel like to give something away when you do not know if you will get something back?

Jigsaw learning

- Decide on an activity, such as completing a group presentation about a topic, and define four to six tasks that will be necessary to complete the activity. Each task needs to be vital to the success of the activity.
- Split the class into home groups with four to six students in each one.
- Ask each group to decide together who will complete which task. There should be one task each. At this stage the home groups can also discuss overall strategy and how they will work best together.
- Next the students reform into task groups (i.e. one member of each home group in each task group). In these groups they carry out the task that they have been assigned.
- Finally the students get back into their home groups, bringing with them the completed task to share with the group. The home group then completes the activity, drawing on the unique contribution of every member.
- Post-activity, the students reflect in their home groups and as a class on the process. Was everyone equally engaged? Did they get all of the information that they needed? How did they solve problems?

Group work evaluation

- Before or after a group work activity, brainstorm with the whole class the different roles that people take in group work. Write them up on the whiteboard. These might include leader, motivator, information-gatherer, challenger, time-keeper, grafter, follower, problem-solver, finisher, etc. More negative roles might include passenger, saboteur and distractor. You could ask if the role of critic is positive or negative to generate discussion of group process.
- After a group work activity, get students to take it in turns to share: one thing they found easy, difficult or interesting; one thing that they are proud of; one thing they would like to improve on.
- One or two members of the group then summarise what has been said. Are there any patterns, commonalities, outliers or surprises?
- Next, group members use the list of group roles listed on the whiteboard to share what they felt their role was in the activity. They can have more than one.
- The group then discuss whether or not they agree with each person's self-evaluation. The teacher can get involved in this negotiation too. Group members should aim to give formative feedback in ways that encourage people to hear what is being said rather than responding defensively.
- Each group member sets a target for how they wish to work in a group next time.

This activity enables a degree of reflexivity amongst students, and it provides a safe vehicle for learning about how certain actions affect other people. These messages are really important to hear, especially if students are struggling to cooperate effectively in a self-directed environment.

Learning about conflict

These activities enable students to share with each other the diverse and damaging effects of conflict, and to gain a greater understanding of the processes involved and ways of working together to avoid destructive conflict and embrace constructive conflict within their school community.

Organisation   a board or large piece of paper, post-it notes, pens, a large cardboard 'label' with string attached, dressing-up clothes and props, talking object

Time   30 minutes or more for each activity

Feelings involved in conflict

- Prior to the start of the lesson, draw an outline of a person onto the whiteboard or piece of flipchart paper.
- Ensure that the group is settled. Tell them that this activity takes place in silence.
- Ask students to reflect on a conflict situation (an argument or fight perhaps) which has involved them personally and to try to remember the feelings they experienced while it was happening.
- Each person then writes or draws the feelings onto post-it notes. Encourage them to remember the full range of feelings, and use one note per feeling.
- Still maintaining the silence, the students then stick the post-it notes onto the flipchart pad.
- Ask one or two students to come to the flipchart and re-arrange the feelings notes into groups of similar feelings.
- Then, either you or one of the students reads out the feelings to everyone. If anyone thinks that they need to be re-arranged, they can come up and do this.
- Discuss what we have learned. Make the point that strong feelings are aroused in conflicts and feelings are as important as facts. Feelings ARE facts.

Another way of doing this activity is for students to write feelings onto a piece of paper. The pieces of paper are then put into a hat or a bag, and they each take it in turns to select one from the hat to read out to the rest of the group. It is unlikely to be their own. A possible extension could be to offer students the possibility of further demonstrating their understanding of the effects of conflict through an alternative medium (e.g. art/music/drama/photography/poetry or songs about bullying and/or conflict in school). Another extension is to ask them to make pledges to each other to ensure that no one in their class gets to feel like this in the future. This could be done as a circle activity, or they could write pledges with a partner, put them in an envelope and open them together at a future date to see if the pledges were kept.

Open your hand

- Students work in pairs. One person makes a fist.
- Their partner has exactly 1 minute to get them to open their hand and show a palm.
- After 1 minute, stop them and get them to swap roles and repeat the exercise.
- Discuss the outcomes and the strategies that were used (forcing, distracting, coercing or bribing, using humour, telling stories, etc.). Do they feel that they often use the strategy that they used today in conflict situations? What are the benefits and drawbacks of their chosen strategy?
- Make the point that all of these strategies have their uses. Whether they are successful will depend on how appropriate they are in a given situation.

'Ideal' enemies

- Split the class into small groups (4–6 students).
- Each group is given a large cardboard label with a ribbon tied to it and asked to create an 'ideal enemy' by writing the characteristics that they dislike in other people onto the label. These should be things like pushing into a queue, and not things that are to do with people's identity, such as gender.
- Ask a volunteer from each group to have the label around their neck, and to personify this 'enemy'. You can use dressing-up clothes and props to add authenticity.
- Each group then presents their work to the others by reading out the list on the label while the person wearing the label mimes some of these.
- When the hilarity has died down, ask the students to get back into their groups and to cross off the list on the label anything that anyone in the group still does or has done in the past.
- The result is usually that almost everything on the list is crossed off so that the students understand that we often project onto others the things that we least like about ourselves.

You could end this activity with some discussion about the people who usually suffer from other people's projections. You could make links with the Jews during the Second World War, or refugees today.

Conflict tableaux

- This activity is best undertaken in an open space (e.g. school hall).
- Get students into groups of four or five.
- Groups choose a conflict situation involving four or five people, possibly a situation that has been experienced by one of the group members. They discuss in detail how each person involved in the conflict might have been feeling in this situation.
- Either the person who experienced the conflict or someone else in the group acts as a leader. He or she uses the other group members as statues to represent what happened in a particular conflict situation. They form a 'tableau' to show what was happening at a given moment in time.
- When the groups are ready to show each other their work, the leader sets the tableau and the other group members 'freeze' in position while s/he describes the situation to the rest of the class.

- The class can then ask various people in the tableau how they are feeling and what they think about the conflict. They answer in role.
- When all groups have presented, the teacher can highlight any similarities and differences, and support the class to reflect on the nature of the conflict in each case and how it could be resolved.
- The small groups can then go back and create a new tableau, this time showing a possible resolution to the conflict.
- The process of presenting, questioning and discussing is repeated.

You can end with discussion about what has been learned about constructive and destructive responses to conflict.

Learning to mediate

These activities teach young people about non-adversarial dispute resolution. This is useful at any level, even if students are not going to progress to be peer mediators, but it is an essential part of peer mediation training. The activities included here enable young people to deduce the ground rules of mediation (and therefore to get a deep understanding of why they are important) and to learn and practise the stages of a mediation process through role play.

Organisation   flipchart or whiteboard, worksheets for peer mediation role play

Time   30 minutes or more for each activity; NB: role play of mediations will need to take place several times as students develop and improve their skills

Attacking problems not people

- Draw two stick people on a flipchart facing each other with a tangled mess at their feet to represent a problem.
- Draw arrows pointing from each person towards the other and explain that this is where each is directing their energy – towards attacking the other.
- Ask the students to call out what normally happens when two people are doing this. The responses usually include shouting, insulting, swearing, hitting, blaming, not listening, threatening, interrupting, etc.
- The responses can be written onto the flipchart surrounding the two stick people.
- Explain that the two people are putting all of their energy into attacking the other person and very little energy into sorting out the actual problem.
- Next draw new arrows showing the people putting energy into attacking the problem rather than each other. Ask the students what will happen now that you have changed the direction of the arrows.
- If they are attacking the problem rather than each other, all of the behaviours listed above (shouting, etc.) will disappear. Tell them that this is mediation!
- They can now suggest what the ground rules of mediation should be. These should be short, simple and positively framed where possible (e.g. listen to each other without interrupting, speak with respect, avoid blaming . . .).
- The ground rules for mediation can then be copied into books.

You might also want to discuss the ground rules for the mediators at the same time. These can be deduced by simply asking the class what they normally need if they are going to trust someone to help them sort out an argument. This would normally include people not gossiping about their problem, taking sides or telling them what to do.

Mediation role play

- Remind the students of the mediation ground rules that were formulated in the 'attacking problems not people' activity.
- They can try to memorise these and test each other in pairs.
- Next go over the mediation process. You could show a video of students mediating to give them an idea of what it looks like in practice, or use mediators from elsewhere (further up the school, from another local school, volunteers from a local community mediation service) to role play a mediation.
- Ask students to get into groups of four – two mediators and two disputants – or groups of five with an observer, and to prepare for the mediation role play.
- The disputants in each group will need a copy of the role play hand-outs, and the 'what's the problem?' hand-outs. The mediators will need the 'mediators' prompt sheet'.
- If you are using observers, they can use the preparation time to decide what they are going to be looking for (body language, language used, summing up, fairness, neutrality, openness to suggestions).
- When everyone is ready the role play can begin.
- Debrief after the first mediation and then get everyone to swap roles and repeat.
- This will need to be done several times before everyone is comfortable with the process.

Wellbeing

This section focuses on how wellbeing can build towards positive peace in schools. Wellbeing is about inner and outer peace, and, while inner peace centres around the need to create affirming spaces in the school day, as well as quiet and calm, outer peace centres around the need to feel accepted and valued by others.

The affirmation activities included here build inner peace through self-acceptance and feelings of entitlement and belonging. Clearly, these are complex phenomena, and there is no magic wand if students are experiencing trauma, isolation or mental health difficulties, but they do offer opportunities to develop feelings of self-worth as an individual and as a group The results, in our experience, are always transformative and extend into every area of school life. In cultures of schooling that place people under so much competition and pressure, these activities can provide real respite and remind everyone, adult and child, that education does not have to be like that. Innate abilities and preferences, personality traits and dispositions are unique for every member of a school community. The drive for conformity and standardised assessment can mask the contributions that each person brings, but these activities can begin to restore the balance, and support a school to reclaim the sense of uniqueness of every child.

Affirmation activities

Too often, students are lacking in language to affirm each other in positive ways. Their vocabulary for insults may be much more extended! These activities redress this by extending vocabulary for positive comments and giving students opportunities to practise acknowledging each other and feeling affirmed by the class.

Organisation and resources   a circle of chairs, a safety mirror and box to contain it, a white-board and pens, large pieces of paper (one for each table of four/five), materials for making a display, paper and clipboards for the class

Time   10–40 minutes each activity

Most special person

- Begin by asking the group to name people we all think are special for whatever reason – sport, music, contribution – and ask them what it is that makes people special.
- Tell them that you have a picture in a box of the most special person in the whole class. You are going to let them pass it around to see who that is, but they must not say anything until everyone has seen it. (This is an important test of impulse control. You could begin by discussing what to do if you feel yourself wanting to shout out or say something. You could also offer it as a challenge with a reward if everyone manages it.)
- Pass round the box with the mirror inside so that students can see that the most special person in the whole class is themselves. (Do not forget to look in there yourself!)
- Celebrate having managed the challenge and reinforce the point that every individual is important, unique and special in your group.

This is a lovely activity, which uses discovery to make a very important point.

Positive words and a display

- In small groups around tables ask the students to brainstorm positive qualities, abilities and strengths that they admire about other people in a range of categories, for example:

  √   personal strengths
  √   practical abilities
  √   sports abilities
  √   artistic abilities
  √   intellectual abilities
  √   social strengths
  √   inner qualities.

- Get the groups to feed back to the whole class. Prompt them to be inclusive (i.e. not all abilities have to be the kinds of things that are recognised in exams or assemblies).
- Make a more permanent display that can remain in the classroom as a prompt and a reminder of the kinds of the strengths, qualities and abilities that they admire.

Ideas for a display include: fruit bowl, where students each write onto a piece of fruit one of the qualities, abilities or strengths that are on the list, and these are stuck onto a big picture of a fruit bowl; affirmation tree, where qualities are written onto leaves stuck onto a tree; footprints, where students write affirmations onto large footprints which they stick on top of the insults that they never want to hear again; friendship chain, where students write the gifts which they bring to the class (e.g. humour, friendship etc.) onto a paper link that becomes part of a class paperchain.

Mr Beautiful

- Draw an ugly 'Mr Beautiful' on the whiteboard. He can be round, with only two teeth, and very little hair, for example.
- Ask the students to shout out words to describe him.
- With every negative comment, rub a bit out and with every positive comment draw a bit in. Try to finish with him all drawn back. You could give him a large smile!
- At the end, discuss how saying horrible things makes people 'disappear', and how saying affirming things brings them back. How can they do this for each other?

This activity was adapted from a resource that was used with children in Northern Ireland by the Ulster Quaker Peace Education Project.

Car wash

- Students stand in two lines facing each other like the two sides of a car wash.
- One volunteer has a turn at being a 'car', starting at one end of the 'car wash'.
- The volunteer walks slowly through and receives pats on the back, applause, affirming comments and cheers.

Fame for the day

- A student is chosen at random to have fame for the day; no particular reason is necessary. (They will all get one turn.)
- He/she is treated as a special person for the day. If there are treats or privileges, they get first option; they get to go out first to play, etc.
- When the student is first chosen, the rest of the class brainstorm the things that they like about that student. This can be done in or out of the circle.
- This can be written up later and presented as a certificate for the student to take home.

Lighthouse activity

- Students sit in a large circle or several smaller circles depending on how they will work best, with paper, clipboard and pen(s).
- Students draw a lighthouse on their sheet (or you could pre-print one) and put their name somewhere on the light bit.
- They pass their sheet to the left.
- They write a positive comment on the lighthouse that has been passed to them about the student whose name is on the sheet.
- The teacher circulates to be certain that no negative comments are written on anyone's lighthouse – if there is a real likelihood of negative comments this activity should not be attempted.
- Students keep passing sheets to their left and writing positive comments until their own returns to them.
- They read their sheets and maybe feed back which comments they particularly liked.

This can be also be done by putting notes into backpacks.

Mindfulness activities

As we explored in Chapter 8, mindfulness is a practice that can be used with young people and also with adults. The activities below are taken from a variety of sources, including Patricia Jennings' thoroughly recommended *Mindfulness for Teachers* (2015) and the highly resource-full website www.mindfulteachers.org.

We present two activities aimed at adults and two aimed at children and young people. What will be clear is that the activities can be adapted for any audience. What will also be clear is that for adults to teach mindfulness to children and young people *authentically*, then they must practise mindfulness themselves. Mindfulness is a simple yet complex practice and we strongly recommend that it is undertaken within a school setting following good quality appropriate training for staff.

Organisation and resources   a chair or a cushion to sit on, a timer, paper and pencil

Time   1–10 minutes for each activity

Setting intentions

Take a moment at the start of the working day or just before that difficult class arrives to set yourself a positive intention. An intention should not be confused with a goal. An intention comes from inside; goals come from outside. An intention is an expression of a valuable way of thinking, feeling or being that can serve as a touchstone when the going gets tough. Examples of intentions that might help in the classroom include: 'Be gentle', 'Respond with kindness' and 'Be present'.

Three breaths

Again, in the midst of the hubbub and high-energy of school life, it can be restorative to take a minute – in between classes maybe – to simply notice when you are breathing in, and then breathing out, breathing in and breathing out, and breathing in and breathing out. Then gently notice how you are feeling.

Hand-breathing game (this game appears courtesy of www.joyfulmind.net.au)

Stand in front of your class. Slowly raise both your arms, bending your elbows slightly as though you are conducting an orchestra. Tell the students to breathe in as you raise your arms. Slowly lower your arms and tell the students to breathe out as your arms lower. The students can either be motionless or raising their arms along with you.

Start with at least three slow, calm rounds. You can then start to vary the speed and the height of the arms. Have fun with it. You can pause your arms mid-raise: the breath is held in. You can stagger the breath by climbing imaginary stairs with your hands. There are endless possibilities and variations for this practice to engage the attention of your students. Always come back to the basic three slow, calm, even rounds.

*Mindful listening (this activity appears courtesy of
www.meditationinschools.org)*

Ask your class to sit in a comfortable posture in their chairs and for 1 minute to listen to the different sounds around them, sitting quietly without talking. Ask them to gently close their eyes while they do this practice, so they can listen without distraction. (Let them know that after this 1 minute they are going to write down all the different sounds that they heard, in and outside the room.)

After 1 minute ask your class to stop listening, take a few breaths and write down all the different sounds they heard. They have 1 more minute to do this practice.

After 1 minute ask your class to stop writing. Ask them to let you know what sounds they could hear. What sounds are written on their list? Ask for a volunteer to get this process started. Go around the class asking. When one child is reading out their list, ask the other children if they also heard the sound. They can acknowledge this by raising their hand.

Facilitate discussion with the group, asking: What did they notice during the practice of listening? What did it feel like? When might it help them?

Learning about emotion

These activities address the affective dimension of learning and support young people to be aware of emotions and to manage them well. Situations of direct violence in schools often have their origin in misinterpretation of signals from other people or in poor impulse control. Although some young people may need more intensive support, these activities aim to build all students' capacity to: understand themselves and their emotions; express emotions; read social and emotional cues; and make more informed decisions to act based on self-awareness and control. Clearly, peace-keeping and peace-making require a certain level of emotional intelligence, but these activities aim to go beyond this into peace-building.

These games develop self-awareness and the ability to differentiate between feelings. They also extend young people's vocabulary of feelings and their ability to recognise feelings in others.

Organisation and resources circle of chairs, a book or small board, various artefacts, cooking materials, art and display materials, graph paper, post cards or index cards

Time 3–5 minutes each game, longer for the cooking activities

Guess my feeling

Name six feelings and model the facial expression accompanying the feeling, for example:

- happy
- sad
- angry
- thoughtful
- afraid
- disgusted.

The students can then try out the facial expressions for themselves. This can become a guessing game, where first the teacher and then individual students reveal an expression for the others to guess.

Pass the face

This game is similar to Chinese whispers, but a facial expression is passed around the circle, hidden behind a book or small board.

Feeling table

Develop a feelings table devoted to one feeling at a time. Students can collect items such as pictures, poems and stories to illustrate the feeling.

Biscuit faces

Students can bake face biscuits and decorate them with icing, sugar strands, cherries, currants, etc., to depict different facial expressions. Look at them together in the circle and talk about their expressions. (The same could be done with plasticine models.)

Feelings wall

Older students often benefit from an extended feelings vocabulary and from a visible reminder of the various feelings they might experience in the course of a day. This activity does both.

- Students brainstorm as many feelings as they can think of. In a circle the talking object can be handed around until all ideas for feelings words have been exhausted. It may help to think of families of words, making lists of words associated with anger, sadness, fear, enjoyment, love, surprise, disgust, shame, etc.
- Students make a display of as many feelings as possible.
- As an on-going activity throughout the day, student volunteers go over to the wall and point to how they are feeling at the moment. If they want to, they can say why.

Feelings graphs

The aim of this activity is to demonstrate that everyone feels a range of feelings throughout the day, and that these can change quite quickly.

- The students draw a graph with happy–sad on one axis, and the times of the school day in hours on the other.
- The students keep a record throughout the day and then compare results at the end to find out who was feeling what and when. The graphs can be a useful guide for the teacher to see what parts of the day students most enjoy or dislike.

Feelings cards

This is a matching game that helps students to develop a useful set of words for linking actions with feelings and to avoid blaming others for their emotional responses.

- Students prepare a set of action cards, which all have a sentence beginning 'When you . . . ' and a series of feelings cards which all have a sentence beginning 'I feel . . . ' on them. An example of an action card might be: When you borrow my pencil without asking, and an example of a feelings card might be: I feel annoyed.

- The students play a variety of card games with them. As an example, they put all cards face down and take it in turns to try to pick up two that match (e.g. 'When you tell me that you like my hair' with 'I feel proud' or 'I feel happy'). If they pick up two that do not match, they have to put both cards back. The winner is the one who has the most pairs after all the cards have been picked up that can be matched.

Sentence completion go-rounds

This is a circle learning activity based on a go-round. Although this is a 'safe' activity, because students are talking about people in general, rather than themselves, inevitably they will draw on personal experience. Students are asked to complete these sentences:

- People feel happy (surprised, afraid, angry, etc.) when . . .
- Something people feel sad about is . . .

One to ten

This activity is also based on a go-round. It is a powerful exercise and helps to develop awareness and empathy. If you feel that individual pupils with low scores would benefit from peer support, this could be set in motion.

In a go-round students give a score to how they are feeling at the moment from one to ten, and explain why in a sentence if they wish to.

Conclusion

We hope that staff working in and with schools will find the range of activities presented useful and at times challenging. The aim of presenting these activities is to refresh the repertoire of activities at people's disposal but also to make explicit the benefits and purposes of these activities. Yes, it is important and enjoyable to have fun with children and young people in schools; the burdensome focus on test results makes opportunities for fun and human connection even more important in our eyes. However, engaging in some of the activities described above is also crucial in teaching and developing the qualities, skills and attitudes that young people need in order to become positively peaceful citizens.

References

Axelrod, R. (1984). *The Evolution of Cooperation*. Cambridge: Perseus Books.
Johnson, D. and Johnson, R. (1989). *Cooperation and Competition: theory and research*. Edina, MN: Interaction Book Company.
Stacey, H. and Robinson, P. (1997). *Let's Mediate: a teacher's guide to peer support and conflict resolution skills for all ages*. London: Sage Publications.
West Midlands Quaker Peace Education Project. (2016). *Learning for Peace: a guide to developing outstanding SMSC in your primary school*. [online] Retrieved 10 September 2016 from www.peacemakers.org.uk/wp-content/uploads/2013/01/Cover-Learning-for-Peace-e1463403949199.jpg

Concluding comments

Out beyond ideas of wrongdoing and rightdoing, there is a field. I'll meet you there.

(Jalal ad-Din Rumi, thirteenth century)

Rather ironically and sadly, peace education has gone out of political favour in many parts of the world. Over the past four decades (in the UK at least) peace education has been variously vilified as either hippy-nonsense or political propaganda. As Page remarks, "[i]t is difficult to avoid the perception that peace education involves some implicit criticism of the existing social order" (2008: 15), so that those in power often become suspicious and hostile to its aims and practices. In our book, therefore, we have attempted to provide a rationale for peace education that will be inspiring for our readers, while remaining mindful of the sociopolitical context in which peace education functions.

We have noted throughout this book that peace education needs to be grounded in processes of dialogue and community-building around preferred futures. This means that its work will never be done. Peace needs to be constantly rediscovered as schools and communities evolve and change. It is this process of peace-building that is at the heart of postmodern peace education and positive peace in schools. Our challenge here has been to operationalise peace sufficiently well that actual people working in actual schools can put peace into practice. At the same time, we have attempted not to operationalise peace to such an extent that it becomes an intervention, a programme or a tool. We have tried to tread the line between peace as philosophy and peace as practice carefully.

Peace education functions at both the micro and the macro level. While it can be tempting to focus only on the micro-level of the individual and the school, it is equally important to look to the macro-level, and the ways in which the school exists and functions within a broader eco-system that extends from the local and the national to the regional and the global. There is a need to take account of questions of agency and structure or, in other words, the extent to which actors are free to bring about change in the structures that make up their social reality. Many in postmodern times have become paralysed by these concerns, unable to take action because of a lack of belief in possibilities for change. We would argue, however, that process is all and that it is possible to reduce conflict in schools (outer peace) and to reduce the stress and hopelessness that maintain it (inner peace).

We hope that we have provided here a sufficiently robust case for why building a culture of positive peace in schools is important and also how such a culture could be built. We reiterate here that we do not hold teachers responsible for healing all of the ills of society, but we do urge people working in and with schools to cast a critical eye over what is done in the name of standards and progress, to name peace as a value and goal and to use this book to work towards it.

We would like this ending to involve looking forward and hope that our book has opened up new spaces of inquiry and enquiry. We wonder what will happen at the ground level in schools, and with teachers, as they seek to engage in crucially important, but potentially counter-cultural, peace-building. We find ourselves asking many questions:

- What happens when school staff feel that crucial tension between their human needs and priorities and the needs and priorities of a schooling system that privileges different concerns?
- What are the spaces and mechanisms that need to be created to enable a focus on peace to come to the fore in schools?
- Whose vision of peace counts in a school and how do we ensure that everyone is heard?
- How can we make use of those critical moments in the life of a school when people are returned to their essential humanity?
- What will be some of the unanticipated outcomes of schools engaging in more explicit work towards peace? What do we not yet know?
- How will the continually evolving face of conflict shape the new possibilities for peace?

We look forward to on-going discoveries as these issues play out. As will be clear by now, we are advocates for peace, for peace education and for peace-building, despite our criticisms of the field at times. We hope that we have been able to communicate our enthusiasm, as well as our concerns, and to inspire other to take up these challenges and delights. We urge adults in schools to engage with the ideas and the practices we have presented through this book and to take heart from the case studies of real schools that have been provided. We will continue to use them ourselves in our work supporting schools and school staff. We will continue to interrogate and refine our own understanding and our own practices. We hope that our readers will interrogate and fashion what we have presented, making use of their own personal and professional perspectives and experiences and taking this work forward in new ways.

In the spirit of postmodernity and peace-building that we have expressed throughout this book, we now turn to the thorny question of how to conclude. There can of course be no conclusion, but rather continuous questions and challenges, for positive peace is not a destination but rather a journey and a dynamic one at that! We return here in our final remarks to the centrality of one of our key points: that it is possible to create transformative moments in schools without the need to transform schools as institutions. While this latter may be desirable, it is not going to happen any time soon. We end with an image – a night sky that is dotted with stars. Each represents a moment of peace in the lives of the adults and young people in a school community. The more stars, the brighter the night sky. The brighter the sky, the easier it is for travellers to find their way. We hope that starlight is a fitting metaphor for the beauty and fragility of education for peace.

Reference

Page, J. (2008). *Peace Education: exploring ethical and philosophical foundations.* Charlotte, NC: Information Age Publishing.

Index